SO-FAJ-416

When the World Turned Upside Down

This book is part of the Peter Lang Education list.
Every volume is peer reviewed and meets
the highest quality standards for content and production.

PETER LANG
New York • Berlin • Brussels • Lausanne • Oxford

Luis Martínez-Fernández

When the World Turned Upside Down

Politics, Culture, and the Unimaginable Events of 2019-2022

PETER LANG
New York • Berlin • Brussels • Lausanne • Oxford

Library of Congress Cataloging-in-Publication Control Number: 2022046978

Bibliographic information published by **Die Deutsche Nationalbibliothek**.
Die Deutsche Nationalbibliothek lists this publication in the "Deutsche
Nationalbibliografie"; detailed bibliographic data are available
on the Internet at http://dnb.d-nb.de/.

ISBN 978-1-4331-9614-0 (paperback)
ISBN 978-1-4331-9598-3 (ebook pdf)
ISBN 978-1-4331-9599-0 (epub)
DOI 10.3726/b20055

© 2023 Peter Lang Publishing, Inc., New York
80 Broad Street, 5th floor, New York, NY 10004
www.peterlang.com

All rights reserved.
Reprint or reproduction, even partially, in all forms such as microfilm,
xerography, microfiche, microcard, and offset strictly prohibited.

Dedication

With love and hope, for my two grandsons, east-coaster Emilio Martínez González and west-coaster Wesley Martínez, born within six months of each other at a time when the unimaginable became daily news.

All history is contemporary history.
Benedetto Croce

History must teach us, in first place, how to read a newspaper.
Pierre Vilar

There comes a time when silence becomes dishonesty.
Frantz Fanon

When you write a book, you are asking someone to make an investment in their time and money. A column can come and go as the weeks pass, but a book needs to be timeless.
Regina Brett

Contents

Foreword

I was in bewildered mourning at the events of 2019 to 2022. Is there any sense to be made? To this confusion, historian/columnist Luis Martínez-Fernández brings clarity. *When the World Turned Upside Down* makes real George Santayana's warning that "Those who cannot remember the past are condemned to repeat it."

As a reader, I want to be mesmerized while being educated. I savor fact-based stories, not pontifications. Martínez-Fernández's book reads like a series of missives from the front, capturing the drama of unfolding, often unpredictable, events. Insights into government and its mechanics are not dry, but fascinating. The author is a master story-weaver, drawing from the warp and weft of our national and global histories to reveal patterns in today's events.

Within each essay, many of which were written in real time, Martínez-Fernández's seems prescient when forecasting about unimaginable events as they evolve. But no clairvoyance here. His grasp of history pinpoints how economic urgencies, world leaders, and myopic policies led to "the unprecedented" in ages past, and recognizable contemporary patterns. How is this possible within each short and engaging essay? This is the gift of "seeing" Luis Martínez-Fernández brings to all his readers.

Suzette Martinez Standring, Author of *The Art of Column Writing* and Past President of The National Society of Newspaper Columnists

Acknowledgments

I am eternally grateful to my parents Celestino Martínez Lindín (1933–2005) and Luisa Martínez, who sacrificed so much to give their children the best education possible. It is on that foundation that I built all my professional accomplishments, including this book.

At the University of Puerto Rico, where I began my formal education in history in 1978, I had the fortune to work with world-class historians, among them my mentor Fernando Picó; and at Duke University, I studied under leading colonialist historian John TePaske. I am indebted to them and many of my other professors. Picó wrote plenty of books but also found the time to write regular opinion columns for the *San Juan Star*. I emulated him, penning occasional op-eds for Puerto Rico's dailies *El Mundo* and *El Reportero* when I was in my mid-20s.

Three-and-a-half decades later, in January 2019, I received an invitation from Fieke Snijder to write an opinion column on a contemporary Cuban topic for the international, online news media outlet *The Globe Post*. Her request opened an opportunity to publish a dozen columns over the next few months. Had it not been for her invitation and encouragement, I doubt I would have become a regular columnist.

After amassing a portfolio of columns, in the summer of 2020, I threw a message in a bottle of sorts; I approached Creators Syndicate to see if they would be interested in carrying my columns. To my surprise—it is incredibly difficult to get into syndication—a month later, they invited me to join their prestigious roster of opinion columnists.

I am particularly grateful to Creators' managing editors Simone Slykhouse and Kelly Evans and editors Alissa Stevens, Alessandra Caruso, and Sam Peloquin. Fifty-one of this volume's essays were originally published by Creators Syndicate. I thank them for the permission to republish them here.

I am also indebted to University of Central Florida students Marena Montes Colón and Alexis Rodríguez who provided thoughtful research support for some of the columns that appear in this book.

My short columnist career has benefited from the encouragement of many friends and colleagues, who have read and commented on my opinion columns and other essays. Too many to be mentioned here, I wish to acknowledge some of them, Rocco Anastasio, Lemuel Aguayo, Jonathan Arnold, Gustavo Arvelo, Anne Beatty, Kristy Brugar, Carlos Chardón, James Clark, Carole Crinshaw, Bárbara Cruz, Pablo Davis, Maggie Favretti, Rick Fernández, Jorge Giovanetti, Nathalie González, Julio Guerrero, Stephanye Hunter, Olga Jiménez de Wagenheim, Paul Koethe, Zenaida Kotala, Asela Laguna, Eduardo Lolo, Grace Leatherman, Andrés Martínez, Daphne Martínez, Pedro Martínez, Herb Margolis, Andy Mink, William Morgan, Hakan Özoğlu, Fernando Rivera, Roselina Rivera, Orlando Rivero, Cecilia Rodríguez-Milanés, Jorge Luis Romeu, Eric Rutkow, Pedro San Miguel, Rafael Saumel, Mercedes Soler, Vladimir Solonari, Soren Triff, José Vázquez, Zulma Vélez, and Jim Wunder.

I also extend my gratitude to Suzette Martinez Standring for graciously agreeing to write the foreword.

Finally, I am thankful to Peter Lang Publishing's acquisitions editor Dani Green for her enthusiastic support for this project and to Jacqueline Pavlovic and the other editors who played a role in shepherding it from manuscript to book.

Abbreviations

ADHD	Attention Deficit Hyperactivity Disorder
AOC	Alexandria Ocasio-Cortez
AUKUS	Australia-United Kingdom-United States security pact
BECA	Basic Exchange and Cooperation Agreement
BIPOC	Black, indigenous and people of color
CDC	Centers for Disease Control and Prevention
CDR	Committees for the Defence of the Revolution
CEIP	Carnegie Endowment for International Peace
CMEA	Council for Mutual Economic Assistance
CSI	Commonwealth of Independent States
CSTO	Collective Security Treaty Organization
DACA	Deferred Action for Childhood Arrivals
EAEU	Eurasian Economic Union
EIU	Economist Intelligence Unit
FCAT	Florida Comprehension Assessment Test
FEMA	Federal Emergency Management Administration
G-7	Group of Seven

GAESA	Business Administration Group (Cuba)
HUD	Housing and Urban Development
ICE	Immigration and Customs Enforcement
IOC	International Olympic Committee
LASA	Latin American Studies Association
LULAC	League of United Latin American Citizens
MADA	Make America Democratic Again
MAGA	Make America Great Again
NASCAR	National Association for Stock Car Auto Racing
NATO	North Atlantic Treaty Organization
NGO	non-governmental organization
NPR	National Public Radio
NRP	National Revolutionary Police
PNP	New Progressive Party
PPD	Popular Democratic Party
PPP	purchasing power parity
PRERA	Puerto Rico Emergency Relief Administration
PROMESA	Puerto Rico Oversight, Management and Economic Stability Act
PRRA	Puerto Rico Recovery Administration
ROC	Russian Olympic Committee
SCO	Shanghai Cooperation Organization
SEATO	Southeast Asia Treaty Organization
STEM	science, technology, engineering, and math
UAE	United Arab Emirates
UCF	University of Central Florida
UPR	University of Puerto Rico
WHO	World Health Organization
WPA	Works Progress Administration
Y2K	Year 2000

Introduction

When the World Turned Upside Down is a collection of 66 essays and opinion columns written between February 2019 and December 2022. Together, they stand at the intersection of historical writing, opinion journalism and chronicling. Readers will recognize each of these modes of thinking and writing, which combined produce a synergy for a better understanding of historical and contemporary realities. The book is an exercise in humanistic journalism, a work informed and guided by the humanistic values of rationality, the quest for truth (evasive as it may be), and appreciation for creativity and felicity of prose.

While each individual essay stands on its own, collectively they were conceived as a coherent collection organized into nine topical sections, each preceded by an introductory essay: (1) American History, Past, Present (Future?), (2) Rough Drafts of History: U.S. Society and Politics, 2019–2022, (3) Culture Is the History That We Inherit, (4) I Never Left the Classroom: Reflections on Education, Books, and Reading, (5) *¡Despierta Latino!*, (6) Puerto Rico, the World's Oldest Colony, (7) Exercises in Cuban Historiographical Maroonage, (8) Not Boring at All: Globalization and World Affairs, and (9) The Oracle of History.

A professional historian for over three decades, I address these subjects from my discipline's perspective, applying its standards of rigor and its research and analysis methodologies. These essays are informed by knowledge of the past but also the recognition that present-day preoccupations guide which historical topics we study, the questions we ask, and even the conclusions we reach. Italian philosopher of history Benedetto Croce encapsulated these ideas succinctly when he wrote that "All history is contemporary history."

Readers will recognize that this book is an apology for the field of history that underscores its usefulness—its urgency, rather—in the grossly utilitarian context of the early twenty-first century. History matters for itself; it matters as a means for a better understanding of the present; it even matters when trying to anticipate future developments.

That said, this book levels serious criticisms against the history profession and some of its practitioners' deviation from truth, well-supported arguments, and even common sense.

I have set a few rules for myself as a columnist besides that universal rule of opinion writing: "Do no harm." First, to write columns only when I have something relevant to say or can offer a unique, hopefully unexpected, perspective (because I am in syndication, that means that every week I must write something of relevance). I agree with what I recently heard Pulitzer-winning columnist John Archibald say: "When we become predictable, we become useless." And while I consciously avoid a moralizing, prescriptive tone, my columns are purposely pedagogic. I want readers to come out having learned something new from each column.

Equally important, I strive for the highest levels of intellectual honesty (this starts with being honest with myself). I follow the advice I give my students: do not make things up, never write things that you yourself don't believe, and never say anything just to come across as cool or to be popular. There is too much of that out there. Ernest Hemingway's admonition for good writing is now more important than ever, have "a built-in, shock proof, shit detector." I carry an extra one for the sake of redundancy.

Another rule I have set for myself is to make my columns not only readable but pleasing to the reader's ear. I spend time Thesaurusing for the right word (yes, often that means making up words that do not appear in the Thesaurus). I resort to metaphors and other figures of speech, vivid imagery, rhythm, and creative structures. I try my best to endow each column with some literary value.

While the opinion column genre offers advantages over the scholarly article and academic book, namely the speed with which one's ideas reach the reading public; word limits (around 750) make it hard to develop and sustain complex arguments in a single column. For that reason, some of this book's essays combine two, three, even five or six separate columns under one title.

How This Book Came About

Rather than a sudden determination, my decisions to become a columnist and write this book came about gradually, the result of an alignment of three factors; serendipity also played a role.

First, Donald Trump was sworn in on January 20, 2017. His first 24 hours as president set the tone for his administration: a dark inaugural speech ghost written by Steve Bannon, promising to deliver us from "carnage"; lies about the size of the crowd gathered at the National Mall "documented" with manipulated images by the ill-suited—remember Sean Spicer? —White House Press Secretary.

Trump's administration turned out to be the motherlode of raw material for late-night comedians and columnists, alike: his anti-democratic antics; serial pathological lying—the *Washington Post* tallied 30,573 lies and misleading statements—appointments of unqualified, inept and often corrupt senior staff and cabinet members; orders to deploy troops to the U.S.-Mexico border and to incarcerate undocumented children; adulation of assassin world leaders—need I say alleged?—(Vladimir Putin, Mohammed bin Salman Al Saud, Kim Jong-un); unending self-enrichment schemes, the Big Lie, his two impeachments (not that unimaginable); and to top the list, his inciting of the U.S. Capitol attack on January 6, 2021.

The years 2019–2022 have witnessed momentous world events some of which motivated several of this book's opinion pieces: the COVID-19 pandemic; accelerated climate change producing massive forest fires in the Amazon, California, and Australia and catastrophic floods in Africa, South Asia, Europe, and the United States; rising authoritarianism and wholesale human and civil rights violations in China, Russia, Cuba, Venezuela, Hungary, Belarus, Myanmar, even in Puerto Rico; violent suppression of protests in Hong Kong, Moscow, Havana and Tehran; Putin's unprovoked invasion of Ukraine starting in February 2022; Ukraine's successful counteroffensive since September 2022; and the Russian leader's repeated threats of nuclear war.

The second factor emerged a few weeks after Trump's inauguration when I accepted an invitation to write a chapter on U.S.-Caribbean relations (nineteenth century) for *The Cambridge History of America and the World*. The project included the study of U.S. domestic and international developments during the Antebellum and the Civil War. It did not take me long to realize that the news I was watching at night mirrored what I was reading in the morning and afternoon. A few of my earliest columns address parallelisms and connections between 1850–1877 and 2008–2022.

The third factor was my decision to reinvent myself at age 59 as a regular opinion columnist, first for the *Globe Post*, and later in national syndication with Creators Syndicate. After three decades authoring academic books and articles on Cuba and the Caribbean, I repurposed my pen, at least for the time being, to write regular opinion columns on contemporary subjects on my primary fields of expertise (Cuba and Puerto Rico) but mostly on developments in the United States and other parts of the world.

When I started writing regular columns, I did not intend to collect them and publish them in book format. That, and the recognition that we had entered a period of unimaginable developments, came later in the process.

To maintain the integrity of each column as a chronicle written without the benefit of much hindsight, I have resisted the temptation to update or make corrections to them. They appear here with only minor changes, mostly stylistic. Readers will find information on place and date of publication following each column title. In a few instances, I have added post-publication updates in the form of footnotes.

The final product is a book, whose essays paint a portrait of a pivotal con-vulsed period in American and global history, a time when the world turned upside down, years of unimaginable events. What can be more unimaginable than the January 6 attempted coup, the overturn of the half-century entrenched Roe v. Wade decision in 2022, serious discussions about the potential for a sec-ond U.S. Civil War, massive protests in Cuba, Iran and China, and the prospect of a Third World War, which as Putin said on March 3, 2022, and reiterated on September 20, will be nuclear—God forbid.

Section I
American History, Past, Present (Future?)

Introduction

During 2017 and 2018, I read extensively on the U.S. Antebellum and Civil War. It soon dawned on me that at night I was watching news that mirrored what I was finding in my research: heightened political polarization, increasing racial hatred and violence, and frightening threats to peace, national unity, and democracy. The parallels I found inspired me to write a handful of essays on contemporary echoes from the 1850s and 1860s.

The past, it is generally accepted, sheds light on the present, think of George Santayana's overquoted admonition "Those who cannot learn from history are doomed to repeat it." Decades later, British historian Edward H. Carr looked at it from the other direction. "Good history," he proposed in *What Is History?* "is accomplished when the historian's view of the past is illuminated by reflections on present day problems."

Whether this book is good history or not I'll leave to readers and critics—some critics don't read—but every essay in this section, in the entire book for that matter, rests on the supposition that history is a continuous dialog between past and present. The nine essays that follow refer to U.S. history, engaging the past in service of the present and the present in service of the past.

The opening essay is the earliest of my regular opinion columns "Trump, Fake News, and Why History Matters More Than Ever," which I wrote in February

2019. It defends history as an indispensable discipline whose primary purpose is the pursuit of truth.

But alas, truth finds itself increasingly in the crossfire between the strangest of bedfellows: on one side, nationalist populists who weave conspiracy theories and speak of "alternative facts" (Giuliani, Bannon, Conway & Co.), on the other side, equally anti-intellectual postmodernists (Foucault & Co.) and assorted new sophists with Ph.D.s who parrot one another.

I have settled for pursuing truth with the understanding that there are multiple perspectives on truth and that historical inquiry evolves in such ways as to reveal new truths. There is no room, however, for falsification, senseless obfuscation and nonsense.

This opening section includes columns that connect historical developments of the 1850s and 1860s with their thundering echoes beginning with the inauguration of Barack Obama as America's first Black president in January 2009 and the election and controversy-ridden presidential term of Donald Trump (2017–2021). Among them are the essays: "'All History Is Contemporary': A 20/20 Look at the U.S. Antebellum and Civil War," and "Polarization, Nationalism, and Secessionism (Past and Present)." Another column, "I Cannot Believe the Things I Have Been Reading in the Pre-election Media," reveals uncanny similarities between the campaigns and elections of 1860 and 2020.

1

Trump, Fake News, and Why History Matters More Than Ever

(The Globe Post, February 19, 2019)

We live in Orwellian times. Truth is fake and fake is truth. Good is bad and bad is good. Fact is fiction and fiction is fact; and as in George Orwell's dystopian classic *1984*, "ignorance is strength," strength for those who insist on keeping the masses ignorant. It's time for historians to step in.

We also live at a time when history, as well as the arts and humanities, are increasingly neglected in schools and universities, sacrificed at the altar of the gods of STEM (science, technology, engineering, and mathematics).

That is largely based on incorrect assumptions about history's lack of practical application and the belief that its study sheds light exclusively on the past. That is simply not true. The training and practice of history provide a long-term (telescopic) perspective and sensitivity toward the interconnectedness of human actions and reactions and foster an intuitiveness that helps understand the present and even anticipate future outcomes.

That said, us historians are generally shy about issuing forecasts. We are trained to avoid it, partly because we focus on the past and write about events and realities from decades if not centuries ago. We are even dissuaded from fantasizing about counterfactuals, what-ifs such as what would have happened if Caesar had not crossed the river Rubicon? or Richard Nixon had won the presidential elections of 1960?

Likewise, we learn to refute the cliched aphorism "history repeats itself." Karl Marx believed it, even if only in a tongue-in-cheek way: "History repeats itself," he wrote, "first as tragedy, second as farce."

The farthest historians are allowed to go is recognize that human beings will respond in similar ways to similar circumstances at different times.

Connecting Developments

German philosopher Friedrich von Schlegel once said that a historian is a prophet facing backward. Centuries earlier, Romans had enshrined Janus as deity of change and time. Janus became a symbol for the field of history, visually represented by a head with two faces, one looking to the past, the other to the future.

Because historians mostly look backward, we develop an unmatched sensitivity to change over time and a telescopic way of connecting developments over different periods of time.

If cultural anthropologists, sociologists, and political scientists are the photographers of human activity and interactions, historians are their videographers. The same telescopes and video cameras we point to the past serve us well when we turn them to the present and future.

These sensitivities manifest themselves as a keen sense of intuition, an instinct that historians develop about the past, present, and future. Intuition, I argue, is as important to history as research, reflection, and analysis.

Devaluating Historians

Shortly after the United States' entry into World War II, Franklin D. Roosevelt, the story goes, gathered a group of historians to pick their brains on the question of how long the war would last. They accurately predicted that it would end in four years.[1]

---

1 On August 5, 2022, President Joe Biden invited a group of historians to the White House that included presidential historian Michael Beschloss and Jon Meahan. Reportedly they discussed imminent threats to democracy in America and the global rise of authoritarianism.

In recent decades, however, historians have been increasingly devalued almost everywhere, from the local middle school to the White House, and even in higher education. This has been to the detriment of our society.

What if—excuse these counterfactuals—foreign policymakers had consulted historians about how they should treat Cuba and its revolutionary leaders, or about the wisdom of going to war in Afghanistan and Iraq? What if financial policymakers and government officials had asked historians about the risks of banking deregulation?

The Donald J. Trump administration is, without doubt, the most hostile ever toward historians, intellectuals in general. It has demonstrated an almost obsessive disdain for truth and carved foolish lapidary phrases such as "alternative facts" and "the truth isn't the truth."

Why Historians Are Needed

Paradoxically, historians have been debased and STEM-bullied to our lowest point ever, precisely at a time when we are most needed. Not only do we provide insights about the present and what may come tomorrow, we also teach students and the general public basic knowledge and skills required for informed citizenship: the ability to read reflectively and critically, the capacity to recognize faulty logic, and the ability to express and defend arguments.

The historical discipline must be protected, lest Orwell's adage become fact: "The most effective way to destroy people is to deny and obliterate their own understanding of their history."

As I encourage my students: Read! Think! Disappoint them! Even if they feel powerless, I also tell them: at least they know that you know.

2

"All History Is Contemporary": A 20/20 Look at the Antebellum and Civil War

(The Globe Post, July 2, 2020)

The historical discipline depends on a continuous conversation between past and present, a dialog—not a monolog—between historians and those about whom we write.

Playing with the ambiguity of the word "contemporary," Italian philosopher of history Benedetto Croce once wrote that "All history is contemporary history," meaning that the weight of present-day needs and circumstances inescapably shapes the way we look at the past, no matter how remote.

Read the *New York Times* or *Washington Post* or turn on CNN or MSNBC any given day and you will read and see eerie echoes of most of the factors that led to the U.S. Civil War 155 years ago.

The parallels are manifold, among them profound political and partisan polarization, the passing or marginalization of political compromisers, a rise in political extremism, the public's loss of confidence in government institutions including the presidency, Congress, and the Supreme Court, intensified nationalism, and escalating political vitriol and racial violence.

Resurgence of Southern Nationalism

The past decade or so has witnessed a resurgence of southern nationalism, a widespread revival of Confederate symbols, the Confederate flag namely, and a growing veneration of Confederate leaders.

This is partly a reaction to successful efforts to remove Confederate flags from public buildings, knock Confederate generals like Thomas "Stonewall" Jackson down from their bronze horses, and uproot generic statues of Confederate foot soldiers as was the case in Durham, North Carolina, in the summer of 2017.

Weeks later, to protest plans to remove the statue of Confederate General Robert E. Lee, militants from various extreme right and white supremacist organizations—including neo-Nazis, neo-Confederates, and the KKK—congregated for the so-called "Unite the Right" rally in one of America's most civilized cities, Charlottesville, Virginia. The city, the nation, and the world watched footage and saw images of violent and ultimately deadly confrontations between those hate groups and counter-protesters.

Racial, social, and political tensions have exploded into mass mobilizations of antiracist protesters, riots, and quasi-military responses from various police departments and National Guard units since the public execution of African American George Floyd by white Minneapolis police officers on May 25.

Since then, Black Lives Matter protesters have knocked down numerous confederate statues and commemorative plaques in Virginia, Alabama, Florida, Kentucky, Georgia, North and South Carolina, and Tennessee, among them one honoring Confederate President Jefferson Davis in Richmond on June 10. Photographs of the toppled bronze Davis, show him on his back, his head smashed and bloodied with paint, and his right arm extended upwards as if begging to be lifted. That same night, demonstrators knocked down the statues of four generic Confederate soldiers in Portsmouth, Virginia.

State and city authorities are pre-emptively removing similar statues. Earlier this week, the City of Charleston brought down John C. Calhoun's; and Virginia's governor has promised to remove General Lee's Richmond equestrian monument.

On June 10, The Lincoln Project, the Republican super PAC that opposes Donald Trump, denounced his public defense of Confederate symbols, asserting that he "is more interested in acting like the President of the Confederacy, than as the President of all Americans." More recently, dauphin and political-humorist-wannabe Donald Trump Jr. suggested that toppled Confederate monuments be replaced with statues of his father's likeness.

Few people know that most of the Confederate statues that are coming down do not date to the Civil War or the immediate decades that followed. In fact, most were erected during the Jim Crow Era (1890s–1950s).

What about the aphorism that victors always write history? Not in this case, where the South lost the war yet won the interpretation of that war and its aftermath.

The "First" Civil War

Historians recognize that the main cause of the Civil War was slavery (essentially a race matter) and more specifically the institution's expansion into new territories and states.

While slavery was the Antebellum Era's most divisive socio-political issue, it was braided into a thicker noose of contentions that included the balance between slave and free states (concomitantly, political balance in Congress); states' rights versus strong federal authority; low tariffs versus protectionism; and commercial or territorial expansionism.

Among the multitude of other causes was the passing (or marginalization) of a generation of compromisers in Congress, the likes of Henry Clay and Daniel Webster (Whig Party leaders both of whom died in 1852), Democratic Senator William R. King of Alabama (who died in 1853), and Democratic Senator from Illinois Stephen A. Douglas, among others; and the parallel rise of extremists on both sides of every divisive issue: northern anti-slavery radicals such as William H. Seward, Salmon P. Chase, and Thaddeus Stevens, and fire-eating pro-slavery secessionists the likes of John Quitman, John C. Breckinridge, and Jefferson Davis.

Other contributing factors include polarization between political parties, escalation of nationalist sentiments (unionism in the North and nationalist secessionism in the South), increased bitter rhetoric and political violence as in the case of guerrilla warfare in Bleeding Kansas, John Brown's raid of Harpers Ferry, and even inside the walls of the Capitol building and on duel ranges in the nation's Capital.

Even bloodier and more vicious was the violence perpetrated against southern free and enslaved Blacks, manifested through more frequent and harsher physical punishments, new repressive legislation, anti-Black riots, and illegal re-enslavement, as exemplified in the diary of Solomon Northup in *Twelve Years a Slave*.

In some northern cities, meanwhile, Irish and German working-class immigrants feared that emancipation would reduce work opportunities and lower salaries; and, on occasion, unleashed violent rhetoric and physical attacks against Blacks. The infamous New York City anti-draft racial riots of 1863 were the period's bloodiest manifestations of white immigrant violence against Blacks. When all was said and done, around 120 individuals, most of them Black, lay dead in New York's streets.

Irish and German Catholic immigrants themselves had been the targets of ethnic hatred nationwide, sentiments that led to the formation of Know-Nothing organizations and the founding of the nativist, anti-Catholic American Party in 1855.

Erosion of Faith in Political Institutions

As is presently the case, the years leading to the Civil War saw an erosion of faith in political institutions, the national electoral system and Congress among many southerners, and the Supreme Court in the eyes of some northerners.

The composition of Congress and the Senate were intimately tied to the number of free states and slave states. Whereas in 1837 there was a balance of 13 free states and 13 slave states, by 1858 the ratio was 17 to 15 in favor of the North's and Far West's free states but that year, Republicans failed to elect a single congressman in any of the slave states.

Those electoral shifts responded to demographic changes, including faster westward expansion north of the Mason-Dixon line and disproportionate growth of the electorate of the North. For an increasing number of Democrats, representative democracy seemed to no longer work in their favor.

In the Supreme Court, also known as the Taney Court, Democrats enjoyed a 7 to 2 majority that overlapped with a southern majority of 6 to 3. Southern Democratic dominance became disturbingly evident to many northerners and Republicans when the court reached the Dred Scott decision in 1857, a ruling declaring that Blacks were inferior and therefore not deserving of U.S. citizenship nor the protections inherent to that status. Exactly 160 years later (in 2017), Maryland authorities removed a statue of Chief Justice Roger Brooke Taney from the State House in Annapolis.

Southern voters saw the federal legislative system as an obstacle to their sectional interests, while their northern counterparts deemed the Supreme Court incapable of protecting theirs.

1860 Elections

Illinois Republican candidate Abraham Lincoln was elected president in 1860, but he won by a margin of only one electoral vote, with less than 40 percent of the popular vote, and without getting a single ballot in 10 southern states.

Just three days after the elections, on November 9, the South Carolina General Assembly declared Lincoln's election a "hostile act"; seceded from the Union in December and was later joined by 10 other southern states in 1860 and 1861.

The Civil War interrupted the expansion of slavery and led to its abolition but did not end the North-South divide and short of reducing discrimination, exploitation, and violence against Blacks, resulted in a failed Reconstruction and long decades of exploitative sharecropping arrangements, segregation, disenfranchisement, and lynching.

In the past few months, the unending dialog between past and present has gotten louder, a shouting match that reminds us that all history is contemporary.

3

Polarization, Nationalism, and Secessionism (Past and Present)

(The Globe Post, August 17, 2020)

On July 14, CDC director Dr. Robert Redfield blamed northerners who had headed south for Memorial Day weekend vacations for the latest surge of COVID-19 cases. Harvard scientists and New York Governor Mario Cuomo retorted that it was not the North's fault, pointing the blame at southern politicians who had rushed to reopen their states prematurely.

States are also divided on mandates to wear masks. The line of demarcation running roughly along the Mason-Dixon line, the same line of contention of the Antebellum, Civil War, and Reconstruction.

Historical Precedents

James Madison, with his extraordinary political wisdom and foresight, could not have anticipated that so many Americans would come to cherish the freedom to not wear a mask as almost worthy of inclusion in the hallowed Bill of Rights. No one would have foreseen even just three months ago, that such issue would divide the nation to the extent that it has.

There is somewhat of a historical precedent, however. During the Spanish flu pandemic (1918–1920) opponents of mask-wearing ordinances organized and marched in protest in many U.S. cities.

Anyone barely familiar with the Reconstruction Era that followed the Civil War and its long conflictive aftermath knows that the peace signed at Appomattox, far from healing the wounds of division, aggravated sectional and interracial tensions, gave way to long decades of systematic exploitation and marginalization of former slaves, often imposed through violence.

The Antebellum South was geographically suited to produce tropical and semitropical staples (tobacco, rice, cotton, sugar), which many landowners believed could only be produced with enslaved labor. While the North imported part of that production, much of it headed toward European markets, thus southern politicians' insistence on friendly relations with Europe and keeping tariffs low.

Contrastingly, since colonial times, the northern economy focused on temperate climate agricultural activities, commerce, navigation, and manufacturing; a system that thrived on high protectionist tariffs and did not depend on slave labor.

Historians have long recognized southern secessionism as a form of nationalism, whereby many white southerners viewed themselves as constituting a different nation with its distinct culture, and therefore deserving of political autonomy, if not independence. The North had its own form of nationalism, which strove to preserve the Union at whatever cost. The Civil War was the culmination of tensions between southern secessionist nationalism and northern unionist nationalism.

Between North and South, a belt of five border states extended west from Delaware through Missouri. Neither slavery nor southern nationalism were particularly strong in that region and none of those states seceded.

Before the secession of eleven southern slave states, the formation of the Confederate States of America, and four years of all-out civil war, the North-South divide had been intensifying for decades, reaching an explosive climax in the presidential elections of 1860, when party alignments overlapped sectional divisions to such an extent that northern Republican candidate Abraham Lincoln carried all free states (northern [except New Jersey] and western) and lost all southern slave states—I had to double- and triple-check the astonishing fact that he did not receive a single popular vote in Alabama, Arkansas, Florida, Georgia, Louisiana, Maryland, Mississippi, North and South Carolina, and Texas.

From the Blue and the Gray to the Red and the Blue

Since the 1990s, but particularly following Barack Obama's 2008 electoral victory, sectionalism, rural vs. urban antagonism, and other manifestations of geographical political rivalry have remerged with a vengeance, intensified during the first years of Donald Trump's presidency, and have reached feverish levels of vitriol and violence in 2019 and 2020. As was the case during the Antebellum, Civil War, and Reconstruction, these conflicts are intertwined with manifestations of nationalism, partisan politics, and secessionism.

While the correspondence between geographical region and political party affiliation is nowhere close to what it was eight score years ago, geography continues to matter. According to Pew Research Center polls, in 2014, there was a clear overlap between region and party affiliation with 51 percent of North-eastern voters identifying as Democratic/leaning (only 31 percent Republican/leaning); Republican affiliation was much stronger in the South at 41 percent, a statistical tie with Democrats (42 percent).

An examination of the 2016 presidential electoral map reflects uncanny parallels with its 1860 counterpart. Map colors are, of course, inverted because the Republican (red) and Democratic (blue) parties had swapped ideological positions on many issues, including civil rights, race relations, and social justice. What has remained constant is the social conservatism and states' rights ideology of the South.

Out of the 29 states voting Republican or Democratic in 1860, all but seven went to the opposing party in 2016. Among them were Michigan, Pennsylvania, and Wisconsin, where Republican candidate Trump won by margins of less than 1 percent and a combined total of only 78,000 votes. Tellingly, the political party inversion rate between 1860 and 2016 was 100 percent in New England, the Southern, and Pacific coast states.

The Countryside Is Red / Cities Are Blue / Let's Split the Suburbs / Between Me and You

During the Antebellum, cities overall leaned more Republican than Democratic—rural areas are still more conservative than urban centers. These political correlations overlap with contrasting demographic and cultural realities: racially diverse and multicultural cities and apple-pie and Chevrolet truck rural settings.

Stanford University Political Science Professor Jonathan Rodden, who studies the growing political divide between urban and rural areas, has gone as far as stating that contemporary political polarization "is all about geography." Perhaps not quite. A 2018 Pew Research Center poll assessing political and ideological differences among urban, rural, and suburban adults found wide gaps and polarization between urban and rural residents in views about Trump, immigration, abortion, and same-sex marriage. Pew researchers concluded that such differences had more to do with party affiliation than with geographic setting.

Urban Republicans are significantly more moderate (more evenly split) than their rural counterparts.

The urban-rural political divide has been growing for a couple of decades. In 2008, defeated red presidential candidate John McCain carried 53 percent of the rural vote; eight years later, Trump received nearly twice as many rural votes (62 percent) as blue candidate Hillary Clinton, who just got 34 percent.

Suburban America, meanwhile, has turned purple, mirroring the Antebellum's frontier states. May the metaphor of battleground states remain a figure of speech.

Three Neos: Nationalists, Confederates, and Secessionists

Just as Lincoln was unacceptable to the white South in 1860, Obama's 2008 election was intolerable to broad segments of the white electorate. His election gave rise to numerous radical conservative groups and movements, starting with the formation of the Tea Party, just days after he took office.

Likewise, the United States has seen an upsurge of neo-confederate militance and racial hatred and violence, far beyond the geographical limits of the old Confederacy. Confederate flags are flying in states like Mississippi and Alabama but also in old unionist states such as Michigan and Wisconsin.

As fringe as they may be, neo-secessionist organizations and petitions multiplied after Obama's election. They have quieted down in the last few years but are likely to resurface if Trump does not win re-election in 2020.[1]

---

1 In June 2022, the Texas Republican Party adopted a new platform that expressed that the state "retains the right to secede from the United States" and that the "Texas Legislature should be called upon to pass a referendum."

Red Caps vs. White Masks

A recent Pew Research Center poll on mask-wearing shows some fascinating, if not completely surprising, correlations. Northeasterners responded that they "always" (54 percent) and "very often" (23 percent) wear masks outside their homes. Numbers are much lower in other regions; the Midwest, for example, where only 33 percent of the adult population wears masks all the time and another 29 percent very often.

There was an even stronger correlation with party affiliation with 94 percent of blues wearing masks either all the time or very often, compared to only half as many reds (46 percent). Only 1 percent of Democrats never wear masks, in contrast to 27 percent of Republicans. It is odd that to wear-or-not-wear a mask is today's single most politicized and polarizing issue.

There have been numerous instances of verbal and physical violence even deaths over mask wearing. Are Walmarts, Dollar Stores, and Waffle Houses our Bleeding Kansas, Harpers Ferry, and Fort Sumter?

4

Race and Politics: Contemporary Echoes of the U.S. Antebellum

(Creators Syndicate, September 9, 19, 2020)

Not a few commentators rushed to celebrate Barack Obama's 2008 election as the advent of a "post-racial America," but the eight years that followed proved them wrong.

In March 2008, false rumors began to spread that Obama had been born in Kenya and was, therefore, ineligible to run for president. Once elected, white supremacists and broad segments of conservatism viewed him the way many white Southerners saw Abraham Lincoln (the only other president hailing from Illinois), as an illegitimate president.

Nearly a century and a half later, Republican congressional leaders did not advocate nor pursue secession but did the next best/worst thing: "secession" by withholding all forms of cooperation and compromise with the executive branch, declaring their priority to make Obama a one-term president.

In 2011, when Donald Trump began to explore a presidential run, he embraced the so-called Birther movement, becoming one of its most vociferous mouthpieces, a move that helped him build the base that later propelled him to the White House. One year after his election, 57 percent of those who voted for him still believed that America's first Black president was either "definitely" or "probably" born in Kenya.

As Dr. Phil is fond of saying, "The best predictor of future behavior is past behavior." Within a few hours of Democratic presidential nominee Joe Biden's announcement of his selection of Senator Kamala Harris for vice president, Trump was at it again, spreading the lie that "she doesn't meet the requirements."

One and a half minutes into his 2016 presidential campaign announcement speech, Trump threw a 72-ounce raw steak at his supporters gathered at the lobby of New York City's Trump Tower and the national audience watching on TV. "The United States has become a dumping ground for everybody else's problems," said the red-tied tycoon. Some in the crowd hollered back in affirmation. "When Mexico sends its people," Trump lashed, "they're not sending their best …. They're bringing drugs. They're bringing crime. They're rapists." More hollering.

That was his declaration of war against immigrant Latinos. Later came the "big, beautiful" border wall that Mexico would pay for; then his verbal attacks on U.S. District Attorney Gonzalo Curiel, who he accused of judicial bias because of his Mexican heritage; then a series of attacks against Dreamers' protections; and, to top it all, the inhumane family separation and caging of thousands of refugee children.

Trump has maligned other ethnic, racial, and religious minorities. In his 2016 candidacy announcement speech, he invoked the threat of "Islamic terrorism," code for the world's 1.9 billion Muslims, including over 3.45 million living in the United States. Once in office, Trump issued an executive order banning the entry of Iranians and nationals of another six predominantly Muslim countries.

A few months later, the president uttered that infamous statement, calling Haiti and unspecified African countries a "shithole." While he claims to love Blacks and that Blacks love him back, his speeches, tweets and other public remarks are filled with dog-whistle calls aimed at stirring the worst anti-Black, racist instincts of many in his political base.

Demographic Changes

In the twenty first century, the proportion of Americans not born in the United States increased to 13.7 percent. As Brookings Institution fellow Philip Wallach reminded us, that parallels the Antebellum proportion of 13.2 percent in 1860. Then and now, such significant proportions of immigrants spurred anti-immigration sentiments and movements: the anti-Catholic Know Nothing organizations of the 1850s and contemporary white supremacism and numerous unabashedly racist groups.

In the three decades since 1990, the population of the United States increased from 249.6 million to 330 million. The sharper growth of the Hispanic population from 22 million to 60 million was responsible for much of the overall population expansion. Official figures from the 2003 census showed that by that year, the Hispanic population of 38.8 million had surpassed the African American population of 38.3 million; Asians lagged at 13.1 million.

The Hispanic population grew by another 10 million between 2010 and 2019 and is now over 18 percent of the population. The latest U.S. census estimates point to an unprecedented phenomenon: the white segment of the population dropped in absolute numbers from 197,845,666 in 2016 to 197,309,822 in 2019.

While it is not clear that the white population will continue to shrink, it will continue to decrease in proportional terms. Currently, whites constitute less than half of the population in Hawaii, California, New Mexico, Washington, D.C., Texas, and Nevada. The same is true in 47 of the largest 100 metropolitan areas, including cities in the battleground states Texas, Florida, and Georgia. This explains why Trump expresses such disdain for the nation's cities and celebrates red states as "patriotic America."

Politics of Race

University of Maryland Professor James G. Gimpel's race and ethnicity analysis of the 2016 presidential campaign and elections produced several important conclusions, among them: "Approaching the 2016 election, immigration policy polarized opinion by partisan identity more than at any other time in contemporary history" and "Election surveys suggest that immigration policy opinion was responsible for moving crossover voters to Donald Trump in the 2016 presidential election, improving his performance over Mitt Romney in 2012."

The 2016 election results also demonstrate a high level of party racialization. Trump edged Hillary Clinton with 306 electoral votes against 232. If we were to count only the votes of non-whites, Clinton would have run the table, with all 538 electoral votes; if we were to count only votes cast by white Americans, she would have carried only 169 electoral votes to Trump's 369. Counting only non-college educated whites—the "undereducated" Trump says he loves—Clinton would have won only six states (and half of Maine), totaling just 64 electoral votes. A few days after the 2016 election, columnist Perry Bacon Jr. wrote that "Whites without college degrees voted like an ethnic bloc."

Even the undereducated can see the simple mathematical formula: the larger the immigrant and ethnic minority population, the more eligible voters from those groups; and because they tend to vote Democratic, the more they vote, the lower the chances of Republicans winning.

A total of over 23 million immigrants and 32 million Latinos are eligible to vote in 2020; 30 million African Americans are also eligible.

A System That No Longer Works for One Major Party

During the Antebellum, Democratic politicians, particularly Southerners, witnessed demographic shifts that pointed to growing northern electoral power and translated into an expanding majority of free states vis-á-vis slave states. These developments produced increasing frustration that historian Robert E. May used to explain growing Southern belligerence in the 1850s, including a wave of expansionist filibustering against Cuba and the outbreak of civil war.

Behind that frustration was a growing sense that the national electoral system no longer worked for white Southerners.

Today's national electoral system, with its increasing number of minority and foreign-born voters, no longer works for a Republican Party whose ideology, actions (and inactions), and rhetoric against such groups have escalated from neglect and disdain to open hostility.

In the aftermath of former President Obama's re-election in 2012, Republican leaders, campaign managers and pundits spoke much about the need to expand the party's tent by making its platform and candidates more appealing to minority and immigrant voters. What sounded like a logical and necessary strategy, however, clashed against the reality of an increasingly anti-minority and anti-immigration Republican Party base.

Trump's strategy was the opposite: to further chastise minorities and immigrants with the goal of energizing and mobilizing a white, mostly rural, mostly non-college educated and predominantly male political base.

It worked for Trump because of Hillary Clinton's trust deficit and because of a finely targeted strategy that delivered Pennsylvania, Wisconsin, and Michigan. While no one can estimate how many red votes resulted from Russian interference, the truth is that Russian operatives engaged in a massive, precisely targeted disinformation campaign that most certainly made a difference in those three states and others. The equation is simple: Political propaganda, regardless of its origin, influences people; if not, why would candidates spend so many millions in advertising? Russian interference made a difference, unquantifiable as it may be.

Most Republicans have resorted to turning a blind eye to ongoing Russian efforts to sow divisions, hurt Democratic nominee Joe Biden's image and undermine democracy. Some Republican operatives are pursuing multiple strategies to suppress and dilute Black and Latino votes through gerrymandering, intimidation, misinformation, legislation that makes it harder for people to vote, and outright fraud, as was evident in 2018 in North Carolina's 9th Congressional District.

Come November 2020, if demographics and democracy are allowed to follow their course, Trump—as virtually all polls suggest—will lose re-election. However, the winds of voter suppression, renewed foreign interference, an uncontrolled COVID-19 pandemic, and shenanigans at the Postal Service may make it work for Trump one more time.

Either way, once the results are in, racial, ethnic, gender, geographical, cultural, and partisan hostilities will intensify, as they did in November 1860. Given Trump's record of falsely denouncing rigged elections and mass electoral fraud, and his persistent calls for political violence, it is hard to imagine a dignified concession and exit from power. Blood will be spilled, not between two armies but in a low-intensity conflict that could last years. May my historian's intuition fail me this time.

5

How Do Lincoln, Kennedy, Obama, and Trump Compare?

(The Globe Post, May 8, 2020)

On Sunday, May 3, 2020, Donald Trump appeared on a Fox News TV "town hall" staged inside the hallowed Lincoln Memorial in Washington, D.C. He used the opportunity to play his favorite instrument: the fiddle of victimhood. He complained that no other president had ever been treated with as much hostility by the press. Pointing at the 20-foot marble statue of Abraham Lincoln, Trump uttered, "The closest would be that gentleman right up there ... I believe I am treated worse."[1]

Consistently ranked as America's best president, Lincoln has often been the object of comparisons: with John F. Kennedy, who was also assassinated; more recently, with fellow Illinoian Barack Obama; and by some, oddly enough, with Trump.

---

1 In an October 5, 2022, speech in Miami, Trump said to the audience: "I remember a very famous pollster, very well known, John McLaughlin, came to my office just prior to the plague coming and he said, 'Sir, if George Washington and Abraham Lincoln came alive from the dead and they formed a president-vice president team, you would beat them by 40 percent.' That's how good our numbers were."

Lincoln and Kennedy

The year was 1976, the United States was celebrating its Bicentennial, and my father decided that it was a good time for a family trip to Washington, D.C. I was 16 years old. We enjoyed the monuments, museums, and ubiquitous stores crammed with presidential and patriotic souvenirs. A small cardboard with a Lincoln penny and a Kennedy half dollar drew my attention.

I still remember the coin set's accompanying text. It listed similarities in the lives of Presidents Lincoln and Kennedy: they were first elected to Congress and 14 years later to the presidency exactly 100 years apart; both were northerners; Lincoln's secretary was surnamed Kennedy and Kennedy's Lincoln. Both were shot in the head by southerners on a Friday. After fatally shooting Lincoln, John Wilkes Booth ran from a theater and was apprehended in a warehouse while Kennedy's assassin fled from a warehouse to a theater. Lincoln and Kennedy were both succeeded by southern vice presidents named Johnson.

Wow! I am still amused by those facts. But when I learned how to think and read like a historian, I came to understand that those parallels short of historical were merely coincidental factoids.

We can recognize, however, clusters of interconnected historical parallels. Lincoln and Kennedy were strong advocates of civil rights for Blacks, positions that earned them wide opposition and animosity among many white voters, particularly in the South.

Both presidencies were haunted by clouds of illegitimacy resulting from either narrow popular vote margins (Kennedy's 0.17 percent) or their failure to receive a majority of the popular vote (Lincoln's 38.9 percent).

The fact that Lincoln was a Republican and Kennedy a Democrat strengthens the historical parallels between them. The Republican Party in Lincoln's era was far more progressive on most issues including human and civil rights than its Democratic counterpart, but today those ideological positions are inverted.

The electoral results of 1860 and 1960 fueled the rising crests of sectional tensions, partisan rancor, polarization, and violence. Lincoln's election precipitated the secession of eleven southern states and a bloody four-year long civil war. And while there was no domestic war during the 1960s, the decade saw a peak in political violence tied to the interconnected issues of civil rights and the anti-Vietnam War movement.

Lincoln and Obama

In 2008, 143 years after Lincoln's assassination, Senator Obama was elected president. They are the only two politicians hailing from Illinois to have won the White House.

Political observers and commentators were quick to find parallels between both presidents. Lincoln and Obama were men of humble social origins who became lawyers. They launched their political careers in Illinois but had been born in other states. They entered politics as state legislators before running successfully for Congress.

Having served just two years in Congress, both decided to run for president as underdog candidates, eventually defeating more popular and experienced contenders, William H. Seward and Hillary Clinton, who coincidentally served in their time as U.S. Senators from New York. Expanding on these coincidences, Lincoln named Seward Secretary of State and Obama appointed Clinton to the same post.

Obama and Lincoln were master wordsmiths and gifted orators. These qualities were largely responsible for their widespread popularity and electoral support. Both, moreover, believed in and forcefully promoted civil rights and economic empowerment, particularly for African Americans.

Some parallels between Lincoln and Obama respond to conscious decisions of the latter, reflective of his profound admiration for the former. Obama emulated Lincoln. Let's start with the symbolism of the inauguration ceremony. Obama chose to arrive in Washington by train, as Lincoln had done. He took the oath of office with his left hand resting on Lincoln's Bible. And invoked "the better angels," that Lincoln had summoned in his Inaugural Proclamation.

There are several contextual cluster parallels between the 16th and the 44th presidents. Both ran in times of profound political and party polarization, and while both were compromisers, their mere election further inflamed polarization, rancor, and even political and racial violence.

Obama's presidential legitimacy came under attack, not because of a narrow victory but because of widespread malicious rumors that he had been born in Kenya and therefore was an unlawful candidate and president. To this day, thousands of American voters hold on to the lie that he was not born in the United States.

While he was president, thank goodness, Obama did not see a single state break from the Union, he did not have to fight a civil war to restore the nation, and he was not gunned down. He faced, nonetheless, a parallel surge in sectional secessionism. Echoing the past, South Carolina led the way, with the formation of the neo-secessionist organization Third Palmetto Republic. Similar groups have emerged in Texas, California, and Vermont.

Curiously, three months after Obama took office, Texas Governor Rick Perry conjured the specter of secession at a Tea Party rally. "We've got a great union," he told the crowd, "there's absolutely no reason to dissolve it. But if Washington continues to thumb their nose at the American people, who knows what may come of that."

One can also read Republican congressional refusal to work with Obama and obstructionism as forms of secession. Republican Senate Majority Leader Mitch McConnell rejected Obama's olive branch and made it clear that his priority was to make him a one-term president.

During Obama's two terms, there was no parallel to guerrilla war in Bleeding Kansas (1855–1859) nor John Brown's raid on the federal armory at Harpers Ferry (1859), but those years saw a dramatic rise in hate crimes and racial violence. Incidents of random and institutionalized violence against Blacks became commonplace.

While Obama was thankfully not assassinated, large numbers of Americans hated him to death, and many still do.

Lincoln and Trump

Halt for a minute. Imagine that you are watching an episode of Sesame Street. The images of Lincoln, Kennedy, Obama, and Trump pop up on the screen as Ernie begins to sing his signature song:

> One of these things is not like the others
> One of these things just doesn't belong
> Can you tell which thing is not like the others
> By the time I finish my song?

Anyone with just the most basic knowledge of presidential history or a minimal amount of common sense would know to respond: "Trump."

Yet in 2018, the Ivy League-educated conservative author Dinesh D'Souza released his film *Death of a Nation: Can We Save America a Second Time?* in which he sought to establish historical parallels between Lincoln and Trump, who two months earlier had pardoned him for the crime of making illegal campaign contributions. For curiosity's sake, I went to see it. I could not stomach it and had to leave around halftime.

The film is a stream of intentional distortions, fake history at its best. During the late antebellum, the film goes, Pre-Trump America was dead—at least agonizing—in both cases because of racist Democrats bent on destroying the nation.

Completely ignoring the political inversion whereby Democrats are now the most liberal and progressive and Republicans have embraced ultraconservative positions, D'Souza establishes parallels between two Republican presidents victimized by Democratic politicians, who according to him operated in fascist fashion.

Numerous critics place *Death of a Nation* among the worst films ever. I'd give it an Oscar for the most dishonest.

D'Souza knows better. But he is also aware that the average American is woefully ignorant about U.S. history and even the nation's foundational jewels, the Declaration of Independence and the Constitution.

A national survey released on the 150th anniversary of Lincoln's assassination, showed that half of all Americans did not know when the Civil War took place. College graduates did not fare much better, with one-third incapable of dating America's deadliest conflagration.

Let's halt for a minute one more time to play another children's game. Look at the photograph of Trump under Lincoln's statue and find seven differences. Better yet, 70, 700, 7,000....

6

I Cannot Believe the Things I Have Been Reading in the Pre-election Media

(Creators Syndicate, October 24, 2020)

The closer to Election Day, the more disturbing the news and more hateful the partisan messages appearing in the nation's newspapers. Read or skim through a handful of daily papers from different regions of the country and you will find plenty of news, actual or fake, that will make you wonder whether we have reverted to a bygone era of political tribalism, social and racial violence, unbridled corruption, and massive electoral fraud.

Let's start with news stories about heightened divisive political rhetoric. One party asserts that it is the best option for saving the Constitution from dangers "greater than any which have threatened it" since the nation's founding. A renowned Ohio politician accuses the party in power of having "corrupted every branch of our government." His own party, another story in the same newspaper says, is seeking to end "the corruptions in which the present debased administration [has] involved the finances of the nation." The author of a letter to the editors of a New York newspaper exacerbates rural-urban hostilities, demonizing cities as godless places and "ulcers in the body politic."

Political rhetoric has escalated to the point that it is not uncommon to read mutual accusations of treason and threats of violence and revolt.

Dead Men Voting

Among the most incendiary pre-election news stories are denunciations of widespread electoral fraud. One story assures readers that Republican operatives found "no less than 935 fraudulent names" on a list of registered voters. A published appeal to Republicans claims that another list includes fake registrations, scandalously enough, among them those of two underaged sons of an immigrant woman.

Another story denounces a brewing mass-fraud scheme in which citizens of one Midwestern state are crossing the border to cast ballots in another state.

There are numerous news stories of scattered arrests and charges of committing or conspiring to commit voter fraud, among them the notorious case of the former private secretary of a large-city mayor.

Government authorities, other newspaper stories tell us, have redoubled efforts to curb electoral fraud and rein in voter intimidation. The mayor of a large Southern city has expanded security around polling places after expressing concern over "recent exhibitions of partisan bitterness." Another Southern city mayor will dispatch additional officers to polling stations, promising that "ample security will be guaranteed to every voter."

Scores of groups of citizens are organizing and mobilizing to guard against political fraud. One story tells of a group that has called for volunteers to intimidate potential "ballot-box stuffers."

Political Violence

It is disturbing to read about the mobilization of numerous paramilitary political action groups, some with histories of political and racial violence. Their names point to their militant and violent proclivities: Minutemen, the Blood Tubs, Rough Skins and Red Necks. One such group, dressed in black capes and wearing "black fatigue caps," staged a torch-lit march in Cleveland.

Merchants, meanwhile, are peddling all sorts of political paraphernalia including party banners and uniforms. I could not believe my eyes when I read an ad in a Louisiana paper with the headline "Torches. Torches. Torches." It offers militants unlimited quantities of high-quality tiki torches.

Rival political gangs—some call them clubs—have already clashed in urban and other settings. Printed news narrate violent confrontations that seem to come out of history books: street battles between groups armed with rifles, axes, even pitchforks.

Stories like these point to a convulsed election, calls for secession and perhaps civil war.

Nothing New Under the Sun

Why do I say this, you may ask? Because it happened already.

All those news stories appeared in the *New-York Daily Tribune,* the *Cleveland Morning Dealer,* the *New Orleans Daily Crescent,* and Baltimore's *Daily Exchange* the day before the presidential election of 1860—yes, 1860, when Abraham Lincoln was elected president.

History does not repeat itself, historians say. But sometimes I wonder.

The Library of Congress has digitized these and other historical newspapers. You can read them online at https://chroniclingamerica.loc.gov/search/titles/

7

Statehood for Washington, D.C., and Puerto Rico in Historical Perspective

(Creators Syndicate, November 13, 2020)

On the long, unforgettable evening of November 3, while millions of Americans were nervously glued to their TVs watching CNN, MSNBC, Fox and other news media, their co-citizens in Puerto Rico watched news of their own elections and a yes-or-no referendum on statehood.

For the residents of Washington, D.C., it was yet another election day in which they lacked the right, as guaranteed to states by the Constitution (Article 1, Section 2), to elect two senators and a representative to Congress.

Puerto Rico's nonbinding referendum is the sixth consultation of its kind since 1967. With slightly over half of registered voters participating, 52.3 percent cast ballots for statehood and 47.7 percent against it. Pro-statehood party leaders, yet again, spun the results as a mandate to seek admission as a state of the Union. "The people have declared that we no longer want this [commonwealth] status," uttered Governor-elect Pedro Pierluisi of the pro-statehood New Progressive Party. "We want equality," he added.

Only around one-quarter of eligible voters supported statehood, hardly a mandate to pursue a till-death-do-us-part commitment with the United States.

The statehood for Washington, D.C., movement, meanwhile, has gained momentum since 2016, when a whopping 86 percent of the district's voters expressed their desire to become the 51st state of the Union. That overwhelming majority was the district's will-you-marry-me? message for Congress.

Democratic senators and congresspeople embraced the proposal and presented statehood-for-Washington legislation in both chambers of Congress. Known for his obstructionist tactics, Senate Majority Leader Mitch McConnell, R-KY, refused to hear it. This summer, all Democratic members of the House, with one exception, voted to pass the Washington, D.C., Admission Act. As has become the norm in these times of extreme polarization, the Republican opposition unanimously rejected it. Statehood for Washington, D.C., and Puerto Rico, McConnell protested, was part of the Democrats' "radical" agenda.

Let's Ask Clio, the Historians' Muse

Discussions about and movements to achieve statehood are not unique to Puerto Rico and Washington, D.C. In fact, almost every state, except for the original 13 colonies, has gone through the same general stages: acquisition through expansion, annexation as territory and, finally, admission to the Union by Congress.

An examination of previous cases of statehood, from Vermont in 1791 to Alaska and Hawaii in 1959, offers valuable insights into current efforts in Puerto Rico and the District of Columbia, as well as the types of challenges they face and will continue to face.

Debates about statehood have generally included five sets of issues, all of which are at play today. First, specifically between 1800 and 1860, the admission of new states was tied to the issue of balance of power in Congress between Northern free states and Southern slave states. The current state of partisan and sectional polarization echoes antebellum levels, resulting in intractable party-line positions on statehood requests.

Historically, matters of race and ethnicity (including language and religion) have also been part of statehood debates. This was true in the vast territories carved out of land annexed during the Mexican American War, in discussions surrounding the proposed annexation of the predominantly mixed-race Dominican Republic (1868–1871), and more recently, in Alaska and Hawaii. This has been the case all along in Puerto Rico. While not openly discussed, the fact that Washington, D.C.'s population is 47 percent Black and 11 percent

Hispanic/Latino weighs into a portion of the electorate and its representatives' positions on the subject.

A third factor relates to civil rights, particularly the moral issue of having second-class U.S. citizens who are denied certain rights, such as the right to political representation, despite paying federal taxes. Proponents of statehood for Washington, D.C., loudly echo the rebel colonists' slogan, "Taxation without representation is tyranny."

Fourth and fifth are the intertwined questions of whether new states can contribute to the federal government's treasury or will become a burden on it, and how statehood would impact state-level finances and taxation.

8

The 2020 U.S. Census: Historical Precedents and What Censuses Tell Us about Populations and Power, Past and Present

(Creators Syndicate, August 21, 28, September 4, 2021)

Every 10 years, as mandated by the U.S. Constitution, the federal government conducts a national census. Earlier this month, the Bureau of the Census released the first detailed results of the 2020 census, which gives a total count of 331,449,281 people. Further details will roll out periodically over the next few months and years.

Censuses are invaluable sources for historians, social scientists and anyone interested in statistical information about a particular population and how it changes over time. A historian or social scientist's reading of a census, moreover, can also shed light on matters of political and social power. Understanding census categories and questions (who formulates them? how they change over time?) is important for an understanding of the results they produce.

Censuses date back to ancient Egypt, where populations were counted primarily for tax purposes. Romans later elaborated a complex system of enumeration—the English word census comes from the Latin "censere," meaning "to estimate." The Roman state was particularly interested in knowing how many men were available to fight in wars. The New Testament mentions one such census, which coincided with the birth of Jesus Christ.

American Censuses

The 2020 census is the 24th in the nation's history; the first one dates to 1790. Its origins and initial purposes were in sharp contrast with earlier ones in other parts of the world. Not only did early U.S. censuses reflect the demographic realities of the newly formed states, but also the worldview—warts and all—of the Founding Fathers who created them. Rather than being used for tax assessments, land confiscation or conscription, American censuses primarily served the republican and democratic objectives of the new nation whose constitution prescribed that the apportionment of congressional seats for each state be based on population.

Most contemporary American social scientists believe that race is socially constructed and maintain that the racial classification of humans lacks any scientific foundation. Human genome and genetic studies conducted over the last three decades, however, point to five genetically distinct human groups clustered around specific geographic regions: Africa, Europe, East Asia, the Americas, and Oceania.

Whatever the case, governments, organizations, businesses, and society still find racial classifications useful. The federal government, for example, uses census information on race and ethnicity for affirmative action purposes; organizations ranging from the Native American Journalists Association to Black Lives Matter to the Asian Law Caucus embrace specific race categories as matters of identity that foster group solidarity.

The creation and subsequent transmutations of racial and ethnic census categories are reflections of political, social, and even individual power. Historically, those who held federal political power, such as legislators and census officials, have determined which racial and ethnic categories are used. Throughout most of the U.S. census' history, enumerators on the ground have enjoyed some discretionary power to ascertain individuals' race and ethnicity. Meanwhile, interest groups from Antebellum slave masters to the League of United Latin American Citizens, or LULAC, have lobbied, sometimes successfully, for the creation or elimination of racial and ethnic categories. And since 1970, individuals have had the power to determine their own race and/or ethnicity through self-identification.

America's First Census (1790)

The first and subsequent censuses up to the Civil War mirrored the reality that while "all men are created equal," not all ought to be counted equally. The Three-Fifths Compromise in the Constitution meant that the 697,625 slaves enumerated in 1790 counted as 418,574 for electoral apportionment purposes. Southern states insisted on counting slaves but denied them the right to vote. America's native inhabitants, with very few exceptions, were ignored until 1860 and seldom counted prior to 1900.

America's early censuses used demographic categories deemed important by federal legislators and reflected the hierarchical and discriminatory nature of society. At the top of the hierarchy were free, white, male heads of household; Black slaves were placed at the bottom.

Federal marshals who conducted the first census were instructed to disaggregate the white population by sex (males and females), and in the case of white males, for military purposes, by age (over and under 16). Age distinctions were not considered important enough among free white females, "all other persons," and slaves. Generally, only the names of free, white male heads of households appeared in census rolls; occasionally, so did those of white female widows and some free people of color.

Because census information is generally presented and used only in numbers and percentages, we lose sight of the fact that those statistics are aggregations of real flesh-and-bone individuals. Let's look, for example, at the 1790 census results for the town of Stratford, Connecticut. Assistant marshal Samuel B. Sherwood counted 3,241 inhabitants in 548 different households. Among the town's heads of households was a man named Stiles Lewis, whose household included another white male over the age of 16, two males under 16, most likely his sons, seven females, presumably his wife and daughters, and one of Stratford's 98 slaves.

Two lines down on the ledger, we see another head of household identified simply as "Toby (negro)," no last name, along with three others classified as "other free persons." Among the handful of white female heads of households, we see a "Hannah Hoyt (Wid.)" who lived with another female (unclear as to whether she was a daughter, a sister or some other woman or girl), and one anonymous slave (sex not specified, presumably female).

Nineteenth-Century Censuses

With the passing of time, census categories were expanded and adjusted to better serve the statistical needs of government, industry, and society. The second census, in 1800, divided the free white population, male and female, into five age brackets. The 1820 census began to break down "slaves" and "the free colored" into sex and age subcategories and opened a new category for non-naturalized foreigners.

In the 1840s, slavery and its expansion became increasingly divisive and politicized issues, pitting northern abolitionists and slaves seeking freedom against increasingly defensive and violent pro-slavery white southerners. The period also saw a peak in anti-immigrant sentiments.

The 1850 census included new questions and categories that reflected the intensifying conflict over slavery and immigration. It further emphasized distinctions between free and slave with the use of two different schedules: "No. 1—Free Inhabitants," and "No. 2—Slave Inhabitants."

In response to contemporary pseudoscientific debates about the effects of racial mixing, the 1850 census introduced the "mulatto" category to distinguish color gradations among slaves. New questions were added on the escape or manumission of slaves and their physical traits and mental capacities.

Slavery advocates called for such information to demonstrate that race mixing produced inferior offspring who were more likely to flee and be "deaf and dumb, blind, insane or idiotic," while abolitionists marshalled that type of information to prove, as William H. Seward put it, the rapid progress of the African race.

Responding to interest in information on the growing proportion of immigrants, particularly Catholics, the 1850 census recorded for the first time information on the place of birth of all free inhabitants. The growth in immigration from southern and eastern Europe beginning in the 1870s led to new census inquiries about "mother tongue" and parents' and grandparents' place of birth.

Beginning in the 1850s, tens of thousands of Chinese workers settled in the United States, particularly in California, where they labored as miners, farmers, and railroad construction workers. In 1860, the census classified Chinese residents as "white" but 10 years later added "Chinese" as a new "color" category which also included other East Asians. As Chinese immigration increased over the next two decades, so did racist sentiments that culminated with the Chinese Exclusion Act of 1882, that suspended further Chinese immigration for a decade. Deemed more likely to assimilate to American society, Japanese immigrants were separated from the Chinese beginning in the 1890 census.

Reconstruction- and Jim Crow-era Southern white supremacist ideology filtered into late-century censuses through a host of new racial categories whose object was to establish even firmer distinctions between white and Black citizens and to implement the so-called one-drop rule, which stipulated that individuals with small and barely noticeable African ancestry be categorized as not white. In 1890, census enumerators received instructions to register as "black" anyone having "three-fourths or more black blood," as "mulatto" those who have "from three-eighths to five-eighths black blood," as "quadroon," anyone having "one-fourth black blood," and "those persons who have one-eighth or any trace of black blood" as "octoroons."

Twentieth- and Twenty-First Century Censuses

After dropping the "mulatto" racial category in 1900, the U.S. Census Bureau revived it in 1910 and 1920, then got rid of it for good in 1930, when enumerators received instructions to designate as "Negro" any person "of mixed white and Negro blood ... no matter how small the percentage of Negro blood."

Curiously, in previous censuses Black and/or mulatto census enumerators tended to apply the "mulatto" race designation more often than white enumerators, who were more inclined to follow the one-drop rule of blackness. W.E.B. Dubois and other Black leaders, for their part, deemed the mulatto distinction as divisive and injurious to solidarity among Blacks.

The 1930 census saw other changes, among them the creation of a "Mexican race." Previously, Mexicans were categorized mostly as white, but some were designated as mulatto regardless of whether they had African ancestry or not. The racialization of Mexicans responded to apprehensions about the growing Mexican population in states like Texas, New Mexico, Arizona, and California. Most of them, however, were neither immigrants nor descendants of immigrants. As some Chicanos are fond of pointing out, it was the U.S.-Mexico border that "migrated" south during the Mexican American War of 1846.

Mexican U.S. residents and lobby groups as well as the Mexican government protested the new "Mexican" racial label because it removed all Mexican-born individuals and those who had Mexican parents from the white category, regardless of their "actual race." Mexican leaders and groups such as LULAC succeeded, forcing the census to revert to the designation of Mexicans as white.

The first half of the twentieth century saw other uses of census information to further separate white people from other groups, denote their racial and social supremacy and promote a homogeneous population of British and Western European stock. The Immigration Act of 1924 sought to reduce immigration from Eastern and Southern Europe by establishing national immigration quotas based on population proportions dating back to the 1890 census. The 1924 law excluded Japanese immigrants altogether, and during WWII, census officials provided information that the military used to round up and intern around 120,000 Americans of Japanese birth or descent.

By 1936, the census had established the race and nationality categories that continue to be used up to the present. It recognized three races—white, Negro, (American) Indian—and various Asian and Asian Pacific Islander nationalities.

The next major change happened in 1980—I was 20 at the time and worked as a census enumerator while studying at the university. Besides the long-established questions about race and nationality, the 1980 census asked individuals whether they were "Spanish/Hispanic" or not. Those who responded affirmatively were required to self-identify as belonging to one of the following: "Mexican, Mexican American, Chicano," "Puerto Rican," "Cuban" or "other Spanish/Hispanic." Much to the consternation of many in Spain, Spaniards are not recorded as white as is the case for other Europeans; Egyptians and Lebanese people, contrastingly, are designated white.

With the passing of time, certain racial labels have changed to align census questionnaires with more current taxonomies. In 2000, "Spanish/Hispanic" was expanded to "Spanish/Latino/Hispanic" and the term "African American" was added to "Black/Negro." Long obsolete and widely considered offensive, the word "Negro" was removed only in 2020.

Since 1970, the U.S. census has offered an "other race" option. The number and proportion of American residents checking that category has increased sharply since 2000, as demonstrated by an exhaustive study which concluded that from 2000 to 2010, 10 million Americans changed their race/ethnicity self-designation; 2.5 million individuals who self-identified as "Hispanic" and "some other race" in 2000 changed to "Hispanic" and "white" a decade later.

The most recent reminder of the fact that census questions and categories are never politically neutral and are often controversial was the Trump administration's attempt to include citizenship questions in the 2020 census. The proposed questions, whose inclusion was blocked by the U.S. Supreme Court in the summer of 2019, paralleled yet another peak in nativism and anti-immigrant sentiment. The administration wanted to know not only who was a citizen and who was not, but also who had been naturalized and whether citizens had been born in the United States, in U.S. territories or in other countries.

In 2004, the journal *Migration News* prognosticated the possibility that "by 2050, today's racial and ethnic categories will no longer be in use." That may happen or may not, but the trend is in that direction.

9

Is That a Constitution in Your Pocket?

(Creators Syndicate, March 20, 2021)

Some of the most unwavering champions of the U.S. Constitution and Bill of Rights have habitually carried printed copies of the nation's law of the land in their pockets or purses. Among them are individuals ranging from eminent past legislators such as African American former Congresswoman Barbara Jordan from Texas and former Senator Chris Dodd of Connecticut—the latter once said that his staff teased him for always walking around with one in his pocket— to jurists such as former Supreme Court Justice Hugo Black and Connecticut Supreme Court's first Black justice Robert Davis Glass, who said in an interview, that he had "worn out several copies"—to non-politician defenders of civil rights such as the late Peter Jennings, who anchored ABC's "World News Tonight."

With varying levels of theatricality, some politicians have pulled out pocket-sized copies of the Constitution and shaken them in the air for visual impact. Former Senator Sam Ervin of North Carolina did it in a hearing of the Senate Watergate Committee. In 1995, during a debate about the line-item veto, then-Senator Robert Byrd of West Virginia raised his dog-eared copy while denouncing some of his colleagues' support for such a provision as an act of "collective madness." With much foresight, he cautioned against its potential abuse by some future "power-hungry president."

Fresher in our memory, Gold Star father Khizr Khan raised a copy of the Constitution during his speech at the 2016 National Democratic Convention. "Have you even read the United States Constitution?" Khan asked America's power-hungry bibliophobe-in-chief. "I will gladly lend you my copy."

While miniature books are almost as old as printed books themselves—one of Johann Gutenberg's assistants is credited with binding one in 1468—I could not find any mention of a miniature or pocket U.S. Constitution printed during the lifetimes of any of its signers. Earlier today, however, I did find a pocket first edition (1791) of the French Constitution for sale on eBay for a little over $500. Tempted, but did not buy it.

George Washington had a specially bound 1789 regular-size personal copy of the U.S. Constitution. The Mount Vernon Library bought it at a Christie's auction in 2012 for a record-shattering $9.8 million.

Khan's famous pocket copy has become a piece of American political history in its own right; it is now housed 83 miles south of Washington's Mount Vernon estate among the holdings of the Virginia Museum of History & Culture. One of its pages bears the handwritten signature of former President Barack Obama.

In 1865, the year of Lincoln's second presidential inauguration and assassination, Taggard & Thompson published a miniature edition of the Constitution that also included the Declaration of Independence, George Washington's Farewell Address and Lincoln's Emancipation Proclamation, along with portraits of the first and 16th presidents.

In the aftermath of World War I, several U.S. publishers included miniature copies of the Constitution among their tiny-book offerings, which were sold for pennies at Woolworth and similar stores. But the mass printing of pocket Constitutions would only come a century later following the resolution of Congressman Wayne Hays of Ohio calling for the printing of thousands of pocket-sized copies by the Government Publishing Office.

Since its dramatic display at the 2016 Democratic National Convention and throughout Trump's presidency, sales of pocket Constitutions have skyrocketed. They became an Amazon bestseller days after said convention.

The pocket Constitution's soaring popularity extends far beyond Democrats and civil rights advocates. Purchases among conservatives increased after the founding of the Tea Party in 2009 and have multiplied because many conservatives invoke it in support of causes such as the protection of the Second Amendment, the so-called American lands movement, opposition to the separation of church and state, and what they claim to be excessive government intervention in people's lives.

Some radical conservatives such as Utah's Senator Michael Lee and not a few among January 6's Capitol Building assailants carry and display apocryphal versions annotated with the words of archconservative author W. Cleon Skousen, whom even notorious Red Scare-era Senator Joseph McCarthy deemed too extreme.

With so many millions of pocket Constitutions in circulation, and dozens bulging and popping in and out of politicians' pockets, one would expect that Americans would have at least some basic knowledge of the nation's constitutional foundations. But survey after survey continue to document the general population's ignorance about the Constitution. The Annenberg Public Policy Center's latest poll on the subject showed that only half of Americans can name the three branches of government.

Carrying a copy in one's pocket is a symbolic action, but unless we read and respect the Constitution, democracy remains at risk.

Ignorance is the greatest domestic threat to our democracy. Teachers are our first responders.

Rough Drafts of History: U.S. Society and Politics, 2019–2022

Introduction

The idea that journalism and newspapers are the first or the rough draft of history is widely attributed to Philip L. Graham, former president and publisher of the *Washington Post*, who once said that "journalism is the first rough draft of history." Etymologist Barry Popik has found, however, earlier iterations of that idea including a 1905 newspaper story that appeared in Columbia, South Carolina's *The State*: "newspapers are making morning after morning the rough draft of history."

I am both a veteran historian with seven scholarly books under my belt and a rookie opinion columnist, my first regular columns appearing as recently as February 2019. Having worked in both capacities I find the connections, and disconnections, between journalism and history intriguing and fascinating. Historians and op-ed writers are expected to aspire to good, dare I say pleasing, prose. Historians actually pride ourselves on being better writers than our disciplinary cousins in sociology and political science—there is no Pulitzer Prize for those fields; and we have a muse named Clio—and some of my colleagues in both fields attempt to infuse literary value into their work.

Research, which is the cornerstone of historical writing, is also essential to good editorial writing. I once heard George Will say that he spent far more time researching than he did writing.

There are differences between my two fields, of course. As a historian who publishes books and journal articles, I have the luxury of revisiting those manuscripts numerous times which allows me to think, rethink, and rethink again my arguments and polish and polish and polish the prose. Historians face deadlines but it is nothing like weekly columnists. As a syndicated columnist I must hit the send button every Friday before 7:00 pm lest I turn into a pumpkin. Dairy farmers must milk their cows every day and columnists must milk out a column (sometimes two) every week. There is no respite.

Another difference is that opinion columnists write mostly about recent or ongoing topics and events, and, therefore, do not have the advantage of hindsight that historians enjoy when we turn in our final article or book manuscripts. By the same token, columns generally have a short shelf life. But these apparent disadvantages endow opinion columns with their own unique value. They become chronicles that capture what seems important at the moment of their creation, information and commentary that might be dismissed with the disadvantage of hindsight.

In journalism, news reporting and editorials are kept strictly separate. But reporting is an integral part of op-ed writing. The eight columns in this section are a combination of reporting, in several instances, play-by-play (even blow-by-blow) and opinion/analysis. Some readers may find that my columns have too much reporting and too little opinion. I intentionally wrote them that way.

Columns in this section offer narrative reporting intertwined with commentary about some of the most tumultuous—the book title refers to them as "unimaginable"—events of 2019–2022: the public execution of George Floyd and the massive protests and riots it sparked, the acrimonious primaries and political campaigns of 2020, and most unbelievable of all, the January 6, Trump-instigated attack on the U.S. Capitol, all this shrouded in a cloud of unprecedented global pestilence.

This section includes the column "Do the Riots in Minneapolis Forebode Greater Civil Unrest?"; and what I see as this section's *piece de resistance*, "Fifty-Five Hours Binge-Watching the Never-Before-Seen and the Unimaginable (America, January 4–6, 2021)" which begins: "Notepad and pen in my right hand, TV remote control in the other, caffeine doses taken as needed. This will be a news-heavy week." That, of course, turned out to be a gross understatement.

10

Democratic Socialism in the United States: Does Bernie Sanders Need Rebranding?

(The Globe Post, February 28, 2019)

Why does U.S. Senator and 2020 presidential candidate Bernie Sanders hold on to the socialist label when so few people know what it means, and so many are repelled by the term? Should he discard it?

Socialism, like many words, means different things to different people in different places, at different times. Karl Marx defined it as an intermediate stage in the process of building a communist society, where a purportedly worker-run state owns all the means of production (factories, warehouses, and croplands) and takes care of all the population's needs.

In Europe, socialism means a capitalist system in which a democratic state taxes and regulates private corporations to limit their excesses, to keep them from exploiting workers, and to protect consumers and the environment. Such societies recognize that private corporations are better at making cars and selling TV sets while governments are better at providing basic services like education and healthcare.

So, What Is Socialism?

In the United States, those who hold positive views of socialism tend to accept the democratic European definition, as in Scandinavian countries, Francois Mitterrand's France, and perhaps even Canada. Only a miniscule minority of Americans sympathize with, let alone embrace, anything that remotely approximates Marxist socialism.

For a substantial proportion of those who hold negative views of socialism, Republicans in particular, the term conjures images of Soviet or Cuban despotism, repression of dissidents, and generalized misery. Marx, Vladimir Lenin, Mao Zedong, Che Guevara, and Fidel Castro are mere ghosts, however, in a world in which only the dictatorial side of communism survives and where oligarchic and state capitalism thrive.

A 2015 Gallup poll demonstrated how unpopular socialism was among U.S. voters. Respondents were given a list of eleven racial, religious, and ideological characteristics and were asked if they would vote for presidential candidates with any of those traits or affiliations (Jewish, atheist, Black, Catholic, gay or lesbian, woman, Mormon, Hispanic, Muslim, socialist, and Evangelical Christian).

Between 91 and 93 percent of respondents said that they would vote for a Catholic, Jewish, woman, Hispanic, or Black candidate. The only category below 50 percent acceptance was socialist. At 47 percent it ranked as the least desirable trait among all ages and party affiliations, below atheist (58 percent) and Muslim (60 percent).

A more recent Gallup poll (2018) asked respondents whether they had a positive or negative view of socialism. Results demonstrated a wide gap between Democrats/leaning and Republicans/leaning, with 57 percent of the first group holding a positive view of socialism versus 16 percent in the second. The poll reflected that for the first time, Democrats/leaning viewed socialism more favorably than capitalism, mostly the result of the sharp fall in favorability of capitalism from 56 percent in 2016 to 47 percent in 2018.

Views of socialism varied widely among age groups, with 51 percent of individuals between 18 and 29 holding a favorable view; down to 41 percent among those 30–49; and sinking below 30 percent among those 50 or older.

Misrepresentations of Socialism

President Donald J. Trump and other Republican politicians are astutely taking advantage of Senator Sanders' and Congresswoman Alexandria Ocasio-Cortez's socialist self-labeling, painting them as extremists and Marxist socialists out to destroy capitalism. That is "fake news." Rather than seeking the destruction of capitalism, Sanders and Ocasio-Cortez want to make it fair and work for all, not just the top 1 or 10 percent.

The democratic socialist label is becoming toxic also among progressive Democratic presidential candidates and potential candidates, who know very well what Sanders and Ocasio-Cortez mean by that term. In recent days, Congressman Beto O'Rourke described himself as a capitalist; Senator Kamala Harris, who is further to his left, categorically denied that she is a democratic socialist; even Senator Elizabeth Warren proudly proclaimed, "I am a capitalist to my bones."

Supercapitalism

The extremism is on the other side of the political spectrum, among those who promote and seek what Professor Robert Reich called supercapitalism: a brutal, unethical, and corrupt get-out-of-my-way economic system, that instead of promoting the much-hailed doctrine of free-market competition seeks to crush it with the establishment of monopolies and crony capitalism.

This radical brand of capitalism, short of amiable to democracy, thrives on the destruction of representative democracy. Russia and China are cases in point. It is not a coincidence that in the United States voter suppression and other threats to democracy have spiked parallel to the rise of extreme capitalism.

At the risk of being labeled a communist, I will say that Marx may have been onto something when he said that capitalism contained the seeds of its own destruction. What an irony that supercapitalists seem to be destroying what Franklin D. Roosevelt himself derided as socialist, saved from a fatal implosion. Eight decades later, Barack Obama, who was also scorned as a socialist, took effective measures to keep the global financial system from blowing into pieces.

What should Senator Sanders do? He should continue to push democratic socialist ideas, ideas that, by the way, are becoming mainstream Democratic agendas, even among those who refuse that label. He should not follow the expedient rebranding steps of most Democratic politicians who, beginning in the 1990s, ran from the "liberal" label, so proudly worn by Roosevelt, John F. Kennedy, and even Jimmy Carter.

Sanders must relentlessly educate voters about the meaning of democratic socialism, sticking to one clear and succinct definition; and go as far as proclaiming that socialism is the best defense of traditional capitalism, representative democracy, peace, and the environment.

11

Do the Riots in Minneapolis Forbode Greater Civil Unrest?

(The Globe Post, June 3, 2020)

I sit down to write in the wee hours of May 29, 2020. The city of Minneapolis is ablaze. Pandemonium broke out four or five hours ago, as thousands of angry, mourning protesters surrounded the headquarters of the police 3rd Precinct. Protesters, some of whom engaged in vandalism and arson, demanded justice for George Floyd, the 46-year-old Black man who was summarily murdered on Monday by Minneapolis policeman Derek Chauvin with the assistance of other police officers.

"Chauvin" is a French word that originally meant militaristic and later came to mean extreme nationalism. It is the root of the word "chauvinism." The cult to all things military, the militarization of police departments, the insatiable self-arming of millions of Americans, and white nationalism are cresting in this polarized and increasingly violent nation.

Earlier this week, the COVID-19 pandemic reached a death toll of 100,000, a lugubrious milestone that had to compete for media attention with the death of a single Black man named Floyd, who like many pandemic victims died because he could no longer breathe.

Around 1 a.m., protesters set the police precinct on fire. It might as well have been Nero's Rome in 64 AD or the Bastille on July 14, 1789. There is also unrest and looting in the city's smaller twin, named in honor of the martyred St. Paul, who was decapitated in the aftermath of the Great Fire of Rome. Contrary to popular belief, Nero did not play the violin—that instrument would be invented in Italy 15 centuries later. As the Eternal City burned, he blamed the disaster on the city's Christian population.

Minneapolis and St. Paul, deemed among the most progressive cities in the United States, border the mighty Mississippi River. But what transpired on Monday, May 25 at the dawn of the third decade of the twenty-first century seems to come out of the annals of post-Civil War Mississippi or scenes from the film *Mississippi Burning* based on the 1964 execution of three Black civil rights activists, James Chaney, Andrew Goodman, and Michael Schwerner by a murderous KKK band.

The Killing of George Floyd

On Tuesday, May 26, along with millions of viewers around the world, I watched the video of Floyd's murder. Unfortunately, we have become used to seeing videos of white police officers killing unarmed Black men, but Floyd's case is especially harrowing.

Floyd was a corpulent tall man capable of resisting anybody attempting to restrain him, yet he remained calm and compliant. His demeanor was that of a meek and friendly person, characteristics that had earned him the nickname Gentle Giant.

Floyd's torment lasted over seven minutes and was captured on video with audio. The footage shows a handcuffed Floyd, lying face-down on the pavement while Chauvin pressed his knee onto Floyd's neck. Another video from the opposite angle shows two other policemen crouched over his body.

And to think that this week had been hyped to be a milestone of American power and civilization with the scheduled launch of a crewed rocket from Cape Canaveral. The launch had to be postponed because of thunderstorms.

Chauvin essentially sentenced Floyd to death by garrote, a method of execution by strangulation that suffocates its victims. The garrote is another gift from first-century Rome. Spanish conquistadors brought it to the Americas and used it to kill the Inca Atahualpa in 1533 and hundreds of other victims, among the last was Venezuelan-born filibusterer Narciso López, commander of ill-starred expeditions seeking to free Cuba from Spain.

"I Can't Breathe"

Equally horrific were Floyd's final words. With an increasingly guttural voice, he pleads repeatedly with his tormentor: "My neck hurts. Everything hurts"; "Water or something, please. I can't breathe."

The agonizing man continues to demonstrate respect for his tormentors: please, please.... Not one curse or angry word comes out of his lips which are taking on the whitish hue of death; he calls his deceased mother as if knowing that he will soon meet her—or has already met her—on the other side. He goes silent, the video capturing the quiet, motionless moment of his passing.

Buildings continue to burn in the Twin Cities. The air is thick with smoke and hundreds of masked protesters chant Floyd's final words: "Please, I can't breathe.... Please, I can't breathe...."

At around 2 a.m. President Donald Trump tweets impulsively, calling the protesters "THUGS," deriding the boyish-looking mayor of Minneapolis as a radical leftist, and vowing to take control of the situation by force. "When the looting starts," he tweeted ominously, "the shooting starts." A couple of hours later, Twitter labeled the president's tweet: "glorifying violence."

On the eve of Floyd's death, I had watched the last episode of the History Channel three-part documentary on another president, Ulysses S. Grant, and teared up at the reconstructed scene of Confederate veterans massacring scores of Black people in Louisiana in 1873. They had been freed 10 years earlier. The film highlighted the unfinished and failed character of post-Civil War Reconstruction.

A few hours later, or 147 years later, I found myself tearing up again at the sight of Floyd's public lynching.

The nation is as polarized as it was during Reconstruction and the parallels between the last 10 years and the Antebellum are glaring and foreboding.

The smell of civil war is in the air.

12

Pandemic, Pandemonium, and the November 2020 Elections

(The Globe Post, June 4, 2020)

This is June 2, the eighth night of mass protests across America and once again I feel compelled to sit down and put pen to paper.

The sun has not yet set on the East Coast. I am watching live TV footage of scores of mass demonstrations. What started as protests in the Twin Cities and a handful of other urban centers, has spread faster and more virulently than the COVID-19 virus. Tens of thousands are marching across America, from Miami to Seattle; from San Diego to Boston; from Houston to Chicago, and in many major cities in between.

If history offers any lesson, these mobilizations will escalate on and after June 4, the day of George Floyd's funeral and June 9, when his burial is scheduled.

There are numerous instances in history in which assassinations and martyrdom, and the burials that followed, have sparked protests and even mass rebellions. The assassination of progressive Colombian presidential candidate Jorge Eliécer Gaitán (1948) ignited a bloody revolt that unleashed a decade of political violence, with a death toll of 200,000.

Twenty years later, Martin Luther King Jr.'s assassination sparked a wave of riots and social unrest, at a level not seen since the Civil War.

More recently, in 1977, the brutal execution by torture of South African anti-apartheid activist Steve Biko was, according to Nelson Mandela, "the spark that lit a veld fire across South Africa."

Cracks in Trump's Coalition

The current protests are no longer solely about justice for the murder of George Floyd. His death has triggered an outpour of collective indignation among masses of Americans of all races but especially among the working poor, the unemployed, and many who live in constant fear of losing their jobs, health insurance (if they are fortunate to have one), and homes.

For all that has been said about the indolence and apathy of millennials and generation Z, they are the spearhead of a progressive movement of the sort not seen since 1968.

The dynamics have changed substantially in the last 24 hours. Marches that started on May 25 as human brooks flowing through city streets have turned torrential—veritable oceans of people—as aerial views attest.

President Trump's bravado, his heavy-handed response toward protesters in Washington, D.C., threats of dominating cities by military force, and his Bible-holding stunt in front of the boarded-up St. John's Episcopal Church have elicited much criticism. The judgment comes not just from the usual voices but from sectors of his loyal coalition, including some Republican politicians, police and military forces, and even from some in his staunchest base, conservative Evangelicals.

Republican Senator Ben Sasse castigated the Commander in Chief for "clearing out a peaceful protest for a photo op that treats the Word of God as a political prop." Even conservative Evangelical leader Pat Robertson criticized the president's actions.

More dramatic is TV footage of police officers and even National Guardsmen warmly embracing protesters, marching arm in arm with them, and kneeling in commemoration of Floyd's murder.

Those are the first cracks in Trump's coalition.

Wrong Direction

It is now 11:40 p.m. and newscasters begin to report on today's electoral results. Voters are speaking loudly. Republican primary voters crushed the re-election plans of the unabashedly racist Congressman Steve King of Iowa; minutes later, CNN and MSNBC report that Ella Jones has been elected as the first Black mayor of Ferguson, Missouri, the city where back in August 2014 a white police-man killed 18-year-old Black man Michael Brown, an event that ignited several nights of rioting and the expansion of the Black Lives Matter movement.

The president's handling of the ongoing peaceful antiracist protests has fur-ther eroded his popularity and electoral support. Today's Monmouth Poll reports that a whopping 74 percent of registered voters believe that the country is head-ing in the wrong direction; tellingly 78 percent of independents feel that way.

Presidential Election

Fast forward to November 3. Looking from today's perspective it is not clear what will transpire on election day. At the top of the Democratic party ticket, it is clear, will be Joe Biden.

Amy Klobuchar, it has also become clear, will not be Biden's ticket mate. In the past 10 days she has gone from apparent front-runner to unacceptable, not because she is white but because as Hennepin County attorney, she earned a tough-on-criminals reputation.

It has also become clear that the Democratic Party and its presidential can-didate will be pushed further left by the Bernie Sanders–Elizabeth Warren wing of the party. Biden will not be allowed to govern as a Wall Street Democrat, that is for sure.

Things do not look good for Trump whose coattails are likely to drag Republican candidates to defeat. That Mike Pence will be Trump's running mate is not a done deal. Known for his lack of loyalty, Trump would drop Pence if he believed that another politician, perhaps a woman, would help him win the elections.

I am not exaggerating when I say that the November elections are in jeop-ardy. First, the anticipated second peak of the COVID-19 pandemic will keep tens or hundreds of thousands of voters home. The vote by mail option has not received funding because of Mitch McConnell's partisan obstructionism; President Trump has repeatedly said, without any evidence, that voting by mail invites fraud and his brilliant son-in-law Jared Kushner has dared to say that it is possible that the elections will have to be postponed. Oh, did I fail to mention Russian intervention?

There is nothing in Trump's personality, value system, and record that guarantees that he will step down from power quietly and gracefully. It is more likely that he will challenge the elections, spew hatred, and mobilize his well-armed base. A smooth collaborative transition is also unimaginable.

It is now 3:15 a.m. on June 2. Everything indicates that today's protests have been more peaceful than yesterday's; that is a good sign. As I am about to turn off CNN news, I see footage of a white Florida policeman kneeling to pray with protesters. That is another good sign.

I anticipate having a better night's sleep tomorrow. For now, I am convinced that if the unimaginable happens in November, larger crowds will flood the streets, and American soldiers, National Guardsmen, and police officers will not fire upon them.

13

June 14–June 20, 2020: Trump's Worst Week to Date?

(The Globe Post, June 22, 2020)

It is 11 p.m. (Juneteenth Day, 2020) on the East Coast of the United States. I was hoping to go to bed earlier but have learned about some new developments in President Donald Trump's administration while watching "The Rachel Maddow Show" on MSNBC.

What a news week! (perhaps Trump's worst to date): COVID-19 cases are rising sharply while pandemic deniers in the White House and in not a few governors' mansions play statistical gymnastics to downplay the number of cases and deaths.

The Supreme Court (where two of Trump's appointees sit) rules to extend employment protections for LGBTQ individuals and then to limit the government's authority to deport immigrants protected by DACA. Those are two major defeats for the Trump administration.

Out of magnanimity, Trump postpones his Tulsa, Oklahoma political rally from Juneteenth—a day he takes credit for making "very famous"—to Saturday, June 20. Oklahoma and Tulsa are experiencing a spike in coronavirus cases.

Some of his most ardent supporters have camped outside the arena for days, willing to sign documents releasing Trump and his campaign from any responsibility in case they contract the coronavirus. Social distancing will be impossible, and neither the president nor many of his supporters will wear masks, in defiance of the recommendations of Anthony Fauci, Deborah Birx, and hundreds of other health experts. The president's campaign brags that one million supporters have acquired tickets to the Tulsa rally.[1]

Wait, there is more. Footage of former National Security Advisor John Bolton's interview with Martha Raddatz has hit the TV waves. Bolton's tell-all book *The Room Where It Happened* is filled with scathing criticism of Trump. In another defeat for the White House, a federal judge ruled against the administration's petition to delay the book's publication, which is scheduled for June 23.

Earlier this week, RealClear Politics published its latest poll averages report. Even more bad news for Trump: he trails behind Joe Biden nationwide (41 to 55 percent) and is losing in the key battleground states of Florida, Pennsylvania, Wisconsin, North Carolina, and Arizona, all of which he carried in 2016. Trump's response: we are winning in our own polls.

In the last quarter of her show, Rachel Maddow presents an exclusive story on the June 17 shakedown at the U.S. Agency for Global Media, which includes the Voice of America Network. Calling it the Wednesday night massacre, Maddow gives a play-by-play account of what transpired at the traditionally nonpartisan agency. Double Pulitzer Prize winner Amanda Bennett, head of the agency, and Sandy Sugawara, the second in command, suddenly resign from their positions; Trump nominates Michael Pack to take over and the Republican-dominated Senate sheepishly assents; he proceeds to fire the heads of all the agency's regional networks and their entire advisory boards.

Neither Pack nor his newly appointed network directors have backgrounds in journalism or diplomacy. His claim to fame: being a mentee of right-wing media executive Steve Bannon and producing poor quality films. As a good friend of mine would say, Pack "is a man of discreet quality."

9:52 p.m. Before the blood of the Wednesday massacre has dried up, more slaughter unfolds. A seemingly shocked Maddow announces that she has received breaking news. After a commercial break, she reports that Attorney General William Barr has announced the resignation of Geoffrey Berman, U.S. Attorney for the Lower District of New York. Berman, who is currently investigating Rudy

---

1 Two days later, media outlets reported that K-pop fans had encouraged others via TikTok and Twitter to make phony registrations for Trump's rally.

Giuliani and other Trump allies, replies that he has not resigned nor intends to do so.

Saturday, June 20 brings new developments: Berman resigns; Barr says he acted on the president's orders; Trump contradicts Barr, says he had nothing to do with that.

8:30 p.m. Tonight I am watching CNN, whose cameras are focusing on the empty areas of the Tulsa arena that sits 19,000. I switch to Fox News to see what they are doing. No camera shots of the empty seats there, only a close shot of Mike Pence addressing the audience in his characteristic bland monotone.

Trump must be fuming at the sight of a partially full arena. Size matters to him, as he made evident on the day of his inauguration in January 2017, when his campaign mouthpieces falsely claimed record-setting crowds. Official photographs of the Mall looked like one of those comb-over images used in ads promising quasi-miraculous hair growth.

It is 8:50 p.m., and Trump is scheduled to speak in 10 minutes. The crowd is not one million, not 100,000, and not even the 19,000 that could fit in the arena. The overflow of 50,000 MAGA folks that was expected, never materialized.

At 9:03 p.m., Trump is still not there, that is the impression I get from watching CNN. "This is an apple," the news network has been telling us, but their coverage of the rally is sort of bannanish. I check out Fox again, and there he is, giving a strident speech that will last almost two hours. Trump is at his best, or his worst, depending on who you ask.

The past two weeks have witnessed a turning point in the United States and Trump's re-election campaign. Some of his old allies, including armed forces generals, have openly criticized him. Many Evangelicals were displeased with his upside-down-Bible photo op. The highest-ranking African American in the administration, Mary Elizabeth Taylor, resigns.

Biden's poll numbers are the highest they have ever been. Mitch McConnell and his Republican colleagues, silent as tombs.

14

Election-Eve Carpet Bombings, Scarier-Than-Usual Halloween Costumes, and Other Things We May See Before and on Election Day 2020

(Creators Syndicate, October 31, 2020)

As I sit down to start this week's column, the general elections are less than a week away. I see them as the most consequential in U.S. history. Columnist Eugene Robinson wrote earlier this week that these elections are a matter of life and death. If democracy is life and tyranny is death, I fully concur.

One of the most repeated aphorisms about history is that it repeats itself. Historians like me reject that idea but some of us recognize the power of historical thinking and knowledge in anticipating future outcomes.

Polling data is so overwhelmingly and consistently in favor of Democratic presidential candidate Joe Biden that one does not have to be a trained social scientist to predict he will win next Tuesday. Democrats will carry the northern battleground trifecta—Pennsylvania, Michigan, and Wisconsin—and will likely win most other battleground states.

There are a few caveats, however. As I wrote in an earlier column, if demographics and democracy are allowed to run their course, we should see those results. Variables still up in the air include turnout, the extent of voter suppression and intimidation, and assorted wrenches that may be thrown into the process by humans or nature.

Turnout statistics, including registration numbers, early voting, and vote-by-mail reports, point to higher-than-usual voter participation and record-breaking vote totals. At this writing (Friday evening), the U.S. Elections Project has tallied 86.5 million early votes, 55.8 million of them by mail. According to the same source, there are another 35 million outstanding mail-in ballots.

Some things may go wrong (or right, depending on which side you are on), such as even slower-than-expected mail delivery, or massive intimidation of voters through robocalls, emails or heavily armed partisans in and around polling places. Earlier this week, a court in Michigan, the state in which an armed mob stormed the statehouse in May and where a militia band allegedly plotted to kidnap and execute Governor Gretchen Whitmer, blocked a ban on weapons in voting places.[1]

We cannot discount the unimaginable: widespread sabotage, foreign and domestic, of electric grids; roadways and city streets; and internet communications through the spread of computer viruses—digital COVID-20, so to speak. A few hours after I wrote this sentence, disturbing news of Russian hacking of U.S. hospital computer systems hit the news. Couldn't our cyberforces retaliate with a 24-hour blackout of Moscow and St. Petersburg? Not with Trump as commander in chief.

Over the remaining days, we can expect an increase in electoral-campaign carpet-bombing, last-minute revelations about the sins and crimes of candidates. They do not have to be true to cause harm.

Democrats and their sympathizers have engaged in a strategic "bombing" campaign. Anti-Trump tell-all and tell-some books have been rolling off the press at the rate of two per week. In the first two weeks of September alone, these titles hit book stands: *Donald Trump v. The United States, Liar's Circus, Melania and Me, The Useful Idiot, Compromised, Disloyal, Proof of Corruption* and Bob Woodward's *Rage*. Similarly lethal have been the *New York Times'* recurrent exposés of Trump's tax evasion maneuvers, debts, and shady international business deals.

Republican return fire has been mostly ineffective. Low-caliber ordnance like the domestic spying investigation against former president Obama failed to detonate. And Hunter Biden's seemingly fake emails were more of a stink bomb than anything else;[2] not even Fox News fell for that. Moreover, Republicans have

---

1   On October 26, 2022, three militiamen were convicted of aiding domestic terrorists who plotted to kidnap the governor.

2   While the story was originally dismissed by the mainstream media and banned by Twitter and Facebook, in 2022, the *Washington Post, New York Times,* and other

no equivalent to then-FBI Director James Comey's 2016 high-tonnage revelation of a renewed FBI investigation of Trump's opponent.

October 31, it is Halloween. In the past, Halloween nights have been propitious occasions for riots. This time, we can expect—I hope I am wrong—far more tricks than treats and more costumes bought at riot-gear stores than at Party City.

Whether democracy will run its course on election night and the following days is not clear. Having decisive results on election night or even during the wee hours of November 4 is increasingly unlikely.

Trump has stated that he does not want votes to be counted past election night. That, of course, is beyond his power, as such matters are decided at the state level. His obsessive desire to pack the Supreme Court with conservative allies may pay off, however, in the possible scenario of close races in Pennsylvania and elsewhere.

We have a system of checks and balances, every middle-school child knows. But who checks the Supreme Court if Congress fails to check the executive? The people!

---

media verified the authenticity of some of Hunter Biden's computer files that reveal malfeasance and perhaps unlawful activities.

15

Fifty-Five Hours Binge-Watching the Never-Before-Seen and the Unimaginable (America, January 4–6, 2021)

(Creators Syndicate, January 9, 16, 23, 2021)

Notepad and pen in my right hand, TV remote control in the other; caffeine doses taken as needed. This will be a news-heavy week.

January 4, Eve of the U.S. Senate Runoff Elections in Georgia

President Donald Trump is scheduled to speak at 9:00 p.m. in Dalton, Whitfield County, Georgia. Neither MSNBC nor CNN are airing the speech. I am curious as to how far (low) he will go. Will he cross the line and openly call his MAGA "patriots" to arms?

Click, click. Fox News is covering it. Tucker Carlson is on. The MyPillow guy sells his made-in-America wares at 20-minute intervals.

Whitfield County is one of north Georgia's solidly red counties, where Trump and the two sitting Republican senators, David Perdue and Kelly Loeffler, won five weeks ago by 40-point margins.

Marine One has landed, and Trump emerges from its entrails. "USA! USA! USA!" chants the adoring MAGA-capped, unmasked crowd. Wait; that's him. I spot the MyPillow guy in the crowd. Will he sleep well tonight? Will he give us our money back?

"Hello, Georgia," salutes the president. "By the way, there is no way we lost Georgia; there is no way. That was a rigged election."

Tonight's litany of lies is more imaginative than usual. It borders on halluci-nation. Trump takes credit for the power of his coattails, but on November 3, his coattails were shorter than those of a bullfighter's jacket. "I won by a landslide," he claimed. "Mexico paid for the wall." "We are rounding the turn because of the vaccine." But there are no Mexican Government checks. On this day, the United States added close to 200,000 new COVID-19 cases and over 2,000 Americans died of it. It is a turn but for the worse.

Deeply concerned about the January 6 congressional certification of President-elect Joe Biden's victory, Trump nudges his ever-faithful VP. "I hope Mike Pence comes through for us," he says half-jokingly.

Trump calls on Senator Kelly Loeffler: "Kelly, I'd love you to come up and say a few words."

Crowd: "Kelly! Kelly! Kelly! ..."

Loeffler: "I have an announcement, Georgia! On January 6, I will object to the Electoral College vote count!" The MAGA crowd cheers on.

Oh, and regarding the anticipated call to arms, Trump did shout out, "We are going to fight like hell!"

January 5, Runoff Elections Day

Click, click. Back to MSNBC and—click, click—CNN. There is footage of a couple hundred Trump supporters already gathering at D.C.'s Freedom Plaza in preparation for tomorrow's Stop the Steal rally. There was a violent dress rehearsal for it on December 13, with four stabbings and 30 arrests. D.C. Mayor Muriel Bowser has requested National Guard troops be deployed.

The clock strikes 7 p.m., closing time for Georgia's polls. Immediately, the first results pop up on the screen, 1 percent in: Raphael Warnock, 52.2 per-cent; Senator David Perdue, 47.7 percent; Jon Ossoff, 52.3 percent; Senator Kelly Loeffler, 47.8 percent. This will be a long night.

Over the next few hours, as results continue to trickle in, I feel I am watching a Duke-UNC basketball game. At 7:41, the blue team is up by 2 points. At 7:48, Perdue up by one. At 7:49, the blues regain the lead.

On MSNBC, Steve Kornacki is back, clad in khaki pants, his white shirt sleeves rolled up literally and figuratively. How he manages to make phone calls, read text messages, listen to producers through an earpiece, speak with Bryan Williams, read his magic board, and look at the camera all at the same time is beyond comprehension.

Click, click. His counterpart at Fox, Bill Hemmer, is no match; Kornacki is winning by a landslide.

You can hear and read it on the faces of Fox pundits and interviewees. They are not happy. Tucker Carlson is visibly and audibly becoming unhinged. He calls Ossoff the "greasiest little fraud" and, as if it were true and as if it matters, castigates him for having worked for the "dumbest" member of Congress. The image of Congressman Hank Johnson, who is Black, is up on the screen. But wait a minute, Carlson, back in March, you said that another congressperson, Alexandria Ocasio-Cortez, was the dumbest.

Sean Hannity, the King of Fox News, is now on, interviewing the soon-to-be former Dauphin, Donald Trump Jr., who denounces "irregularities" and dead men voting.

Karl Rove tells Hannity that DeKalb County scares him the most, and for good reason, as tens of thousands of early votes are still pending count in one of Georgia's bluest counties.

11:18 p.m.: A large number of DeKalb votes come in, cutting Perdue's lead to 20,000 votes. Warnock has now edged his opponent. An overoptimistic Dana Perino claims that the elections can still go either way.

11:50 p.m.: Vote-count reports continue streaming in. It has become clear that Warnock will win the disputed Senate seat. Ossoff, meanwhile, will likely squeeze a victory of his own. TV networks and news agencies are not yet ready, however, to project winners.

And what if Ossoff's victory margin is less than 0.5 percent? That translates into an automatic recount that can prolong for days, if not weeks of uncertainty about which party will control the Senate.

Click, click. At Fox News, interviewers and interviewees look and sound increasingly somber. It is evident that they have given up hope of keeping the Senate red and have turned their attention to tomorrow, when Congress is scheduled to count the official state elector votes and certify the next president's election.

Senator Marsha Blackburn from Tennessee justifies a congressional overturn of the results by praising the 1876 political deal that ended Reconstruction and opened the floodgates to disenfranchisement, Jim Crow, and lynching. In her state alone, 233 Black people were lynched between 1877 and 1950.

But tonight, the eyes of the nation are on another state, Georgia, incidentally second only to Mississippi in number of documented lynchings, with 589.

It is midnight, January 6, Epiphany Day. At 12:37 a.m., MSNBC and CNN air Warnock's victory speech, much of it a grateful celebration of his parents: his father, a pastor like him, and his 82-year-old mother, whose hands, he tells the audience, "Used to pick somebody else's cotton," and who raised 12 children, of which he was the 11th.

News commentators have repeatedly used the word "historic" to describe Warnock's impending victory. He is about to become Georgia's first Black U.S. senator and one of only three Southern Blacks ever elected to that body. The first was Hiram Revels (1827–1901) from Mississippi—like Warnock, a preacher and a preacher's son.

Two other Black Georgians are in Warnock's and many other Georgians' minds: Martin Luther King Jr., who had pastored Warnock's Atlanta Ebenezer Baptist Church, and the late Congressman John Lewis, Warnock's friend, civil rights giant, and member of his congregation.

Warnock ends his speech quoting Psalm 30: "Weeping may endure for the night, but joy comes in the morning."

Morning of January 6, Washington, D.C.

Trump is scheduled to speak at the so-called Stop the Steal rally around 11:00 a.m. One of his opening acts is his lead personal lawyer, Rudy Giuliani. "This was the worst election in American history," the former "America's Mayor" says. He calls for a "trial by combat."

Fox News is covering the rally. MSNBC and CNN are not. The soon-to-be former president harangues the cheering crowd of several hundred. "Our country will be destroyed," he roars before pointing his followers up Pennsylvania Avenue and saying, "[W]e are going to walk down to the Capitol.... History is going to be made."

Before Trump is finished speaking, hundreds of his followers march toward Capitol Hill to protest the election certification ceremony presided by Vice President Mike Pence, heretofore Trump's most loyal lieutenant. "I hope Mike is going to do the right thing," Trump had just told the crowd. "[I]f Mike Pence does the right thing, we win the election." But newscasts are reporting that Pence has promised to follow the Constitution.

Click, click. PBS is covering the day's events with one eye inside the Capitol, another on the building's periphery. House Majority Leader Nancy Pelosi gavels the joint session into order. First to speak on the side of the count objectors is Republican House minority whip from Louisiana, Steve Scalise. In June 2017, the National Rifle Association A-plus-rated congressman and three other individuals were shot and wounded while at practice for that year's Congressional Baseball Game.

The story unfolding outside the Capitol is outshining the certification debate, and all news networks are now focused on the protest. A couple-thousand-strong sea of Trump supporters lay siege on the nation's—arguably, the world's—most visible monument to democracy. This veritable human moat threatens to overflow inside the building.

The crowd gets larger, louder, and angrier by the minute. Protesters carry a wide assortment of flags: several variations of the American flag, including some with Trump's face and name; several state flags (Arizona's, Maryland's, South Carolina's); scores of Confederate battle flags, yellow "Don't Tread on Me" banners and even ensigns of conspiracy-theory group QAnon.

12:52 p.m., Insurrection

Just eight minutes before the joint session of Congress is set to start, dozens, soon hundreds, of rioters breach the first of several Capitol Police barriers.

TV journalists and commentators on CNN and—click, click—MSNBC are no longer calling this a protest. Some are speaking in what just a few hours ago were unspeakable terms: "insurrection," "sedition," "coup d'état attempt."

What makes this most horrific is that the thousands-strong mob is marching to the orders of the sitting president. Trump promised he would walk with them to the Capitol. But his imaginary Vietnam-era bone spurs seem to have conveniently sprung back. He will sit this one at the White House.[1]

---

1 As evidenced by testimony in the January 6 Congressional hearings of 2022, Trump intended to join his supporters at the Capitol, but Secret Service agents refused to drive him there.

The mob seeking to take the hill includes hundreds of Trump's beloved "undereducated" foot soldiers. "USA! USA! USA!" they say. "Stop the Steal! Stop the Steal!" they scream. "Whose house?" "Our house!" they respond.

Before nightfall, Trump will tell them that he loves them one more time.

But the throng is motley. It appears to be a cross-section of American conservatism. I see couples of grandparents dressed as they would for a church picnic, rubbing—actually, bumping—shoulders with vociferating thugs.

Many are clad in intimidating camo or Black assault military garb. Yet others seem to have made a stop at Party City. I see a lady, seemingly in her eighties, wearing a QAnon T-shirt and a foam Statue of Liberty crown; a short, stout man sports a Revolutionary-era outfit, three-cornered hat, and all. Had he not been dressed in British Army red (MAGA red), he could have passed for Benjamin Franklin.

The fact that Trumpism has brought together trailer-park residents and CEOs, Klansmen, and church ladies, the monosyllabic and the articulate, shall remain one of the century's most astonishing political feats.

Around 2:11 p.m., hundreds of rioters break into the Capitol, injuring police officers along the way. Footage shows a policeman smashed against a glass door, gasping for air; others are hit mercilessly with hockey sticks, flag masts, fire extinguishers—anything that can hurt or kill.

At one point, we see a bloodied blonde woman emerge out of the Capitol on a stretcher. Later, we will find out that she is the riot's first casualty, a rioter herself. Click, click. On Fox, Carlson opines that she does not look like a protester, and the screen shows footage of this summer's Black Lives Matter riots; the network's way of saying "that's what rioters look like."

Within a few hours, another four fatalities are reported, one of them a police officer. The Capitol has become a multiple murder scene.

The mob, whose spiritual leader appears to be the buffalo-skin-clad self-ordained QAnon shaman, thirsts for more blood, none more precious than House Speaker Nancy Pelosi's. Her office has been breached and occupied. A grinning MAGA soldier rests his booted feet on the Speaker's desk.

Some are chanting, "Hang Mike Pence! Hang Mike Pence!" A noose on makeshift gallows awaits outside.

History is invoked repeatedly. Echoing former President Franklin D. Roosevelt, some are referring to the day as one that shall live in infamy. Indeed, January 6 is joining the calendar of American history's fateful and tragic days: September 11, November 22, December 7.

Comparisons are being made with the burning of the Capitol and White House by British troops in 1814 and the Confederate assault on Fort Sumter in 1861.

Back on July 11, 1864, Confederate General Jubal Early and his raggedy troops marched toward Washington, D.C. On the way, they captured Silver Spring, Maryland, and then Fort Stevens. The Confederates came within sight of the Capitol. The soon-to-be martyred President Abraham Lincoln came close enough to the line of fire that eyewitnesses reported enemy bullets flying past his signature top hat.

Trump watches his troops from the comfort and safety of the White House. A middle-aged Delawarean can be seen fulfilling General Early's dream. He walks proudly inside the Capitol waving a Confederate flag.[2]

4:29 p.m., CNN: Any other day, it would have sucked the oxygen out of the nation's newsrooms, but given the unfolding carnage at Capitol Hill, the projection of Jon Ossoff's U.S. Senate victory goes barely noticed. It is another historical event. He is Georgia's first Jewish senator, and his election will make another Jewish man, Charles Schumer, Senate majority leader.

Sundown

Flash bombs explode. The acrid smell of tear gas envelops the hill. Union troop reinforcements pour in.

Once the rioters are dispersed, news cameras turn to the White House. It is midnight, the exterior unlit; a barely visible amount of light comes out from the inside. It is the capital city's darkest night ever. Click, click.

---

2 On June 15, 2022, a federal judge found him and his son guilty of felony obstruction of an official proceeding.

16

Happy 2021 Valentine's Day, Mr. Trump

(Creators Syndicate, February 13, 20, 2021)

I assume that I am not alone in appreciating former President Donald Trump's withdrawal from the public eye, the public's ear, and the public's hair. After five years (since the start of his first presidential campaign in 2015) of continuously flowing lies, lawlessness, mean-spirited rhetoric and nonsense, many Americans welcome this reprieve. I am grateful for Twitter's and Facebook's gag orders.

Having penned several columns on Trump's exploits, I did not anticipate writing on the subject anytime soon. But I could not resist composing this Valentine's Day column.

Trump is a man of few words—not that he speaks little but that his vocabulary is slim. We know that he does not read, not even in self-defense. Megyn Kelly, also gone from the public eye, once asked Trump about the latest book he had read, to which he responded: "I read passages. I read areas. I'll read chapters. I just—I don't have the time." Do you use a thesaurus? I would have asked. Who needs a prehistoric reptile? I can imagine him saying. "I have the best words," he once bragged.

We became accustomed to his overuse of certain best words: "perfect," for example, as in that perfect call with the Ukrainian president, and "beautiful," as in the beautiful letter from Kim Jong-un. But the four-letter word "love" ranks highest among his most abused.

I scoured Trump's speeches and tweets—check out rev.com—in search of the word "love," and this is some of what I found:

For Love of Country

Judging from Trump's communications, nobody loves America more than him. On scores of occasions, he has reminded us that he loves the country. "I ran because this country has been good to me. I love America," he told a crowd in St. Augustine, Florida, shortly before the 2016 election.

Trump holds in highest esteem Americans who love their country, such as the patriots, as he calls them; veterans and police officers; the bikers, "great people who truly love our Country"; and newly adopted America lovers, like Venezuelan exiles who "love our country." "We'll take care of the Venezuelan people," he promised two days before St. Valentine's Day 2020.

"Others," he has bitterly denounced, "do not love our country. In fact, they hate our Country!" This includes virtually all Democrats. He once singled out Somali-born Congresswoman Ilhan Omar, she "doesn't love our country."

Got to "Love the World"

Despite his beautiful and perfect nationalism, in matters of love, Trump is an indiscriminate globalist.

During his 2015–2016 campaign, he repeatedly expressed his love for Mexico and Mexicans. I lost track of the number of times. After getting elected, he sort of fell out of love with the Mexican people.

Curiously, whenever Trump said that he loved Mexicans, he often added statements such as "I've had thousands of … Mexicans working for me." But he loves some Mexicans more than others: "[T]he rich Mexicans, they're great people—friends of mine. They buy my apartments." No love for Mexican "bad hombres," border crossers, drug dealers or rapists, and certainly not for the children he ordered torn from their parents' arms.

It is curious that Trump only loves Latinos from places that have significant numbers—read: voters. "I love Puerto Rico," he said in August 2018. In a speech he gave in Miami, he posed the rhetorical questions: "Do we love Cuba?" Applause. "Do we love Nicaragua?" More applause.

And Canada? O Canada! Trump has expressed his love for our northern neighbors, their "taking advantage of the United States for many years" notwithstanding.

As for Turkey, he offered the exact same words: The country has "great people" but "has taken advantage of the United States for many years."

The Irish—everybody loves the Irish. Trump calls them "strong and resilient." As he said in Shannon, Ireland in June 2019, "I think I know most of them because they are my friends." No data offered as to how many reside in Trump's many towers.

Trump has repeatedly said he loves China, but it is more like a love-hate relationship. "I love China. In fact, they're my tenants in New York," he said early in his first campaign.

Russia is a sour topic for Trump. But at least once, he said in public, "I love Russia." Russian President Vladimir Putin has been Trump's favorite valentine. Someone should make a film about their lasting romance. What about "From America with Love" for a title.

A quick internet search of the name Donald Trump and the word "love" generates an avalanche of the former president's statements about love: the things he loves ("I love free trade"; "I love Hershey chocolate"), the human objects of his affection ("I love winners"; "I love the poorly educated") and the individuals he loves, from Tom Brady to former Sheriff Joe Arpaio. We also find numerous claims about those who love him (i.e., bikers) or those about whose love he fantasizes (African Americans and Mexican immigrants).

"I love people," Trump has said numerous times, but his polyamory is selective and conditional. In his speeches, tweets, and assorted pronouncements, he proclaims love for particular demographic groups, such as rural Americans; professions such as mining and trucking; and other categories—the "deplorables," for example—all of which constitute key pillars of his coalition.

He Loves Men in Uniform

Trump has a particular attraction for men in uniform, be they soldiers, police officers or border patrollers. Psychologist Midge Wilson has explained the unconscious sources behind the uniform fetish: tapping into "father figures, heroism, protection and power."

Trump loves war, he once told us, and all things military (parades and arma-ment). He loved the military's top brass so much that he appointed four generals to his Cabinet, Michael Flynn, John Kelly, James Mattis and H.R. McMaster—"my generals," he affectionately called them. He extends his love to all branches of the military: "I love the Air Force. I love those planes. I love buying those planes at a reduced price"; "We love our Navy SEALs. They've [sic] very special, very incredible people."

Judging from his numerous comments about veterans, Trump has them in a special place in his heart—particularly "wounded warriors," John McCain excluded. Likewise, he loves "angel moms"—"great people"—as long it is not Ghazala Khan, wife of Khizr Khan, who chastised Trump in a speech at the 2016 Democratic convention.

Trump is infatuated with others who wear uniforms. He often expresses his love for police officers: "We love them. They're all over. They're the greatest peo-ple." The same holds true for ICE agents and "firemen."

Trump has repeatedly said that he loves workers, particularly of the blue-collar sort, people who work outdoors, be they farmers or construction workers. And, for some reason beyond my areas of expertise, he is attracted to—let's call them "macho types": hunters, outdoorsmen, people who make machines, bikers. During his campaigns, he loved farmers when he visited rural areas: "I love rural America. All that red." When he signed an order reversing Obama-era environ-mental regulations, he said: "We love our coal miners. Great people." He showed similar affection for steel workers in a speech on trade in Granite City, Illinois.

Trump has a crush on machines, those who make them and those who run them. "I love mechanical things," he said at a Made in America event. "I love the whole thing," proclaimed Trump at his first 2020 campaign rally, "the world of tractors and all of that stuff." Truckers are also on his list of valentines.

"I Love You, [If] You Love Me / We're a Happy Family"

I apologize—well … not really—if I have reincepted Barney's song in the brains of readers who may have undergone years of therapy to delete that hypnotic ditty from their heads.

Trump, it is well known, sees life as an unending business negotiation, where everything is a transaction. Love is no exception. His speeches and tweets reflect the conditional nature of what he calls love. It is always "you scratch my back and I'll scratch yours."

Here are a few examples: "I love the American farmer…. They backed me," he once said. He loves the miners: "Oh, West Virginia was good to me." He also loves the *New York Post* because it treats him well. And NASCAR? Well, he loves NASCAR because they endorsed him in 2016.

Although notorious for not paying back his debts, Trump is not shy about demanding love from those he loves. "Pennsylvania has to love Trump," he tweeted in August 2018, "because unlike all of the others before me, I am bringing STEEL BACK in a VERY BIG way." And Puerto Ricans, he claimed after signing a hurricane relief bill, "have to love their President."

But does Trump pay his own love debts? Russian President Vladimir Putin may be able to vouch for him.

Happy Valentines, Mr. Trump!

17

Tucker and the Talking Heads: Anatomy of a Fox News Show Built on Deceit and Demagoguery

(Creators Syndicate, April 3, 2021)

I am not in the habit of watching the Fox News Channel, except when investigating what the network is up to in news coverage and commentary.

Earlier this week, on Tuesday, March 30, I tuned into "Tucker Carlson Tonight," which, according to Nielsen Global Media's latest report, registered the largest viewership of any prime-time program, averaging a daily audience of 3.4 million for the quarter.

Prompted by the release earlier that day of a report by a World Health Organization team of scientists on the possible origins of the COVID-19 pandemic, Carlson dedicated the lion's share of the program to the subject.

The WHO report examined four scenarios on how the virus spread to humans:

No. 1: Direct transmission from bats.
No. 2: Transmission from an "intermediate (animal) host" who received the virus from a bat.
No. 3: Contagion through the food chain.
No. 4: Accidental escape from a research lab in Wuhan, China.

While none of those theories were dismissed, the report leaned toward the first two explanations, stating that the lab leak option was an "extremely unlikely pathway."

By most accounts, including those of scientists, journalists and government officials, the report is incomplete and lacks transparency. Its authors were the first to recognize the need for further research. White House Press Secretary Jen Psaki criticized it for its lack of "crucial data, information and access."

China, as expected, does not only reject the idea that the COVID-19 virus was intentionally manufactured in Wuhan, but Chinese officials have been floating the idea that it originated in the United States. A spokesperson for China's Ministry of Foreign Affairs made the preposterous suggestion that the U.S. Army brought it to Wuhan.

After showing footage of an interview of Dr. Peter Daszak, a zoologist and the only U.S.-based scientist joining the WHO team that investigated the origins of the pandemic, Carlson summoned his own "expert" on the subject, Bill Gertz from the *Washington Times*, who is neither a scientist nor a journalist of science. He may not be the best source—certainly neither fair nor balanced—to speak on things China, given his acknowledgment of having received large sums of money from a financier associated with controversial Chinese exile billionaire Guo Wengui. Gertz, who covered Guo for the *Washington Free Beacon*, described the payment as an "advance" for the publication of his highly critical book *Deceiving the Sky: Inside Communist China's Drive for Global Supremacy.*

Gertz is convinced that China created the virus and started the pandemic. He also claims that China has "ethnic weapons," biological weapons that can target ethnic groups. Anglo-Saxons, beware.

Per usual, Carlson used the occasion to attack his archenemies in the mainstream media. Pivoting from the virus story to its coverage by CNN, MSNBC, and other news organizations, he accused his rival colleagues of "dutifully" repeating claims by scientists and others that the COVID-19 virus could not have been manufactured in a Chinese lab. His assertion, however, rests on a false premise, as the WHO report does not dismiss the possibility of a lab escape.

Carlson proceeded to use half-truths and out-of-context quotes to build his case against NPR and National Geographic, two organizations with well-deserved reputations for integrity and intellectual honesty. To demonstrate that NPR has uncritically embraced and is irresponsibly disseminating one of the animal-origin theories, he puts up on the screen a quote from an NPR story from January 2020 that reads, "A 'wet market' in Wuhan, China, is catching the blame as the probable source of the current coronavirus outbreak." But the quote itself includes the qualifier "probable."

Likewise with another quote from a National Geographic story. On the screen, it reads "'Wet markets' likely launched the coronavirus," but Carlson does not even bother to read the quote correctly, leaving out the word "likely."

Carlson and other dishonest journalists are counting not only on our ignorance but also on our incapacity to read and listen carefully and critically.

Read! Think! Disappoint them!

Section III
Culture Is the History That We Inherit

Introduction

Culture, it is widely believed, consists of what I call the four usual suspects: food, music, dance, and ethnic costumes. This is, of course, a limited definition that includes only a few tangible manifestations of material culture.

But a wider definition of culture includes a universe of intangibles shared by people in a particular place at a specific time, their way of life: customs, beliefs, values, diversions, forms of expression and entertainment, and much more.

The world is moving toward a uniform global material culture, dominated by mostly American influences: technological innovations, fashion, Hollywood and the celebrity culture it promotes, hip-hop, and rock 'n' roll. But the pervasiveness of the trappings of American culture obscures the central cultural paradox of globalization: people around the world may wear, eat, and listen to American products, but they retain their deeply ingrained values, beliefs, and underlying assumptions. They may embrace the material products of modernity, but they cling tenaciously to their own underlying cultural cores—which remain vibrant and resiliently distinct.

Even with the United States' success in spreading its material culture globally, those underlying values, mores, and habits persist. Being unaware of them—that is, lacking international cultural fluency—hurts Americans both individually and as a country, whether we try to seal a business deal with Mexican executives, penetrate the Vietnamese consumer market in Los Angeles, or build a real coalition for war or peace in the Middle East.

The eight essays in this section view culture as the history that peoples inherit, ways of life that include aspects of material culture such as ancient summer Solstice rituals in Eastern Europe and plantain-based foods in the Caribbean. They also approach intangibles such as the practice of haggling in a Moroccan market, the concept of honor in Latin America, and the evolving use of words like "hero" and "patriotism" in the United States.

These essays and columns resort to several concepts and perspectives on world cultures, among them *cultural diffusion*, the movement of aspects of culture from one human group to another (i.e., the trajectory of the Cuban sandwich from Cuba to Tampa/Ybor City, to Miami, and then to most countries around the world); *syncretism* and *hybridity*, the amalgamation of cultural traits and practices from different cultures (i.e., the observance of Spanish, local, and U.S. holidays in Puerto Rico); *transculturation*, a concept and term coined by renowned Cuban anthropologist Fernando Ortiz (1881–1969) that explains the complex cultural interactions among Indigenous Cubans, Europeans and their descendants and enslaved and free Africans and their descendants (i.e., the evolution of the *ajiaco*, Cuba's traditional stew); *cultural translating*, which I define as having knowledge of a culture other than one's own with enough fluency to understand actions, values, beliefs, symbols and meanings, and having the ability to translate them between cultures (i.e., how to haggle in different parts of the world); and *cultural resistance*, as in the recent removal of Queen Elizabeth as Barbados' head of state and Horatio Nelson's statue from Bridgetown's main square.

18

"Epic," "Heroic," "Patriots": Words We Have Abused into Meaninglessness

(Creators Syndicate, September 8, 2020)

I advise my students to avoid starting their papers with hackneyed platitudes—
"Most historians agree …," or worse yet, "When the going gets tough …"—
and to stay away from cliche opening sentences, such as "*The Merriam-Webster Dictionary* defines …."

Today, I will breach one of my own rules, however.

The Merriam-Webster Dictionary defines "hero" as "a person admired for
achievements and noble qualities" and "one who shows great courage." According
to the Oxford English Dictionary, a patriot is "a person who vigorously sup-
ports their country and is prepared to defend it against enemies or detractors."
In recent years, those two words, along with "epic," the verb "curate" and many
other words have been misused and abused to the point that they have become
almost meaningless.

Words change meanings. In Chaucer's time, the word "girl," for example,
referred to both girls and boys; "meat," "clue," and "fizzle" used to mean food in
general, a ball of yarn, and the release of intestinal fumes, respectively.

The secular prophet George Orwell, best known for his timely (then and
now) novel *1984*, wrote the excellent essay "Politics and the English Language"

in 1946. He decried the decay of the English language, which he largely blamed on political speech: its vagueness, its pretentiousness, its insincerity, and the meaninglessness of certain words.

He recognized the bidirectional connection between language and thought. "It becomes ugly and inaccurate because our thoughts are foolish," Orwell wrote, "but the slovenliness of our language makes it easier for us to have foolish thoughts."

Among the abused, meaningless, and pretentious words Orwell denounced in the wake of World War II were "socialism," "fascism," "democracy;" and yes, "patriotic" and "epic." If, in Orwell's words, the English language in Great Britain was in a "bad way," in America today, it's in far worse shape: foolish words lead to foolish thoughts, which lead to even more foolish words and thoughts.

Everything Is Epic

Let's start with "epic." The word entered the English language in the late 1500s, meaning lengthy heroic poem, as in Homer's *The Iliad*. In the 1700s, it became an adjective that meant heroic and grandiose. The Battle of St. Quintin, the Battle of Gettysburg and the invasion of Normandy qualify as epic, and so do the 1956 film *The Ten Commandments* and even the "Star Wars" film series.

In the twenty-first century, "epic" has transitioned from regular word to slang, morphing to mean great, huge, or awesome. Advertising and magazines helped popularize the word's newfound meanings. In 2008, the Epic Burger chain opened in Chicago; a 2013 *Cosmopolitan* cover offered advice on how to have "epic sex." Anything can be considered epic: a prom dance, a wedding cake, even a slice of pizza.

Of Heroes and Patriots

Something epic used to require heroes and heroic actions, but the word "hero" has also lost its meaning. In the late 1300s, the word crossed the English Channel from France. Originally from the Greek language, "hero," was first used in reference to demigods. Later, it was applied to human beings who displayed extraordinary courage in the face of danger or death. "Being a hero," Will Rogers said, "is about the shortest-lived profession on Earth."

As in Orwell's time, politicians are partially responsible for the deterioration of the English language, starting with President Donald Trump. Imagine him as a spelling bee contestant. He is asked to spell "hero." That's an easy word for him: h, e, r, o. But can he use it correctly in a sentence or two? Let's see: "John McCain is 'not a war hero.'" "I should be considered a national hero." One endured five and a half years as a prisoner of war; the other dodged service in the same war claiming he had foot bone spurs.

Trump and those who parrot him bestow blanket patriotic status on entire groups of people. All those who serve in the military, regardless of their actions, are heroes. So are all members of law enforcement bodies, whether they act heroically or abusively. Farmers and ranchers who feed America are heroes, too. Border Patrol agents are "superheroes."

What about teachers, many of whom are being deployed to schools in the face of potential COVID-19 infection, perhaps even death? When does a pandemic cross the line to become a genocide?

"Patriot" has run a similar course. Trump once claimed, "there is nobody more Patriotic than me." He declared disgraced former Sheriff Joe Arpaio and former presidential candidate Herman Cain patriots and gave FOX's Sean Hannity the title "Great American Patriot." He has bestowed the same honor on anti-Black Lives Matter protesters. Former national security adviser John Bolton was a patriot until he no longer was. Red states and rural America are patriotic; cities and blue states are not, according to Trump.

Orwell has the final word: "When the general atmosphere is bad, language must suffer."

19

The Diplomacy of Haggling

(Creators Syndicate, December 12, 2020)

Travelers are, to some degree, diplomats who willingly or unwillingly represent their country abroad. I have seen and heard my fair share of tourist misbehavior: obnoxiousness, arrogance, inappropriate clothing, and penny-pinching avarice demonstrated while haggling over the price of a straw hat or ugly T-shirt.

Here are four real-life stories of tourist haggling intertwined with tips on how to avoid being an ugly tourist.

Grenada, West Indies, 1992

I am a guest speaker on one of Cunard's vessels cruising the Caribbean. We dock in St. George's, the picturesque port and capital of an island appropriately nicknamed Spice Island.

As passengers disembark, local women peddle their wares, much of which consists of herbs, spices, and bottled extracts. I observe an American tourist haggling over a bag of spices. The seller names her price, and the tourist counteroffers half that amount. Following universal haggling rules, the peddler offers to meet the costumer halfway (75 percent of the original asking price). It should have ended there, but the tourist turns ugly, insisting on a deeper discount. The seller agrees, but her pouted mouth expresses displeasure, perhaps disgust.

The grinning, red face-tanned tourist does not realize that he fought tooth and nail over a couple of quarters with an aging Black woman whose income was probably 5 percent of his—two more quarters to feed the ship's slot machines. "Would you like something to drink, sir?" "Yes, a piña colada." "It will be $15 (plus tip), sir." This is precisely why Antiguan author Jamaica Kincaid projects such visceral anger toward run-of-the-mill English or American tourists in her book *A Small Place*.

Mérida, Yucatan, 1992

The city is hosting a Caribbean studies conference. Two anthropologists, experts on Belize, and a Cuban historian walk into a restaurant. (No, this is not a joke.) We are having margaritas and appetizers and, suddenly, a hammock peddler swings by our table. He shows his wares with pride and talks anthropologist No. 1 into buying a hammock for $40. Twenty minutes later, the vendor comes back, and after some low-intensity haggling, anthropologist No. 2 buys one for $30.

I am the only potential costumer left, and the hammock man is going for the trifecta. I offer $20; he agrees. We exchange smiles and winks. My anthropologist friends, especially No. 1, are not amused. There is no such thing as a free meal nor a free in situ lesson in ethnography.

Morocco (Somewhere between Ceuta and Tangier), 2010

I am doing archival research in Spain and take a weekend to visit Morocco. The tour takes us to a crafts market. It is described to us as a villagers' cooperative enterprise. On the market rooftop, a middle-aged, tunicked man approaches me and inquires where I am from. Cuba, I say; without pause, he tells me "I have a brother who lives there."

He invites me to the building basement to see a variety of woven goods. There they offer me tea, and then we haggle a bit over some sashes and bed covers. I know that I could continue negotiating but pay close to the asking price; the textiles are beautiful, and it is a bargain—a win-win.

I return to the rooftop to rejoin my tour group, where I overhear the man with a brother in Cuba ask another tourist: "Where are you from?" "Oh, I have a brother who lives there."

Beijing, 2010

I am part of a delegation of educators visiting China. Most of us, at one point or another, go to the city's famous Silk Market and snake the sinuous interior of the 7-level mall in search of bargains. Name it and you can find it there: pearl earrings and necklaces; Folex watches; fake designer eyewear; and an immense variety of products, from edible roasted scorpions to copies of Mao's *Red Book*—I got one for myself—and, of course, a multitude of silk products.

My belt had come undone, and I need a new one. I approach a young woman standing next to a rack of leather belts. I don't know what possesses me; I get carried away with the haggling and realize that the young vendor's smile vanished from her face.

Realizing what I have done, I immediately try to redeem myself, purchasing the belt at the original asking price. The smile returns to her face, and I still get the belt at a fraction of what I would pay in the United States. She even offers to fix my old broken belt.

"Losing" a negotiation can be a victory. On-site anthropology lessons should not be free. Every tourist is a diplomat, to some degree.

20

"Ask Them to Spell Their Names" and Other Real-Life Blunders in Transcultural Communications

(Creators Syndicate, December 19, 2020, February 12, 2022)

"The single greatest barrier to business success is the one erected by culture," said Edward T. Hall and Mildred Reed Hall. I agree.

Someone who wishes to purchase goods and services in the international marketplace may get by with English only and little understanding of foreign cultures, but if you want to sell in an increasingly competitive global market, you must be able to communicate effectively across linguistic and cultural boundaries.

But there are not that many functionally bilingual people in the United States. "What do you call a person who speaks many languages?" the joke goes, "A polyglot." "Someone who speaks two languages?" "Bilingual." "And someone who speaks only one language?" "An American."

Here are some stats. According to the American Community Survey, in 2018, only 1 in 5 Americans were bilingual. I suspect that most of them were immigrants who learned English in this country. By contrast, nearly two-thirds of Europeans know a second language. Europe's rate of trilingualism (22 percent) is higher than America's rate of bilingualism (20.6).

Not too long ago, a Florida legislator—where do they find them?—proposed that coding be included among Florida schools' language options.

Curiously, but not surprisingly, the United Kingdom is Europe's most monolingual country, with roughly half of Europe's rate of bilingualism. I once heard a fellow scholar use the phrase "the linguistic arrogance of all English-speaking peoples."

International cultural interest, let alone fluency, is another American weak flank. Recent statistics demonstrate that under 20 percent of Americans follow international news closely and the major TV network-news programs devote less than 4 percent of airtime to foreign news—an airplane crashed yesterday off the coast of the politically troubled nation of San Marcos (wink, Woody), 200 dead, three of them American.

Over the years, I have compiled notes about instances in which failure to know the local language and the most basic aspects of another country's culture and norms has led to disastrous consequences. Here are five examples.

Case No. 1: Mr. Ñemerson's Spelling Bee

A few years ago, a know-it-all executive from Chicago—let's call him Mr. Ñemerson—traveled to Puerto Rico to train the San Juan office sales staff. With an insufferable air of superiority, he instructed the attentive "natives" to demonstrate interest in their potential customers by asking them, "How do you spell your name?"

No doubt that being interested in your clients is an important ingredient in sales success. You do not need an MBA to know that. Even those who are not genuinely interested may gain an advantage by pretending to be, as Mr. Ñemerson advised his trainees.

My late father, Celestino Martínez Lindín, who was always generous with advice, gently pulled Mr. Ñemerson aside and explained to him that Spanish is a phonetic language, meaning that it is spoken just as it is written. He dismissed the advice.

If you are in Topeka, it might be a good idea to ask a client who says her name is Katherine to spell it, as it may be Catherine, Kathryn, or some other variation. For a Spanish-speaking person to ask another named González how it is spelled is ridiculous and makes that person sound foolish, just like Mr. Ñemerson, MBA.

Case No. 2: "Yes" Is Not Always "Sí"

An Anglo pastor arrived at a predominately Latino town in Texas. He wanted to communicate to the town's Hispanics that they were welcome at his church. He called residents on the phone and invited them to a church picnic. He heard an encouragingly large number of yeses; he was delighted and planned accordingly.

Picnic day came, and to his disappointment, almost no one showed up. "Oh, Lord, what am I going to do with all of these tortillas?"

He shared the experience with a fellow pastor—call him Pedro—who was Hispanic. Why had his guests been so untruthful and ungrateful?—"I have three months' worth of tortillas!"

Pedro gave Reverend—let's call him Charles—a brief lesson on culture: Latinos generally have a high regard for authority figures such as priests, and even teachers. They were not trying to mislead you. They simply did not feel comfortable telling you "no."

I have been in this country 36 years. I am grateful for that, but it's been only recently, that I learned to say "no" without an accent.

Case No. 3: Are Latino Students More Dishonest?

A few years ago, researchers at a large midwestern university conducted a study about honesty and dishonesty among university students. They employed a survey with sociodemographic questions about race and ethnicity and questions designed to gauge the students' level of honesty. One of the survey's questions was—I am paraphrasing—if you see another student cheating on a test would you notify the professor? The research team concluded that Latino students were not as honest as their non-Hispanic peers.

The researchers had failed to understand that distinct cultures—and social classes, for that matter—define honesty in different ways; and that among many Latino students "snitching" on fellow classmates, short of a sign of honesty represents lack of solidarity.

Case No. 4: Let Me See Your Purchase Ticket, Señora

A large U.S. warehouse chain store opened new branches in a Spanish-speaking country. Local managers were instructed to follow the company's U.S. practice of checking purchased items against receipts at the exit. Many customers were offended by such scrutiny which they perceived as an affront on their trust and sense of honor. The ensuing outcry created a public relations crisis and the chain had to adjust its policy.

Store policy makers and managers would have avoided bad publicity and loss of business had they understood their customer's Iberian-derived sense of honor.

Case No. 5: An Encyclopedia of Cuban Musicians and Athletes?

A group of scholars edited an encyclopedia of Cuba. They made a concerted effort to include entries on a wide range of topics (Biotechnology, Philharmonic Orchestra, Chinese Contract Laborers, etc.) and a diverse list of notable individuals of different races (painter Wifredo Lam, track-and-field star Ana Fidelia Quirot, and nineteenth-century patriot Ignacio Agramonte, etc.).

The publishers designed covers for each volume of the encyclopedia. One cover included a picture of four Black rhumba dancers making child-like grimaces. The other had a picture of a mulatto Cuban baseball pitcher. The encyclopedia sold poorly among its natural demographic, South Florida Cubans. Those stereotypes can be offensive, we told the publishers. But they knew best.

The publishing house would have sold far more encyclopedias had its editors listened to us (I was one of the editors) and designed covers that reflected Cuban diversity and conveyed the message that Cubans can be good athletes and musicians but scientists and architects as well.

21

Lost in Cultural Translation

(Creators Syndicate, March 13, 2021)

As a professor and columnist, I am always on the lookout for information, images and artifacts that someday may come in handy in the classroom, in my writing or just in everyday conversation.

During a trip to China, I huffed and puffed up the steps of the Great Wall, whose construction cost an estimated one million lives. I was amused by some of the bilingual metal signs posted along the way. One of the signs warned, "Speaking cellphone is strictly prohibited when thunderstorm." Another read, "Please protect caltaral relics." Odd translations with typos and bad grammar, but passersby who understand English get the message, even the Tarzanesque iterations.

Translation is not easy. It is a profession that requires years of study and demands fluency in the languages you are translating to and from. But for some reason, many people think that anyone with basic knowledge of the required languages can translate.

"Do you know anyone who can translate this into Spanish?" "Yes, I have a cousin, who took Spanish in high school." That often leads to botched translations like one I recently saw (and photographed) at a construction site. In English, it said, "This area is a designated constrution [sic] site and anyone trespassing on this property upon conviction shall be guilty of a felony." The Spanish translation is a barely intelligible mess: "Esta zona es una construcción designado sitio y violación a nadie en este propiedad convicta que fuere será culpable de un delito." If the sign does not keep you away, the bad grammar will.

In 2006, the almighty and omniscient Google created Google Translate. A gift that human translators welcomed with the same enthusiasm airport "maleteros" (porters) accepted the innovation of wheeled suitcases. But Google translates the Spanish word "maleteros" into trunks, as in car trunks in which you can place luggage.

There is another form of translation for which the wizards of Silicon Valley cannot create programs, webpages, or apps. It is cultural translation, requiring a deep understanding of cultures, not just material culture but also the intangible: beliefs, values, social norms, and cultural assumptions.

In these times of increased attention to cultural awareness and sensitivity, all kinds of institutions, including government entities, colleges and universities, and corporations are seeking expert advice from individuals and agencies that offer help on matters of transcultural communications.

But as is the case with purely literal translation, you can do it on the cheap—ask the niece who spent two weeks in France—or spend a couple of hours cruising Wikipedia to gain superficial knowledge of another culture.

Here are two examples of attempts at cultural translation, first, one of cultural translating gone awry.

Perhaps you have heard this one. Some "multicultural experts" use the example of Chevrolet Novas selling poorly in Puerto Rico and other Spanish-speaking countries because "Nova" sounds like the Spanish phrase "no va," which literally translates to "does not go." To begin, the presupposition that Nova cars did not sell well in Puerto Rico is wrong—"fake news," in today's parlance. That model was actually very popular; it was our family car.

That little story may be cute and likely to generate a quick laugh from an audience in a multicultural awareness session. But when you think of it, it is offensive, a suggestion that Latino or Latin American consumers make major purchase decisions based on such silly considerations. The Nova, "sí, va"—it goes.

Here is an example of a thoughtful cultural translation. When a Spanish language U.S.-Mexico coproduction of the "Sesame Street" children's program was launched in 1972, instead of using the literal translation "Calle Ajonjolí," or "Calle Sésamo," they named it "Plaza Sésamo," with the accent mark on the letter é and all.

This was a culturally sensitive decision, reflective of the understanding that in the Hispanic tradition, a town's central plaza is significant as a place of encounter, socialization and community building. In the United States, by contrast, the main street is usually the center of a town or city's social and commercial life.

And what does Google Translate have to say about that? As expected, when I type "street," the result is "calle." But when I input "Sesame Street," it is translated into "Plaza Sésamo." The program translated it that way, not because it is culturally aware but because it "learned" it by gathering linguistic metadata and identifying common usage patterns.

Experts agree that Google Translate is not as accurate as human translators, especially when it comes to vocabulary selection.

Will I someday receive a Google Alert informing me of the launch of Google Opinion Column Generator? I hope not.

22

The Summer Solstice, Kupalo/ Kupala and St. John the Baptist

(Creators Syndicate, June 26, July 10, 2021)

In case you have not noticed, this is summer solstice week.

Week? You may ask. Well, not quite, but as I recently learned, the longest day of the year (or the shortest, if you live in the Southern Hemisphere) is not always June 21; it can also fall on either the 20th or 22nd: between the just-officially-declared U.S. federal holiday Juneteenth and the 23rd, eve of St. John's the Baptist Day.

The solstice marks the beginning of summer, but it is also known as Midsummer Day. In ancient Greece, some viewed it as the start of a new year. Because it is the time of year when the sun is closest to the surface of the tilted earth's Northern Hemisphere, it should be among the hottest days, but it's not the case because temperature changes lag, producing variation even within the United States. The hottest days of the year strike first in southern Nevada and New Mexico and Western Texas around the last week of June and two months later in coastal California.

As someone born and raised in the tropics, I am drawn to the sun. Thus, every year I look forward to summer solstice day, which brings the longest hours of daylight, little over 15 hours in Central New Jersey, where I used to live, and shy of 14 in Central Florida, where I now reside.

Because the summer solstice is the peak of solar radiation in the Northern Hemisphere, it also marks the moment when days begin to get shorter and shorter over the next six months. By the same token, I find comfort in the arrival of the winter solstice (circa December 21) because thenceforward days get longer until they peak again in six months.

I am also fascinated by the summer solstice because I lived many years in the San Juan metropolitan area, Puerto Rico's capital, whose patron saint is St. John the Baptist. The eve of the Día de San Juan falls on June 23, very close, and not coincidentally also, to the year's longest day.

Agrarian societies from the Neolithic level to the present have been far more attentive to astronomical cycles of the sun and the moon than we are because their livelihood (and lives) depended on it: figuring out which is the most propitious time of the year to plant specific crops, for example. Prehistoric religions sacralized the earth, practiced numerous fertility rituals and imposed divinity on the sun as source of life.

Historically, throughout many cultures of the Northern Hemisphere, Midsummer Day has been a time of celebration characterized by common themes, some of which are still observed today. Those recurring themes include fertility rituals and the belief that that day marks beginnings, as in the start of a new year, a propitious time to break with the past, cleanse oneself of the influence of evil spirits or bad luck, and look forward to new happy and prosperous beginnings.

In pre-Christian Europe, summer solstice celebrations invariably included the elements of fire and water. Bonfires lit on the eve of that day were believed to further strengthen the sun and at the same time scare away evil spirits. Pre-Christian Celts' summer solstice festivities, known as Litha, included lighting bonfires and setting wheels on fire to be rolled down hills. Men in ancient Greece jumped over bonfires to gain luck and demonstrate bravery. Likewise, Slavs in Russia and other parts of Eastern Europe practiced Midsummer fire rituals on the day of Kupalo, a Slavic god of fertility, connected to the sun.

Water, which is as important to successful farming as sunlight, was another key component of pagan solstice celebrations. Kupalo is also represented as a female deity, Kupala, goddess of water. Slavs and other European peoples engaged in rituals of purification by water that included swimming and submersion. Solstice Day swimming was believed to have curative powers. The more times someone plunged into a river or lake, the better the results.

Ancient and pre-Christian medieval solstice celebrations in which fire and water played protagonist roles were intimately tied to fertility rituals across different parts of the world. Because of their critical role in procreation, women figured prominently in solstice rituals of courtship, marriage, and childbirth. Female deities, mother goddesses, often represented as voluptuous figurines, were central to the religious beliefs and practices of early agricultural peoples.

Ancient Egyptians celebrated the summer solstice and aligned pyramids and other constructions along the sun's trajectory on the year's longest day. They saw the solstice as a signal of the impending reappearance, after around 70 days of invisibility, of the star Sirius that marked the start of a new year that coincided with the annual flooding of the Nile basin and thus a cycle of agricultural abundance. The star, known to Egyptians as the goddess Sopdet (meaning skilled woman), was a deity of fertility and a mother goddess.

On the second week of June, ancient Romans held festivals and celebrations honoring the virgin goddess Vesta, deity of the hearth, home, and family. Once a year, married women entered her temple to give offerings seeking blessings for their families.

Another Roman deity, Juno, was goddess of marriage, human fertility and childbearing. The month of June—named after her—was believed to be propitious for weddings and happy, fecund, and prosperous marriages. In the United States and elsewhere, June is still a popular month for weddings.

One of the keys to the success of the expanding Roman Empire was its purposeful ability to merge its power structure and culture, especially its religious pantheon, with those of peoples it conquered. A salient example of this phenomenon known as religious syncretism is evident in the still-standing Roman-built temple in Bath, England, where Romans paired their goddess of medicine Minerva with Sulis, a local goddess of healing who exerted curative powers through the local thermal waters.

After three centuries of persecution and martyrdom, Roman Emperor Constantine legalized Christianity, which in 380 A.D. became the empire's official religion. The spread of Roman Christianity in Europe, Asia Minor and Northern Africa rested largely on syncretic strategies that aligned or overlapped with pagan deities, rituals, and religious calendars. The Roman church, for example, adopted December 25 as the day in which Jesus was born, aligning it with existing pagan winter solstice festivals.

In similar fashion, the Roman Church and later the Orthodox Church syncretized St. John the Baptist by assigning him a June 24 birthdate that made it easy to merge him and the sacrament of Baptism with pagan summer solstice festivals such as the Celtic and Anglo-Saxon Litha along with deities such as the Slavs' Kupala. When Orthodox Christianity entered the Slavic world, the Kupala festival was renamed Ivan Kupala; Ivan is the Slavic word for the name John.

Christianity, meanwhile, has adopted its fair share of pagan practices, such as the celebration of Easter, originally in honor of the pre-Christian Germanic deity Eostre, a goddess of the spring equinox and nature's rebirth, venerated in the month of April and syncretized with the resurrection of Christ. The symbols of rabbits and eggs and the eating of hot cross buns in contemporary Easter celebrations are remnants of ancient Germanic and Scandinavian spring rituals.

Other similarities facilitated syncretism. Baptisms, like pagan water purification rituals, were carried out in bodies of water. The cleansing of sins through baptism was conflated with ancient practices in which ritual baths were used to cast evil spirits and bad luck.

Fast Forward and Head Southwest

Spanish conquistadors brought Catholicism to the Americas beginning in the 1490s. It was, to be sure, a syncretic religion that combined influences from a wide array of peoples and cultures that passed through the Iberian Peninsula over many centuries: Phoenicians, Iberians, Celts, Romans, Visigoths, Jews, and Muslim Moors.

Over five centuries after the conquest and start of colonization of Puerto Rico (where I spent the most important formative years of my life), residents of San Juan (a city named after John the Baptist), and other parts of the island engage in a variety of syncretic rituals whose origins and meanings are unknown to most.

The custom, which is similarly practiced in many parts of Spain, from Catalonia to the Canary Islands, includes going to the beach on the eve of St. John's Day, and at midnight plunging into the ocean three (as in the name of the Father, Son, and Holy Spirit) times, or seven. This pagan "baptism" is also practiced in swimming pools in the Orlando Metropolitan Area of Florida, where an estimated 385,000 Puerto Ricans reside.

23

The Ajiaco, the Cuban Sandwich, and Other Cuban/Caribbean Foods for Thought

(Creators Syndicate, October 23, 30, November 6, 13, 20, 2021)[1]

There is much truth in Jean Anthelme Brillat-Savarin's famous 1826 aphorism, "Tell me what you eat, and I will tell you what you are." After decades of studying the history of Cuba and its diasporas, I am convinced that what Cubans eat (and have eaten in the past) tells us much about their history and culture, including the encounter of its three foundational roots (Indigenous, Spanish, and African), how those cultures merged to form a creole society, and how its diasporas diffused Cuban culture, in turn weaving it into cultures of other receiving societies. What Cubans eat—and do not eat—also sheds light on where they stand on the social ladder, the island nation's economic health and its relations with foreign countries.

---

1 This essay includes excerpts from my book *Key to the New World: A History of Early Colonial Cuba* (Gainesville, 2018).

First Course: The *ajiaco*

Our Cuban meal begins with an *ajiaco* (a'xjako), a soup that originated among the Tainos, Arawaks who arrived in the island around A.D. 550 to 600. Before the Tainos, more primitive Indigenous peoples inhabited Cuba. They were semi-nomadic and foraged for mollusks, nuts, and seeds. The Tainos were agriculturalists who cultivated *yuca* (manioc), a variety of other tubers, *ají* peppers, maize, tomatoes and guavas and other fruits. They complemented their diet with animal protein from fish, shellfish, iguanas, some types of birds and rodents named *jutías*. They cooked these meats over hot coals called *barbacoas*—yes, that is the origin of the English word barbecue. They also prepared meats by drying them on wooden racks called *bucanes*—and yes, that is the root of the word buccaneer. French pirates adopted the cooking style and the word from natives who inhabited the island of Hispaniola. Jerky, as in beef jerky, comes from the Inca word "charque."

World-renowned Cuban anthropologist Fernando Ortiz has told us that the *ajiaco* was one of the primary dishes of the Tainos before the Spanish conquest and colonization. It was a soup that included various indigenous tubers and *ají* peppers, hence the word *ajiaco*. Tainos dipped insipid *casabe* cakes made from *yuca* paste in pottery bowls filled with *ajiaco*.

Rather than staying fixed, the *ajiaco* recipe as well as its counterparts (*sancocho* in Puerto Rico and the Dominican Republic and *callaloo* in other Caribbean islands) has evolved over time as new waves of European settlers and enslaved Africans tossed new ingredients into the pre-Columbian pottery bowl.

Ortiz and other scholars after him recognized the slow-cooking *ajiaco* as a metaphor for the multiple and compounding processes of transculturation that have produced ever-evolving Cuban cultures. He coined the term transculturation in 1939 to signify complex cultural interactions among Indigenous Cubans, Europeans and their descendants, and enslaved and free Africans and their descendants.

"Transculturation" more accurately reflects the manifold hybridization processes unfolding in Cuba since the 1500s than the term "acculturation," which denotes the assimilation of a new group into an existing culture or society.

Cuba's historic transculturations, rather than producing a blended soup where new ingredients are lost or absorbed into a dominant broth, generated a stew in which various ingredients (from different parts of the world) retained their flavors, aromas, and textures while at the same time infusing one another.

Cuba's first Spanish colonists brought their food preferences, ingredients, and recipes. But they also had to adjust their palates to the island's geographical and agricultural circumstances, accepting—sometimes reluctantly—substitutes such as *casabe* cakes in place of wheat flour bread, or wine made from pineapples rather than grapes. Cubans still use the phrase "a falta de pan, casabe" (if there is no bread, cassava cakes will have to suffice) as an expression of resignation.

Spain Enters the Cuban Kitchen

Spaniards conquered Cuba and established its seven original villages between 1511 and 1519. The largest number of early Spanish immigrants hailed from the South, Andalusia, a region enriched culturally over centuries by multiple waves of immigrants and invaders.

Carthaginian settlers brought the cultivation of olives to Andalusia. Centuries later, Romans introduced wine and chickpeas and turned Southern Spain into their empire's primary producer of olive oil. Spanish cuisine was further enriched when beginning in 711 Arabs and Berbers invaded the Iberian Peninsula, bringing along a host of exotic ingredients originating from as far away as Persia and India. Moors introduced the cultivation of oranges, lemons, almonds, dates, apricots, and coffee as well as spices such as saffron, cumin and black pepper. They also popularized the practice of deep-frying, which appears to have begun in the ancient Middle East.

Islamic dietary restrictions banned the consumption of two of Iberia's dietary mainstays: wine and pork products including ham, *chorizos*, and lard. Eating pork and drinking wine were considered evidence of "limpieza de sangre" (purity of blood), a sign that one was Christian as opposed to Muslim or Jewish. Jews and Muslims who resisted conversion were expelled from Spain in 1492 and forbidden to travel to Spain's new colonies. Originating among Romans, the practice of roasting pigs spread throughout the Iberian Peninsula and became an affirmation of Christianity. It is not a coincidence that roast pork became the centerpiece of Cuba and much of Latin America's traditional Christmas Eve feasts.

Cubans, Puerto Ricans, and Dominicans are avid consumers of fried foods (*frituras*). Among Puerto Rico's most popular are *bacalaitos* (codfish fritters), direct descendants of the popular Andalusian *tortillas de bacalao*; and *alcapurrias*, or fried dough of *malanga* (sago) and green plantains stuffed with meat or shellfish. If you have seen a Middle Eastern falafel, you know what an *alcapurria* looks like; they taste different because falafel paste is made of mashed chickpeas instead.

Early Spanish settlers introduced a broad catalog of new ingredients and recipes. Imports included animal protein like pork, beef, chicken, and eggs. They also brought garlic and onions. Some European crops did not fare well in the Caribbean, such as wheat, olive trees and grape vines; other imported crops like sugar cane and bananas thrived.

Nitza Villapol (1923–1998) is Cuba's best-known celebrity chef of all time. Her *Cocina al minuto* cookbook, first published in 1954, is considered the bible of Cuban cuisine. Her *ajiaco* recipe includes several indigenous ingredients—*ají* peppers, corn, chunks of *malanga, yuca, boniato* (sweet potato) and tomato puree. Spanish settlers contributed ingredients of their own: garlic and onions to make the *sofrito*, a Mediterranean-derived preparation sauteed in olive oil; meats in the form of beef, pork, chicken and *tasajo* (beef jerky); and lime juice. According to Villapol, early versions of *ajiaco* included chickpeas.

Africa Gets Dragged into the Cuban Kitchen

Africans were imported as slaves as soon as Spanish colonization began. They were forced to work in mines and construction, in the cultivation of sugar cane, in sugar manufacturing, and other hard labor tasks.

Aspects of West African culture underwent transculturation, thus expanding the hybrid nature of an emerging Cuban creole society. African contributions were evident—still are—in speech, religion, music, and diet, as well as in numerous other manifestations of material and nonmaterial culture.

African slaves and their descendants tossed their own ingredients into the *ajiaco* bowl, primarily plantains. Other African dietary contributions include yams, Guinea hens and okra.

With the growth of the Black population, plantains, whether green or ripe, replaced *yuca* as the staple of the Cuban and Spanish Caribbean diet. Villapol's *ajiaco* recipe includes two pounds of green plantains and two pounds of ripe plantains. Curiously, sixteenth-century Portuguese merchants took *yuca* (also known as manioc) to West Africa, where it became, and still is, a major staple.

Besides being a suitable metaphor for Cuba's hybrid culture, the *ajiaco* has also been a source and symbol of national pride, even patriotism—somewhat like the French onion soup in France. In a 1951 episode of her popular TV cooking show "Cocina al Minuto," Villapol claimed that the *ajiaco* became a truly Cuban dish when it no longer included chickpeas.

The scarcity of foodstuffs and ingredients going back to the establishment of food rationing in 1962 and further aggravated by severe food shortages since the start of the so-called Special Period in 1993 make it virtually impossible for Cubans on the island to prepare anything resembling an *ajiaco*. One must travel to Miami rather than Havana or Santiago de Cuba to enjoy a truly Cuban *ajiaco*. Members of the Communist elite, of course, have access to all the necessary ingredients.

"Black Foods"

Throughout the history of African slavery, masters and overseers largely determined the basic diets of slaves, which were often prescribed by slave codes. But as with many other impositions, slaves resisted. They altered and supplemented their diet, adding their own recipes and ingredients, yams and okra, for example.

In Cuba, Puerto Rico and other past slave societies, the diet of the enslaved resulted from a combination of two opposing forces. On the one hand, imposition; imposed foods consisting of mostly imported staples such as dried, salted codfish, *tasajo*, rice and locally cultivated plantains, corn (for cornmeal) and *chícharos* (split peas).

On the other hand, was the force of resistance, foodstuffs produced by slaves when, and if, they had access to provision grounds, where they raised pigs and chickens and cultivated plantains, okra, corn, and other vegetables. Slaves pressured their masters, often successfully, for access to provision grounds and free time on Sundays to work on those plots and sell produce.

A fellow Cuban historian shared with me a humorous (but also sad) story of the day he visited a Cuban sugar mill to give a historical talk to an audience of workers. All was going well until he quoted from Manuel Moreno Fraginals' book *El Ingenio* (*The Sugar Mill*). The average slaves' daily diet, my friend told the audience, consisted of 200 grams of *tasajo* or salted codfish, 500 grams of cornmeal or rice, 70 grams of other animal protein, and 13 grams of fat.

When the workers heard that—it was probably around lunchtime—they exploded in *choteo*, the African-derived—according to Fernando Ortiz—Cuban practice of intense mockery, shouting back phrases like "bring slavery back!" and "I want to be a slave!"

It was the early 1990s, the start of the economic crisis of the Special Period. Beef was scarce, as it had been for decades—only individuals diagnosed with cancer and other debilitating diseases received prescriptions allowing them to buy small amounts of beef; codfish was a distant memory; plantains were rationed, when available, and so were limited amounts of substandard Vietnamese rice. One slave diet item was still reasonably available in ration bodegas, *chícharos*, the unwelcome staple food of the Special Period.

On Becoming Bananafied

Of all the "black foods" of the Caribbean, none is more ubiquitous than the plantain. Immigrant peasants from the Canary Islands helped popularize plantains in the Spanish-speaking Caribbean, turning them into the staple food of a predominantly white peasantry.

The plantain became a symbol of creole identity and even nationalist sentiments. "Aplatanarse" which roughly translates into "becoming bananified," is a derisive metaphor for creolization. One of Puerto Rico's most iconic paintings, Luis Paret's *El Jíbaro* (the peasant, 1776) is a self-portrait in which the painter appears dressed in peasant garb, carrying a bunch of green plantains over his right shoulder. *El Jíbaro* is the Spanish-born painter's certificate of bananafication. José Martí, the martyred leader of the Cuban War of Independence, used the symbol lyrically and politically. He wrote about Cuban wine made from plantains—another Cuban food metaphor. "Even if it turns sour," he stated, "it is our own wine."

Plantains are a versatile foodstuff that can be consumed when green, half-ripened or ripe. Just like the human body turns starch into sugar, ripening turns starchy green plantains into sweet plantains. Unlike fruit bananas, which are eaten ripe without processing, their larger cousins must be cooked by frying, boiling or roasting.

Fried slices of green plantains are signature foods in the Spanish-speaking Caribbean's cuisine. *Tostones* are made by frying small chunks of green plantain that are smashed to make them flat and then fried one more time. Lightly fried chunks of green plantains are also mashed and mixed with fried pork rinds (*chicharrones*) salt, garlic and olive oil, and cooked onions to create the sphere-shaped *mofongo*, one of Puerto Rico's—and my—favorite dishes. Their counterparts in Cuba (*fufú*) and the Dominican Republic (*mangú*) are similar but made with half-ripe plantains. Those last three dishes retain names of obvious African origin.

Talk about transculturation and bananafication…. Cubans creolized the Spanish tortilla (omelet), substituting potatoes with fried slices of ripe plantains; Puerto Ricans are fond of *pastelones*, essentially lasagnas with elongated slices of fried plantains in place of boiled lasagna pasta strips. Another Puerto Rican dish, the *pionono* (a deep-fried, batter-drenched ripe plantain stuffed with ground beef), is said to be named after Pope Pius IX (Pio Nono, in Italian), but a more plausible explanation is that the Puerto Rican *pionono* got its name from a Granadian pastry that goes by the same name.

Other "Black Foods"

Sociologist José Luis González, author of the insightful and acclaimed *Puerto Rico: The Four-Storeyed Country*, challenged the prevailing representation of Puerto Rican culture that privileged Spanish cultural contributions over those of Afro-Puerto Ricans, who he claimed built Puerto Rico's first—and thus, foundational—story. "When people speak today for example of 'Jíbaro food,'" González wrote, "what they really mean is 'black food': plantains, rice, codfish, etc." That is also the case in traditional Cuban and Dominican cuisine.

Rice, the primary starch of Hispanic Caribbean cuisine, figured prominently in the slaves' diet. When accompanied by beans (legumes of Mesoamerican origin), they produce what nutritionists call a "complete protein" rich in iron and containing several essential amino acids. While variations of the rice-and-beans combination are consumed around the globe, they sit prominently on the front burners of Latin American and Caribbean stoves, especially in what some historians call "Plantation America."

If we follow the arch of Plantation America, starting in Louisiana, we find creole red beans and rice; further east, Hoppin' John (Carolina peas and rice). Several variations developed in Cuba: rice with black beans in the West; with kidney beans in the East; and combinations of rice and beans mixed and cooked together, that is, *moros y cristianos*, or simply *moros* (with black beans), and *congrís* or *congrí* (with kidney beans). Said to have come from Haiti, *congrís* is a dish of captivating etymology: "cong" (from Congo beans) and "ris" (from riz, French for rice—sounds like "rrrrih"). Further east, we can taste the Dominican version of *congrí* (called *moro*) made with pigeon peas. Its Puerto Rican counterpart, *arroz con gandules*, is perhaps the island's most emblematic dish. In Jamaica and other English-speaking West Indies, "rice and peas" are the staple food. And to conclude the journey, at the southern end of Plantation America we find the slavery-derived Brazilian *feijoada* (a bean and meat stew) served over rice.

The two primary sources of animal proteins in the nineteenth-century slave diet, dried codfish and dried beef (*tasajo*), also found their way into traditional Cuban and Puerto Rican cuisine. They happen to be among my favorite foods.

When I was a student at the University of Puerto Rico, I used to crash the faculty club dining hall on Fridays because they served codfish dishes such as *serenata*. By then, codfish, which had been a food for poor Puerto Ricans, had become prohibitively expensive, especially for an undergraduate student, but the faculty club was generously subsidized, and they did not check IDs.

Tasajo served with rice and fried plantains is my favorite dish. To enjoy it, however, I must drive 240 miles to El Versailles or other Miami Cuban restaurants, whose menus also include *ajiaco* and a variety of "black dishes": *funche* (yellow cornmeal stew), split pea pottage and plantain *fufú* with chunks of pork.

Second Course: The Cuban Sandwich

While an *ajiaco* by itself is a full meal, I have offered it in a cup rather than a bowl as a first course to leave room for a Cuban sandwich, which constitutes a full warm meal by itself.

At the risk of trivializing Fernando Ortiz's use of the *ajiaco* as metaphor for Cuba's history and culture, I propose the Cuban sandwich as yet another manifestation of Cuban transculturation, another example of the Cuban culture's ability to transmutate by incorporating new cultural ingredients, and as metaphor for Tampa and Ybor City, where tens of thousands of Cuban exiles settled beginning in the 1880s.

Like the *ajiaco*, the Cuban sandwich combines ingredients from different food cultures, and like the former's ingredients, the latter's components retain their specific flavors and attributes while igniting a multilayered explosion of mutually fortified aromas, flavors, textures, and temperatures.

But unlike the *ajiaco*, with its undisputed Cuban birth certificate, the Cuban sandwich is a transnational (trans-Florida-Straits) creation, with original recipes of Cuban extraction (the *mixto*, or mixed sandwich) imported by exiled Cuban workers to Florida, where they were transculturated with new layers of ingredients from the pantries and delicatessens of Italian, German, and Jewish immigrants.

There is one essential item in all sandwiches: the bread. From peanut butter and jelly sandwiches to Reubens (one of my favorites), they consist of combinations of items layered between slices of bread. It is even possible to have a sandwich—of sorts—with nothing but bread. I recall the stories of a wise man from West Virginia who during the Great Depression ate his fair share of air sandwiches and later went on to become the state's governor. In the case of the Cuban sandwich, the bread must also be Cuban, and the only air in them is inside the holes in the slices of Swiss cheese.

Now, here is where I can get into trouble with some of my Miami compatriots. Nothing new, given that I wrote—"dared" to write, said CBS South Florida—a comprehensive, and may I dare say fair, history of the Cuban Revolution and the diaspora it generated. Cuban bread, most sources point to, and I agree, originated in Ybor City, Florida—not in Miami, and not in Cuba.

Cuban bread, according to most accounts, was first developed in Ybor City, a town founded in the 1880s by Spanish-born cigar manufacturer Vicente Martínez-Ybor. Formally annexed to Tampa in 1887, Ybor City attracted thousands of immigrants from Cuba, Spain, and Italy. A substantial portion of these immigrants came to work as cigar manufacturers. The city also attracted German workers, many if not most of whom were Jewish.

According to various sources, Cuban bread was first baked in 1896 at La Jóven Francesca bakery, an establishment owned by a Sicilian named Francisco Ferlita. His elongated loafs of bread resembled Italian bread but had thin, hard crusts and soft centers. Cuban bread was distributed early in the morning the way milk used to be. Because they were delivered without paper bags, single loaves were impaled into a long iron nail sticking out of the door of workers' homes. A couple of those old cigar-worker homes, prefabricated Sears models purchased in installments, are still standing in Ybor City, door nail and all.

Like the *ajiaco* we tasted earlier, the Cuban sandwich developed gradually with different groups of newcomers adding their own ingredients. Its origins are in Cuba, where *mixtos* included ham, cheese, and various other ingredients. But the evidence points to the *mixto*'s maturation into what we call a Cuban sandwich in Ybor City/Tampa sometime around the start of the twentieth century.

In preparation for this story, I spoke with Andrea Gonzmart, fifth-generation owner and operator of the Columbia Restaurant chain, whose flagship restaurant is in Ybor City. She concurs with the Tampa origins theory.

This is Columbia Restaurant's recipe for the Cuban sandwich. It begins with a 9-inch piece of Cuban bread (Ybor City's contribution). Three types of meat are layered inside: 4 ounces of thinly sliced smoked ham (Iberian contribution), 1

1/2 ounces of roasted pork loin (Cuban contribution), and a thin slice of Genoa salami (Italian ingredient). Note that salami slices are only used in the Tampa/Ybor City version and are considered culinary heresy in Miami. Then come the German and Jewish contributions: sliced Swiss cheese, yellow mustard, and thin slices of pickles.

That's just the assembly phase. A true Cuban sandwich must be served hot and pressed in a sandwich grill, like a panini but without the grooves. To add flavor and crispiness, the crust is slightly buttered before pressing. And there is one more item. Remember the "bananafication" discussion earlier in this column? It is customary to serve Cuban sandwiches with a side of *mariquitas*, thin, crispy fried slices of green plantains.

From its localized origins in the multicultural working-class neighborhood of Ybor City, the Cuban sandwich has gained popularity around the world. Its globalization is a metaphor for the Cuban diaspora of over two million. Cuban restaurants and cafeterias in virtually any city in the world offer variations of the Cuban sandwich. Since 2012, Tampa has held an annual International Cuban Sandwich Festival with a contest for the best Cuban sandwich. August 23 has been designated National Cuban Sandwich Day.

In Havana or any other Cuban city, however, one would be hard-pressed—pun intended—to find anything resembling a Cuban sandwich.

No Cuban meal is complete without something sweet. I suggest one of my favorite desserts: guava paste with fresh white cheese.

Then, *café*, either black or *con leche*.

¡Buen provecho!

24

Barbados: The Caribbean's First Slavery-and-Sugar Plantation Complex and World's Newest Republic

(Creators Syndicate, December 4, 11, 18, 2021)

I would have not known that it was about to happen had I not been watching "The Rachel Maddow Show" on Monday night (November 29). It was a news-heavy day—these days every day seems that way: anticipation over a potential government shutdown later in the week, Supreme Court oral arguments over Mississippi's abortion law, the new omicron variant of COVID-19, the ongoing Congressional January 6 investigation, and MAGA General Michael Flynn peddling QAnon-themed products online. That is why I was surprised to see Maddow devote her show's opening five minutes to a major development in Caribbean history, which is my primary field of interest and expertise.

When the clock struck midnight a few hours later, Barbados, the United Kingdom's second-oldest former Caribbean colony (1627), independent since 1966, removed Queen Elizabeth II as head of state, replacing her with a Black woman named Sandra Mason who was inaugurated as first president of the newly established Republic of Barbados. Another Black woman, Prime Minister Mia Mottley presided over the ceremony; she had spearheaded the push to sever the four-centuries-old bond with the British Crown.

The following morning in my Caribbean history class, I shared the news with my students. We had read about Barbados earlier in the semester when we studied the 1600s "sugar revolution" and had discussed the fact that Barbados had earned the nickname "Little England," for being the most English of the West Indies: most English in religion (Anglicanism is still the official national church) and education (aligned with the British system); in public architecture (i.e., the Parliament Building and St. Michael's Anglican Cathedral); most English in great house architecture (still-standing Jacobean-era Drax Hall and St. Nicholas Abbey); in politics (Westminster-style democracy); and until this week, in monarchism.

Reflective of Barbados' Englishness was the construction of a Trafalgar Square and erection of a statue in honor of Admiral Horatio Nelson in Bridgetown decades before it happened in London. More on the square and statue later.

In class we searched "Barbados Head of State" and there it was: Wikipedia had already dethroned the British queen.

For an island of its size (only 167 square miles) Barbados has figured prominently in the history of the Caribbean. It was there that the region's (actually, the world's) first sugar revolution took place. First settled by a predominantly white population, half of them indentured servants who cultivated tobacco, cotton and indigo in small farms, the number and proportion of Black slaves remained small, some 800 out of a total population of around 30,000 in 1644. At that point, Barbados, by itself, had a larger population and was a greater source of wealth than all of England's North American colonies combined.

Dramatic changes swept through Barbados starting in the mid-1640s when sugar cane began to swallow most of the island's arable land. This was the start of what historians call the "sugar revolution," a profound, interrelated transformation of the economy, society, and government. Renowned historian of the Caribbean B.W. Higman has summarized the process succinctly: "a shift from diversified agriculture to monoculture, from small to large farming units, from low to high value output, from sparse to dense settlement patterns, and from free labour to slavery."

From Barbados, which was the Caribbean's entry point for the sugar virus, the disease spread gradually to almost every island in the region. Everywhere it came to depend on African slave labor; everywhere it led to the consolidation of land ownership into a few hands; everywhere it produced aristocracies that gripped both economic and political power; everywhere it fostered colonial dependency; everywhere it bred corruption; everywhere it led to violence and moral degradation; and everywhere it sparked slave resistance and rebellion.

First published almost 50 years ago, Richard S. Dunn's *Sugar and Slaves* is perhaps the best history of the English-speaking Caribbean during the 1600s and 1700s. I still assign it to my students because it takes us beyond economic, demographic, and political changes. Dunn invokes the "beyond the line" metaphor to explain the moral degradation of British settlers, who "flouted European social conventions." The sugar islands' average Briton was lazier, more cruel, greedier, and drank more and prayed less than his European counterpart.

Barbados' political transition to a republic responds to numerous factors. Some take us back centuries to the reign of Charles I of England (1625–1649), others, even further back to the West African kingdoms of the Akan and Kongo. There are other more contemporary factors like the worldwide decolonization process that followed World War II. And there are immediate causes, such as the globalization of the Black Lives Matter movement and the killing of George Floyd in the spring of 2020.

The Caribbean was forged by two powerful, mutually reinforced institutions: colonialism and slavery. That's only half of the story, the other, being resistance to slavery and struggles against colonial rule. Knowledge of these forces and counterforces helps us understand why Barbados (the most English of Britain's Caribbean colonies) has broken ties with the British Crown.

Footage and pictures of the November 30 ceremonies evidence the fact that Barbados is a Black nation (around 95 percent of the population); almost all Barbadians descend from slaves. Only one white person was present in the transition ceremony—more on him later.

British settlers brought the island's first six African slaves in 1627. With the sugar revolution in full gear, by 1655, 20,000 slaves toiled on the island. Ten years later, there were as many Black slaves as white settlers. The number of Black people continued to grow while the white population dwindled—much of it emigrating to South Carolina, where tobacco plants fared better; 1684 Barbados census records reflect a population of almost 20,000 white settlers and 46,500 Black slaves.

Historians agree that Barbados saw some of the most brutal treatment of slaves in the region. As elsewhere in "Plantation America," the slaves of Barbados resisted and fought for their freedom. But geographic conditions, namely the island's predominantly flat terrain, made flight from plantations difficult and slave rebellions easy to suffocate by colonial militia forces. In mountainous islands like Jamaica, escaped slaves established long-lasting maroon settlements powerful enough to fight prolonged wars against the British and to secure freedom and land concessions through successfully negotiated treaties. In Jamaica, their descendants live in towns founded by eighteenth-century runaway slaves, preserve close-knit communities rich in African culture, and still call themselves "maroons."

As the sugar industry gobbled up forests, turning them into cane fields, large-scale slave flight became increasingly difficult and those who managed to escape were usually quickly captured. As far back as at least 1675, Barbados' slaves revolted but an inauspicious geography condemned insurrections to failure, followed by harsh punishments, including beheading or burning revolt leaders alive.

Execution by beheading was a common English practice long before French revolutionaries mechanized it and turned it into a wholesale practice. Oliver Cromwell's republican Roundheads decapitated Charles I in 1649; his son Charles II avenged his father with a-head-for-a-head justice. Long dead, Cromwell was exhumed and posthumously decapitated.

No heads rolled in the Barbadian transition to republic, and another Charles, the Prince of Wales, who attended the peaceful "removal" of his mother as head of state is an unlikely candidate to head—pun intended—another war of restoration. In all seriousness, the prospect of the Prince of Wales becoming head of state invigorated Barbadian republicanism.[1]

Among all of Barbados' failed slave insurrections, the largest and best organized was Bussa's Rebellion (1816), named after its African-born leader. Bussa commanded around 400 slaves. He and another 119 rebels died in battle with the colonial militia; 144 were executed.

When the bells inside the clock tower of Bridgetown's House of Parliament tolled midnight and fireworks lit the sky above on November 30, Bussa's statue—also known as the Emancipation Statue—looked down on the joyous ceremony unfolding at the National Heroes Square, so renamed in 1999 after nearly two centuries of bearing the blatantly colonial name Trafalgar Square.

It is paradoxical that the Caribbean's "most English" island with its deep-seated monarchical tradition has become a republic before other former British colonies with longer and deeper anti-colonialist trajectories. A more rebellious Jamaica, homeland to maroon leaders Captain Cudjoe, Quao and Queen Nanny, along with Marcus Garvey, Harry Belafonte, Bob Marley, and Michael Manley, retains the British monarch as its head of state.

---

1 Queen Elizabeth II died on September 8, 2022, and her son became King Charles III. On that week, politicians in Jamaica and in Antigua and Barbuda began preparations for referenda to remove the new king as their head of state.

Barbados may have perhaps begun a global pandemic of republicanism that may very well spread to Jamaica and beyond, to Australia and Canada, to Kenya and Sierra Leone, all the way to Pakistan and Sri Lanka.

Barbados joined the small club of former British-American colonies turned republics (Trinidad and Tobago, Dominica, and Guyana). And let's not forget that the club's founding member was the United States.

While still a teenager, in 1751, George Washington visited Barbados with his ailing half-brother Lawrence. Twenty-five years later, when Great Britain cut trade ties between its loyal Caribbean domains and its wayward continental colonies, disaster struck Barbados. Britain's sugar islands had become monocrop economies, dependent on food imports from North America; when those trade connections were severed, hundreds of slaves starved.

Historically, Barbadians have been ambivalent about monarchical rule largely because two often-conflicting strains of monarchism have manifested themselves on the island, one British, the other African. During the English Civil Wars (1642–1651), Barbados' House of Assembly (mostly composed of slaveholding plantation owners) remained loyal to the English Crown, reluctantly accepting the Commonwealth's authority only in 1651 when the Rump Parliament deployed an invading force and blockaded the island.

In 1675, slaves of the Akan ethnic group, known as skilled warriors, planned a revolt with the objective of gaining control over Barbados and installing a slave named Cuffee as king, enstooling him—the verb exists—in the fashion of the Akan whose descendants inhabit present-day Ghana. British authorities learned of the plot and executed dozens of its leaders. While Ghana gained its independence from Great Britain in 1957 and became a republic three years later, kings, princes and nobles still play important social and symbolic roles and are enstooled as their ancestors have been for centuries.

Bussa's 1816 slave rebellion was Barbados' largest and best organized. Like Cuffee 141 years earlier, Bussa was to be enstooled in the Akan regal tradition, but he was killed in battle. Symbols in one of the rebel slaves' captured flags reflect the abolitionist, pro-independence and African monarchical orientation of the revolt and at the same time show reverence for King George III, who they believed approved of the rebellion. Another revolt leader had the suspiciously republican name Joseph Pitt Washington Franklin. King George III's subjects executed him, something Britain was unable to accomplish with his American namesakes.

In 1998, when Barbados established its Order of National Heroes, it bestowed that honor on Bussa. He was the first to receive that distinction and has been since joined by 10 other Barbadians, most of them politicians and union leaders, pop music star Rihanna, and cricket legend Sir Garfield Sobers, who until recently opposed the queen's removal. Nonetheless, he was one of the transfer (unstooling?) ceremony's guests of honor.

Queen Elizabeth II and Prince Phillip visited Barbados in 1966, 10 months before it became an independent nation. Barbadians warmly greeted them. Except for a few poets and intellectuals there were no expressions of anti-monarchical sentiment at the time. In fact, Oxford-educated Tom Adams, leader of the Barbados Labor Party and second prime minister (1976–1985), held a staunchly monarchist position.

Serious considerations of turning Barbados into a republic began in the late 1970s, but the Cox Commission advised against it. Later commissions opined that the establishment of a republican government was feasible and favorable.

Republicanism gained momentum beginning in 2014, when the Black Lives Matter movement (formed in 2003) swelled in the aftermath of the police killing of Michael Brown in Jefferson, Missouri. By the end of the year, the movement had gone global. In 2015, Barbados' Prime Minister Freundel Stuart advocated for a referendum but it did not materialize.

Then came 2017 with the infamous "Unite the Right" rally in Charlottesville, Virginia. That was the year when Confederate statues began to fall like the proverbial row of dominoes. That year on the eve of Barbados' independence anniversary someone defaced the statue of Horatio Nelson, painting it in yellow and blue, the island's flag colors.

Prime Minister Mia Mottley, elected in 2018, presided over a ceremony to remove Nelson's statue in 2020. The bronze admiral had stood there since 1813.

On November 30, 2020, six months after the execution of George Floyd, Mottley announced that Barbados would become a republic. In her transfer ceremony speech, Mottley quoted another National Hero, the nation's first Prime Minister Errol Barrow, who had warned against "loitering on colonial premises after closing time." For Prince Charles, who represented the British Crown that night, and Admiral Nelson, it was definitely long-past closing time.

25

Puerto Rico: The Holiday Island with the Longest Christmas Season

(Creators Syndicate, December 25, 2021, January 8, 2022)

It is not entirely clear to me how they figure it out and with such precision, but polls and country rankings have recognized Puerto Rico as one of the happiest places in the world. In 2005, one year before the start of the recession that still cripples the island's economy, Puerto Rico ranked first in happiness according to the World Values Survey.

This coincides with its considerable number of holidays and festive days. Puerto Rico has a total of 18 holidays (19 on election years), the most of any Latin American country. Its Christmas season, which de facto begins after Thanksgiving Day, runs into January 24, the end of the *Octavitas* (eight days after the *Octavas*, another eight days of festivities that begin on January 9).

Before the internet, it would have taken me days of work at a good library to find how many public holidays are observed in each country, but thanks to Wikipedia—as President Ronald Reagan said about the Soviets, "Trust but verify"—I found what I was looking for with a few keystrokes, clicks and scrolls.

Online listings of public holidays by country provide different and expectedly inconsistent sets of information. But let's stick with Wikipedia, whose list is topped by Myanmar, with 32 public holidays—this surprised me given the country's long history of military dictatorship; followed by Nepal with 30. Other sources recognize Cambodia as having the largest number of holidays. Cambodia, Myanmar, and other countries with overwhelming Buddhist majorities tend to observe large numbers of holidays. They do not rank high on the happiness list, however.

At the bottom of the "most public holidays" list are the Netherlands and England with eight. Protestant nations in contrast with Catholic countries tend to observe few holidays—the Dutch's Belgian neighbors, who are Catholic, observe 14.

Think about Max Weber's classic book *The Protestant Work Ethic and the Spirit of Capitalism*. Each holiday means one less day of work, which translates into one less day of profits and/or salary. "An idle mind," the aphorism goes, "is the devil's workshop." And besides, holidays bring many expenses, and each English pound spent is one less English pound saved.

Tied with the Dutch and the British are Mexicans—another surprise from the country that has gifted the world with mariachi music, piñatas, and margaritas. Mexico is, of course, Catholic but had a prolonged and deeply anti-clerical revolution (1910–1920). Its official holidays are mostly patriotic: Independence Day, Constitution Day, Revolution Day…. Mexicans, however, celebrate numerous religious feasts, for example, Virgin of Guadalupe Day, which are not official. This in contrast with the Day of St. Willibrord, the Netherlands' patron saint, which passes virtually unnoticed.

Puerto Rican Holidays

The large number of holidays observed in Puerto Rico reflects the island's complex history and bitterly contested political status: a former colony of Catholic Spain; territory, since 1898, of the predominantly Protestant United States; a Hispanic society with a Catholic culture, with close cultural ties to the United States and more churchgoing Protestants than churchgoing Catholics; and a country divided into partisans of three different political status formulas: commonwealth, statehood and independence.

The fact that Catholic societies observe more public holidays than Protestant ones stems in part from the Catholic veneration of numerous saints and the Virgin Mary. A secular, culturally Catholic nation, Puerto Rico mandates commercial closings on six religious holidays, which apart from Good Friday and Easter, have become profoundly secularized: Three Kings Day, Thanksgiving Day, Christmas

Eve, and Christmas Day. Thanksgiving Day is more commonly referred to as *Día del Pavo* (Turkey Day).

Though not official holidays, Puerto Ricans are also fond of celebrating *fiestas patronales* (week-long festivities in honor of the patron saints of each of the island's 78 municipalities). Each February 2, for example, Mayagüez and three other municipalities celebrate the Virgin of La Candelaria Day, a tradition with roots in the Canary Islands; and on July 25, which is also Constitution Day, five towns have Santiago Apostol (St. James) Day. Santiago Apostol Day festivities in Loiza Aldea reflect the strong African cultural presence characteristic of the village.

After nearly four centuries of colonial rule under Catholic Spain, in 1899 Puerto Rico became a U.S. colony, a transition that opened the floodgates to efforts to "Americanize" the population, the most ambitious—and most disastrous—of which was the overnight imposition of English as the language of school instruction.

Unfortunately, almost every issue gets politicized along party lines. The holiday calendar and the way state officials celebrate certain holidays are not immune to partisanship.

Take, for example, last week's official New Year's celebration, the dramatic midnight raising of a glowing star (as opposed to a dropping ball) culminating in a display of fireworks. Video of the spectacle makes evident the use of pro-statehood imagery—watch and judge for yourself. Rather than the star of Bethlehem, spectators saw a rising American flag star (symbolizing the desire to turn Puerto Rico into the 51st state) surrounded by sparkles forming the shape of coconut-tree leaves. The coconut tree is the pro-statehood New Progressive Party's emblem.

Puerto Rico's political code of 1902 established the island's official holiday calendar, which as would be expected was a politically and culturally hybrid list. It removed most Spanish Catholic holidays, Corpus Christi Day, for example; retained New Year's Day, Good Friday, and Christmas Day; and added four other federal holidays: George Washington's Day, Memorial Day, Independence Day, and Thanksgiving Day. Two other territorial holidays completed the nine-holiday calendar: March 22 (Spanish abolition of slavery in Puerto Rico) and July 25 (Day of the U.S. invasion in 1898).

Every new federal holiday is observed on the island, which adds several no-work days to the calendar. I will take a holiday any day of the week but find it odd that Puerto Ricans observe both the Discovery of America (October 12) and the Discovery of Puerto Rico (November 19); the Abolition of Slavery in Puerto Rico (March 22) and Juneteenth. Yes, the Commonwealth's holiday calendar reflects its political schizophrenia.

During the twentieth century, the government of Puerto Rico added numerous holidays, all political in nature, four of them commemorating the birthdays of political leaders who championed one of the three political status formulas: Eugenio María de Hostos and José de Diego (independence), Luis Muñoz Rivera (autonomy), and José Celso Barbosa (statehood); and starting in 1952, on July 25, the commemoration of the Commonwealth's Constitution.

In 2016, Governor Alejandro García Padilla of the pro-commonwealth Popular Democratic Party signed into law a bill that slashed the number of official holidays from 20 (21 on election years) to 16 (15). "We cannot take Puerto Rico out of its economic morass," the governor said, "sunbathing at the beach." The birthdays of the aforementioned politicians were now bunched together on the third Monday of January, along with the birthdays of five new—let us call them "notables"—once again, representing each of the political status options. Previously known as "Presidents' Day," henceforward it would be "Presidents' and Puerto Rican Patriots' Day." For the sake of gender balance, 10 Puerto Rican women have been added to the pantheon of patriots.

In blatantly partisan fashion, García Padilla's successor, Ricardo Rosselló, of the New Progressive Party, eliminated the Commonwealth Constitution Day and added (on March 2) U.S. Citizenship Day. In 2021, his pro-statehood successor, Pedro Pierluisi, reestablished Commonwealth Constitution Day and the birthday of pro-statehood leader Barbosa.

When the Popular Democratic Party regains power, we can expect Barbosa to be thrown back into the generic Patriots' Day.

The Longest Christmas Season

As I write these words—it's January 7, the day after Three Kings Day—in the United States, the Christmas season is over. In the Protestant countries' tradition, it ended on January 1. On the next day, many of my neighbors in Windermere, Florida, began to haul their Christmas trees to the curb for collection.

On many-holidayed Puerto Rico, the Christmas season started early and will not be over until January 24. As the popular Christmas song "Lechón [roasted pork], Lechón, Lechón" goes: "As November comes to an end, I am already well prepared … and following January 6, we continue the tradition and the *octavitas* [sic] begin." *¡Felicidades!*

It's only 10 days before the next holiday (beach day), Martin Luther King Jr. Day. Another 15 holidays will be observed during the rest of 2022.

26

A Russian Soldier Put a Bullet Through the Poet's Head

(Creators Syndicate, April 16, 23, 2022)

Before retreating from the smoldering cities of Bucha and Borodyanka in the first week of April, Russian soldiers raped, tortured, and massacred countless civilians. Upon inspection of the carnage, International Criminal Court chief prosecutor Karim Khan declared the obvious: "Ukraine is a crime scene."

Civilian deaths in those two cities alone are in the thousands, among them a poet in Borodyanka shot in the head by a Russian invader.

There is something about poets, perhaps their gentle sensitivities, that makes them favorite targets of fascist and communist brutality. Like canaries in the dark mine of history, poets are often the first to inhale the deadly fumes of violence and war; they stop chirping, and pandemonium ensues.

Spanish poet and playwright Federico García Lorca was among the early victims of Spanish fascism. He was executed point blank in 1936 by a fascist insurgent who put a bullet through his bulbous, verse-filled head, not before telling him why he would kill him: "for being red and gay" (expletive used).

Four years later, with Generalissimo Francisco Franco's regime firmly in place, a fascist judge sentenced to death another Andalucian poet, Miguel Hernández, who had regaled Spain with some of the most tender (also trenchant) verses ever written, among them the poem "Menos tu vientre" (except for your womb), inspired by his wife's pregnancy; and verses to his unborn child whom he anticipated "clenched fisted will be born." His execution commuted, Hernández died in prison consumed by tuberculosis in 1942. He was 31 years old.

Nazis, sprouting from the same soil as Johann Wolfgang von Goethe and Rainer Maria Rilke, silenced European poets wholesale, brutally so. Take the case of Russian Jewish poet Elena Shirman. In July 1942, Nazi soldiers captured her and her family in Rostov; killed her parents in front of her; ordered her to undress and bludgeoned her to death with the shovel she had used to dig her parents' and her own grave.

Hungarian fascists forced captive fellow Hungarians to mine copper to feed the Nazi war machine; among the thousands of conscripts was poet Miklos Radnoti. "I'm a poet and nobody needs me," he wrote while on a forced march, "prying devils will sing relentlessly." Too exhausted to be of any use, in November 1944, Hungarian devils shot him along with 20 others, then shoved their remains into a mass grave.

Also in 1944, German poet, journalist, and satirist Erich Knauf aroused the ire of none other than Dr. Joseph Goebbels. The Third Reich's infamous propaganda minister hand-picked a Nazi judge who convicted Knauf of "denigrating the Fuhrer," and had him guillotined at the Brandenburg-Gorden Prison. Judicial authorities presented Knauf's widow with a bill for court and execution costs.

Russian poet Ioseb Jughashvili was born in 1878. Under the pen name Soselo, he authored romantic poems about nightingales and the moon ("spreader of light upon the earth"). He is better known by his other nom de guerre (Stalin). He is estimated to have been responsible for 40 million deaths, 10 million more than Hitler. But who is counting? As he put it lyrically, "One death is a tragedy; one million is a statistic."

Call them tragedies or statistics, in 1952 Stalin ordered the killing of 13 Jewish intellectuals, four of them poets (Peretz Markish, David Hofstein, Itzik Feffer and Leib Kvitko). Following years of imprisonment and torture the 13 were executed on what came to be known as "the Night of the Murdered Poets," August 12.

Sensitive and tender as they may be, poets (like everyone else) have moral blind spots of their own. Bafflingly so, some of the Spanish-speaking world's best poets wrote odes to the poet/seminarian turned mass murderer. In the poem "Russia," Miguel Hernández sang praises to Stalin, under whose command the Andalucian poet wrote "huts were transformed into granite houses." In 1941 with World War II underway, Afro-Cuban communist poet Nicolás Guillén wrote an ode to Stalin entitled "Stalin Capitán." Hands down, his worst poem ever. And upon learning about Stalin's death in 1953, future Nobel prize-winning Chilean poet Pablo Neruda credited the Russian tyrant with "peopling [Russia] with schools and flour, printing presses and apples."

But dissident Russian poet Yevgeny Yevtushenko knew better. In his poem "The Heirs of Stalin," he warned: "No, Stalin has not given up / He thinks he can cheat death / We carried him from the mausoleum / But how do we remove Stalin's heirs from Stalin?" "While Stalin's heirs walk this earth," Yevtushenko closed the poem, "Stalin, I fancy, still lurks in the mausoleum."

Russian dictator Vladimir Putin is an unabashed heir to Stalin: cult to personality, militarism, disinformation, political assassinations, dungeons, expansionist wars, mass graves, genocides, and all.

Among the victims of the savage Russian attack and temporary capture of Borodyanka in March and April of this year was a renowned 47-year-old intellectual, whose head was pierced by a bullet in the middle of the city's Central Square. Of peasant stock, his pro-Ukrainian poems had earned him persecution, imprisonment, and even conscription into the Russian army.

But persecution, imprisonment, and conscription not under Stalin's heir but under two of Stalin's predecessors, Tsars Nicholas I and Alexander II. Among Ukrainians, he needs no introduction. He is Taras Shevchenko, born in 1814 in the village of Morintsy, Ukraine.

Deported from his beloved Ukraine, Shevchenko died in St. Petersburg not this March but in March 1861. And the poeticidal bullet did not pierce his head but rather his statue's.

Nine decades later, Putin was born in the same city, then called Leningrad and since renamed St. Petersburg. He grew up in the streets and lived in a rat-infested apartment, resentful of the Nazi's who brought misery upon his family, starved to death one of his siblings, and severely wounded his father. When he calls President Volodymyr Zelenskyy and other Ukrainian leaders "Nazis," Putin is channeling a deep-seated emotional charge. In his cross-wired mind, Ukrainians are to blame for the death of his brother, his father's incapacitation, and his immiserated childhood.

Shevchenko was born a peasant serf, namely a slave, along with the rest of his family, property of a local landlord. After working for several masters, he was taken by a new owner to St. Petersburg, where he studied drawing and painting. Members of St. Petersburg 's artist community raised funds to purchase Shevchenko's freedom when he was 24.

While the Russian soldier who shot Shevchenko's statue was most likely clueless of his victim's identity, the action is highly poetic. Shevchenko was a life-long Ukrainian patriot, proud of his nation's Cossack origins. He grew up hearing stories of Zaporozhian Cossack ancestors, escaped serfs who rose against Russian and Polish/Lithuanian domination in the 1600s and 1700s. The Russian occupation of the Zaporozhian Nuclear Plant (Europe's largest) a few weeks ago echoes old battles between Russians and Cossacks.

In the poem "My Friendly Epistle" (1845) Shevchenko sang ancestral praises: "Our history was bathed in blood / And slept on corpses in the mud, / On Cossack corpses, no more free / But here despoiled of liberty!"

A long-time opponent of servitude and Russian oppression of his native Ukraine, Shevchenko died just one week before the 1861 announcement of the abolition of serfdom. Initially buried in St. Petersburg, his remains were transported to Kanive, Ukraine, where he was re-interred two months later according to his will: "My tomb upon a grave mound high / Amid the spreading plain, / So that the fields, the boundless steppes, / The Dnieper's plunging shore / My eyes could see, my ears could hear / The mighty river roar" ("My Testament," 1845).

Testament to Shevchenko's immortality was Russia's continued persecution of the dead poet and his literary legacy. Tsarist officials banned the publication of his works in the Ukrainian language in 1863 and again in 1876 and dispatched troops to his tomb near the Dnieper Rivers' plunging shore in 1914 to avert potential disorder among pilgrims commemorating the hundredth anniversary of the poet's birth. Later in the century, Stalin's kommissars banned the study of Shevchenko's works.

Earlier this month, when Ukrainian soldiers and civilian authorities returned to the desolated city Borodyanka, they found hundreds of dead civilians; many of them executed, some with their hands tied behind their backs. They embarked on the grim task of corpse identification, then giving them dignified, if temporary, burial.

One anonymous man took it upon himself to bandage the bronze head of the dead poet, whose final verses forecasted: "Dnipro and Ukraina we / Shall recollect, gay villages / In woodlands, gravehills in the steppes, / And we shall sing right merrily" ("Last Poem," 1861).

I Never Left the Classroom: Reflections on Education, Books and Reading

Introduction

"I Never Left the Classroom." Someday I may publish a book with that title. From 1978, when I entered the University of Puerto Rico as a freshman until the present, as full professor at the University of Central Florida, I have always been either a student or a faculty member.

This section goes back even further to 1969, when I was a nine-year-old student at San Marcos Apóstol School in Lima, Peru. The section's opening essay is a re-reading of my favorite schoolbook, a 1966 edition of the *Philips' New School Atlas*. The atlas offers a collection of "still photographs" of the world as it was then and provides an opportunity to reflect on how much it has changed since: two Germanies became one, the Soviet Union disbanded, Yugoslavia unraveled into seven new nations.

Another column, "My Offshore Library," is my time machine travel to the University of Puerto Rico of the late 1970s and early 1980s, a tribute to that institution's intellectual effervescence, and a public thank you letter to its world class faculty.

Two essays offer criticisms to what education has become. One is a defense of the arts and humanities and a call to arms to stop STEM bullying. The other denounces what I call the "seven deadly sins of the modern American

University": STEMism, bureaucratism, metricsism, assessmentism, grantism, credentialism, and footballism.

Two other essays address challenges faced by contemporary students and call for the recognition of different academic strengths and creative assessment of student work. Colleges and universities are plagued by a heartbreaking mental illness pandemic. I see it as the single largest obstacle to student success in higher education.

The section's penultimate essay, "Would You Like to Have Coffee with the Author?" is an invitation to an intimate conversation with some of my favorite Caribbean writers. And the section closes with a trip down memory lane punctuated by newspaper headlines from the 1960s through the year 2002.

27

The Schoolboy's Old, Red English Atlas

(Creators Syndicate, February 27, March 6, 2021)

I love books. It is a love I learned from my father, who, many a Saturday during the late 1960s, took me to one of Lima, Peru's bookstores. I was not even 10 years old.

Of the couple thousand books in my personal library, there is one that I have held on to for the longest time. It has survived all my moves and the sporadic weeding of my home and office library stacks.

I have it in front of me. It's a 64-page, red-covered 54th-edition *Philips' New School Atlas*, published by George Philip & Son in 1966. First issued in 1903, the atlas is now in its 99th edition.

My parents bought me that atlas around 1969; it was required reading at my primary school, San Marcos Apóstol, a Catholic school that followed the British National Curriculum.

My old Philips' atlas captures what French Annales school historians called the longue durée, slow-changing climate patterns, ocean currents and the like, as well as shorter-term changes such as the post-World War II decolonization process and founding of scores of new nations portrayed in the volume's political maps.

As far as the size, shape and location of the world's land masses, not much had changed in the previous five million years. Tectonic geological changes are among the slowest; they are barely perceptible. The Mid-Atlantic Ridge, for example, expands by around one inch per year, and the Himalayas grow taller at the rate of two feet per decade, not enough to render my childhood atlas obsolete or make Mt. Everest's peak harder to reach.

Because it has gone in and out of so many U-Haul boxes, my atlas shows signs of stress. Its covers are coming undone, despite the masking tape I applied to its spine at some point in the 1970s. More than five decades later, like its owner, it is showing signs of aging, including some foxing (humidity spots) as a result of spending a substantial part of its life in humid places like Puerto Rico; foxing is the equivalent of liver spots that appear on the skin of humans once they get as old as my red atlas.

The atlas begins with six pages of average surface temperature and rainfall graphs, one for each continent. The average temperature was 58 degrees Fahrenheit during the coldest month of the year in Lima; almost 10 degrees higher in my birthplace, Havana; and a chilling 37 degrees F in London, where the book had been published. At 48.5 inches, Havana had the highest amount of rainfall, twice as much as London and 23 times more than Lima.

It is—well, it should be—undeniable that the world is undergoing accelerated climate change. The average temperature across the globe in 2019 was 1.71 degrees F higher than the twentieth-century average. This January, the U.S. National Oceanic and Atmospheric Administration confirmed that 2020 was the second-hottest year on record and that 10 of the hottest years ever have occurred since 2005. With regards to temperatures and precipitation, the 1966 Philips' atlas is indeed outdated, and we humans are the only ones to blame.

Curiously, when the atlas was published, the main climatological concern was the opposite: global cooling that began in the 1940s attributed to the widespread use of aerosols.

One degree or two may not sound like a lot, but the increase has been enough to cause global havoc: hotter and more frequent heat waves; melting of polar ice caps and a concomitant rise of ocean levels; widespread flooding; droughts; and far more instances of extreme weather, including tornados and hurricanes.

Since the 1960s, Peru's average temperatures have risen, particularly ocean temperatures, made warmer by periodic El Niño events, which have led to substantial drops in plankton levels, resulting in shrinking fish populations. According to the World Bank, in a matter of 10 years, Peru's climate change doubled the number of "intense rainstorms, mudflows and forest fires."

Turning the page to the Caribbean, we find a dramatic rise in the number of Atlantic-named storms and hurricanes. The yearly average number of hurricanes rose from 4.7 in the 1950s to 1970s to 5.8 from the 1980s to 1990s, jumping to 7.3 in the next two decades. With 30 named storms and 13 hurricanes, 2020 is the stormiest year on record.

And in Great Britain, where Philips' and Son is poised to publish the 100th edition of the school atlas, heat waves and flooding have increased dramatically. The U.K.'s Met Office reported that in August 2020, the country experienced "five tropical nights" during a record-breaking hot spell.

When I started working on this column, my 1966 atlas was holding up precariously. After two weeks of frequent consultation, its front cover has finally fallen off.

I continue to peruse it, now turning my attention to its polychromatic political maps. While the shelf life of a physical map is a magnitude of millions of years, political maps are redrawn with certain regularity, be it on battle fields or around treaty tables.

My old atlas shows countries that no longer exist, others whose borders have been reconfigured and yet others whose names have changed. Yugoslavia, a country artificially cobbled together in the aftermath of World War I, began to disintegrate in 1990; the ensuing, prolonged series of bloody wars culminated with the creation of Bosnia and Herzegovina, Croatia, Serbia and four other new nations. In 2014, the former Ukrainian Soviet Socialist Republic lost over 10,000 square miles of its territory when the Russian Bear bit off the Crimean Peninsula. Ceylon became Sri Lanka in 1972; Rhodesia was renamed Zimbabwe in 1980; and, more recently, in 1999, the Republic of Venezuela was rechristened Bolivarian Republic of Venezuela.

When my atlas rolled off the press, the United Nations had 122 member states. Today, there are 193. During my birth year (1960) alone, 18 new countries joined the organization, and before decade's end, another 28 were added, 17 of them former African colonies.

The growing number of independent nations reflected the decolonization process that had begun in earnest at the end of World War II. It was most evident in Africa, which Europe's imperial nations had sliced as if it were a birthday cake, and in my neck of the woods, the Caribbean, where modern colonialism began as early as the late 1400s.

When my family left Cuba on June 30, 1962, the entire insular Caribbean, except for the Dominican Republic, Haiti, and my homeland, was still under colonial rule. Jamaica and Trinidad and Tobago gained their independence a few weeks later. But in my proud English atlas, the U.K. still held on to most of the rest of the arch of islands from Grenada to the Bahamas.

The geography I learned in school came in handy when my family left Lima in 1970. We flew on a propeller plane that should have had one of those signs that reads, "Caution! This vehicle makes frequent stops." It flew north to Miami along an almost-straight line, stopping to refuel in Quito and Panama City. It is hard to envision this without looking at a map, but the Pacific coast city of Lima sits on a longitude that is farther east (about 3 degrees) than Miami, which is off the Atlantic.

During the 1950s and 1960s, with the Cold War's polarizing winds raging worldwide, nations had to take sides. Under Soviet pressure, in 1949, Central and Eastern European nations formed the Council for Mutual Economic Assistance (CMEA); its military equivalent, the Warsaw Pact, was established in 1955. Their Western counterparts are NATO, created in 1949, and the European Community that began forming in 1958.

Before the century was over, the theretofore-seemingly invincible Soviet Union unraveled into 15 nations including Ukraine, Belarus, Georgia, Lithuania, Borat's adoptive Kazakhstan and another four "stan" nations. In Central and Eastern Europe, meanwhile, the Soviet Union's former satellites saw the collapse of their communist regimes, from Poland to Albania and everywhere in between.

On the other side of Europe, the European Community continued to expand, and in 1992, exactly 500 years after Columbus' fateful voyage, its members signed the Maastricht Treaty that created the European Union. It is now composed of 27 nations, including three former Soviet Socialist Republics, six former Warsaw Pact nations and two former components of Yugoslavia.

On page 8, my atlas has a map of the world with political borders as they stood then. It also includes a series of white bands that represent the world's ocean trade routes; the thicker the band, the more tonnage carried. Among those bands, the widest by far is the one connecting the two coasts of the North Atlantic. Next in volume is one linking Western Europe's major ports with eastern South America's (Rio de Janeiro, Buenos Aires, and Montevideo).

But at some point, in the early 2000s, the Pacific displaced the Atlantic as the world's main trade and navigation axis: Japanese cars, Korean smartphones, Chinese toys and clothing, and, for goodness' sake, drinking water sourced from Fiji, 6,000 miles away.

The more the world changes, the more attached I grow to my red English atlas.

28

My Offshore Library: University of Puerto Rico, 1978–1985

(Creators Syndicate, April 24, May 1, 2021)

I love books. I am fond of them for the words they speak and the ideas they convey, for the stories they tell and the manifold characters that spring out of their pages.

But some of us also enjoy books for reasons beyond their contents, as artifacts, tridimensional objects that readers admire visually, thumb through and even smell.

For all their convenience, e-books do not provide sensorial gifts akin to caressing creamy-textured pages or smelling the aroma of a new book—that enchanting combination of scents emanating from paper, ink, and glue.

Physical books have lives of their own and sometimes (as artifacts) become unique texts in their own right. As single volumes or as part of a collection, they contain memories, even secrets, and if we are willing to listen, they can tell stories as well.

I have three libraries: one at home, one at my university office and one that is a smaller, offshore collection of books I left at my parents' home when I emigrated from Puerto Rico almost 35 years ago.

When I visited my mother, who still lives on the island, this spring break, I spent a few hours examining my unexiled library. The exercise transported me to my years as an undergraduate and graduate student at the University of Puerto Rico (UPR), whose gates I crossed for the first time in 1978, awestruck and starry-eyed.

I pull a small, golden-orange-colored book from a shelf inside the closet that houses my collection. Its slightly discolored spine contains the author's name, Héctor Óscar Ciarlo, and the title, *Las ideas del Renacimiento* (The ideas of the Renaissance, 1974). The smell it emanated as a freshly printed book has long been replaced by the musty whiff of dust, its 180-odd pages showing the unmerciful effect of nearly half a century of tropical heat and an average humidity of 75 percent.

The book brought back fond memories. It was January 1978. I was preparing to enter the University of Puerto Rico at Río Piedras, and my father had the foresight to invite for dinner a neighbor, Professor Ciarlo, an Argentine who held a deanship at the university.

I vividly remember that night's conversation. I told Professor Ciarlo that I was planning to become a high school history teacher. As the good professor he was, he asked where my true passion lay: "Is it in education or in history?" In history, I replied instinctively. "If that is the case," he responded, "you should go to the College of Humanities rather than the College of Pedagogy."

Shortly before leaving, Professor Ciarlo pulled out a copy of his *Las ideas del Renacimiento*, opened it to its title page and handwrote a personal dedication: "For Luis Martínez, with the cordial wish that this reading accompanies your vocation for History." He was the first scholar I ever met, and his wise advice placed me on the right track to become a professional historian and author.

Is it possible for an author to write a personal dedication on an e-book?

I pull out another book, this one much bigger in size and number of pages (589). Titled *Los nuevos sofistas* (The new sophists, 1979), it is the work of one of my UPR humanities professors, the Austrian-born and University of Vienna-trained Dr. Ludwig Schajowicz.

We were fortunate to have such a wise man on UPR's faculty, to which he arrived circuitously. He had fled Nazi Austria in 1939 and resettled in Cuba, where he joined the faculty of the University of Havana. Two decades later, he had to flee again, this time from Castro's dictatorial regime.

I pull out one more book: *Las vallas rotas* (The broken barriers, 1982). Co-authored by my mentor, historian Fernando Picó, political science professor

Milton Pabón and student leader Roberto Alejandro, the book chronicles the UPR strike of 1981 that shut down the campus when I was in my junior year. I transport myself to the day I purchased my copy of *Las vallas rotas*. That afternoon in the spring of 1982, a handful of Picó's students—he insisted that we call him Fernando—gathered in front of the university museum and waited for him. We were going to have dinner at the Jesuit seminary where the priest-scholar lived.

I congratulated him on the publication of the book and showed him the copy I had just purchased. He had not seen one yet—was not even aware that it had come out. And before I finished my sentence, he turned around and began trotting toward the nearest bookstore, La Tertulia, like a schoolchild chasing an ice cream truck.

In 1976, Italian historian Carlo Ginzburg delighted readers with his oddly titled book *Il formaggio e i vermi* (The cheese and the worms). Soon becoming a model for cultural history and microhistory, it recreated a sixteenth-century northern Italian miller's religious beliefs and cosmovision by, among other things, reconstructing his small library and compiling a list of other books he likely read.

Menocchio, as the miller was known, owned a few books and had access to several others, among them Boccaccio's *Decameron* and a book about the adventures of fourteenth-century English knight Sir John Mandeville.

Book collections and reading lists are, indeed, useful sources for recreating individuals' culture, and perhaps the extent of their knowledge, values, and worldview.

A time capsule of sorts, the library I left behind in Puerto Rico in 1986 reveals what I read in the late 1970s and early 1980s, but because that collection is mostly composed of books required in humanities courses at UPR, it also reflects the university's curriculum and the exciting historiographical developments of a time when la Nueva Historia (New History) was at its peak.

Founded in 1903, UPR had the fortune of being forged between two worlds. On the one hand was a combination of European and Spanish intellectual traditions reinforced by numerous exiled anti-fascist Spanish scholars such as Nobel laureate Juan Ramón Jiménez and poet-essayist Pedro Salinas. On the other, was the influence of the modern American (meaning U.S.) university. At the same time, UPR was an institution of higher learning in the Latin American tradition—Marxism and all—with a rich measure of insular nationalism.

My offshore library is testimony to UPR's transatlantic genealogical tree—bush, rather—and the multiple intellectual grafts that have enriched it over the decades.

As a humanities student, I was simultaneously exposed to the canon of Spanish literature—Miguel de Cervantes (*Don Quixote*), Lope de Vega (*Fuenteovejuna*), José Zorrilla (*Don Juan Tenorio*) and Federico García Lorca (*Bodas de sangre*), among other books and authors; the canon of U.S. literature—Herman Melville, Emily Dickinson, John Steinbeck, Ernest Hemingway; a healthy dose of works by modern European authors, most of whom I read in English; a book about a man who turned into a cockroach (by Franz Kafka); a book about an entire nation metamorphosing into rhinoceroses (by Eugene Ionesco); and one about a house guest poet who, to the protagonist's chagrin, overstayed his welcome and never wrote a single verse (by Heinrich Böll).

Colombian Gabriel García Márquez, Peruvian Mario Vargas Llosa and other stellar figures of the 1960s and 1970s Latin American literary boom were widely read at the time. I still hold on to a Spanish-language copy of García Márquez's *No One Writes to the Colonel*, which he once deemed his best book (I recall reading it in one sitting), and a copy of Vargas Llosa's *Los Cachorros*, which, to my surprise and delight, was set in the Lima neighborhood where I grew up during the 1960s.

Since I majored in history and later pursued a masters in the same field, most of my unexiled collection consists of history books. The pages of many of those published before the 1980s have turned brown and brittle because they hail from a time when book printers used acidic additives in paper pulp.

I thumb through profusely underlined copies of books on history and the philosophy of history, among them Spanish-language editions of R.G. Collingwood's *The Idea of History* and Eric Hobsbawm's *Primitive Rebels*.

In Puerto Rico, the late 1970s and early 1980s were times of historiographical splendor. Spearheaded by Puerto Rican historian Fernando Picó (my thesis advisor), student of the nineteenth-century sugar industry Andrés Ramos Mattei, labor historian Gervasio García and historian of slave resistance Guillermo Baralt, the period saw a peak in historiographical effervescence, productivity, and creativity.

Their works, largely inspired by the French Annales school of history and British and American new social history, broke with traditional Puerto Rican historiography by bringing to the forefront those previously "without history": peasants toiling in the island's highlands; fiery torch-bearing, rebellious slaves; socialist cigarmakers; and other proletarians.

By no means a wealthy institution, UPR offered my generation as fine a university education as one could get anywhere in the world; and at $5 to $15 a credit, it was a hard to beat value.

It was there, in a history seminar taught by Picó, that I first heard of Ginzburg and *The Cheese and the Worms*. Just a few years ago, I finally got around to reading it and assigning it to my own students. Tried by the Roman Inquisition for heretical views, an unrepentant Menocchio was burnt at the stake in 1599.

29

The Seven Deadly Sins of the Modern American University

(Creators Syndicate, May 8, 2021)

My 40-odd years in university classrooms—including the past 14 months in the "Alice in Wonderland"-ish Zoom environment—give me a long-term perspective on higher education and what anthropologists call "participant observation" experiences on the changing roles, values, and culture of American higher education.

While the term "ivory tower" (Merriam-Webster: "a secluded place that affords the means of treating practical issues with an impractical often escapist attitude") is generally meant as criticism, I argue that a healthy dose of seclusion and impracticality, even a bit of escapism, are needed more than any time before, given society's overriding obsession with the practical—the utilitarian, the vocational, the profitable, the quantifiable, the STEMish, the faddish and the crude.

Lest I be misunderstood, I am not calling for a return to the 1970s, much less the Middle Ages, when the first universities emerged. I confess that I engage in these friendly, from-the-inside criticisms with some trepidation knowing that the sworn enemies of higher education may use them for nefarious purposes.

A few years ago, I presented the conference paper "The Seven Deadly Sins of the Modern American University." While I have since identified at least twice as many additional sins, these were the original seven: STEMism, bureaucratism, metricsism, assessmentism, grantism, credentialism and footballism.

1. STEMism: The extreme fixation on researching, publishing, and teaching science, technology, engineering, and mathematics threatens to reduce universities to tech centers tasked with training students in narrow utilitarian fields while neglecting and marginalizing the humanistic core of a university education. STEM without the flower is just a stem.

2. Bureaucratism: Over the past few decades, universities have taken on a whole range of new responsibilities beyond their core missions of teaching and research, some necessary, others actual hinderances to learning and scholarship. According to the National Center for Educational Statistics, between 1980–1981 and 2014–2015, the proportion of expenditures in university instructional costs dropped from 41 to 29 percent. Administrative costs, other studies reflect, have since surpassed teaching-related expenses in some universities.

3–5. Metricsism, Assessmentism and Grantism: These are interrelated, compounding obsessions that devaluate the importance of the intangible, unmeasurable and transcendental. Metricists—I do not mean scholars of poetic metrics—believe that almost everything can be reduced to numbers by which universities must live and die. Mr. Bean Counter, can you tell me how to quantify the value of inspiring or transforming the life of a single student? How many points does that get me in my yearly faculty report?

The assessmentist—the root of the word is a giveaway—is equally obsessed (anally so) with numbers but delights in using buzzwords such as "institutional effectiveness" and "accountability." All institutions, particularly those that receive public funds, should strive for effectiveness, and all members of a university community should be accountable, but assessmentism means an unending quest for data, much of it nonsensical, gathered to justify bureaucratic sprawl and satisfy politicians, donors, sports fans, and others. Much of this data is gathered through inopportune, time-consuming surveys—"it only takes 20 minutes to complete," they tell us. I, for one, have unilaterally declared a moratorium on surveys. That one, by the way, took more like 40 minutes. Let's take the "ass" out of "assessment"!

Grantism is yet another numbers fetish. The number and monetary value of research grants has replaced the actual importance of research and publications. Just thumb through any glossy university yearly report and you will see the exaggerated value placed on the amount of grant money received by that particular institution. Some refer to the group of most-grant-money-getting professors as the "millionaire's club." How foolish! As a historian, I belong to a paupers' club, and proudly so.

6. Credentialism: Call me recalcitrant if you wish, but I am not giving up the belief that universities are, at their core, places of teaching and learning. Most everyone needs a job, and universities provide professional credentials necessary to pursue a variety of employment opportunities. But most faculty believe that we are educating students for more than a diploma and paycheck—to become fulfilled, socially conscious citizens who see learning as a lifelong trajectory.

And to close, No. 7: footballism. I will be brief and, lest I get in trouble with one of universities' most powerful constituency, will just paraphrase American philosopher Rodney Dangerfield: "I went to a football game the other night and a university sprung out."

30

Diverse Pathways in Education and Life: Seven Real-Life Stories

(Creators Syndicate, August 7, 14, 2021)

Those of us who teach, whether at the K–12 or college levels, cross paths with thousands of students during our careers. They are all different, each with his or her own strengths and weaknesses. Yet after decades of tinkering with grading systems and standardized tests, we have not produced adequate—or fair, I would add—assessment tools that take into consideration, and adjust for, a host of factors including the much-talked-about "learning styles" (verbal, visual, auditory, etc.).

Students with the learning challenge of attention deficit hyperactivity disorder (ADHD), for example, generally do not receive grades that reflect their often-extraordinary academic and social abilities. They may write the most imaginative paper but get a low grade because they turned it in late or lost it in the bus.

In my more than 35 years of teaching, at high school first, and at the college level later, individuals with ADHD have stood out as my brightest and most creative students.

Pedagogical research has demonstrated that some students, males in particular, lag months if not years behind in maturity; yet we assess their academic performance, skills, and behavior as if all students of the same age are equally mature.

Scores of studies on brain development have demonstrated that key parts of the brain do not reach maturity until around the age of 25, particularly the pre-frontal cortex, which regulates emotions and impulses and allows individuals to assess risks accurately and make long-term plans.

Yet by the age of 25, we are all expected to make mature decisions about some of the most important aspects of our lives: where and what to study, where to live and work and, in many cases, with whom we hope to spend the rest of our lives (or according to marriage expectancy statistics, seven to eight years).

Real-Life Stories

The following are real-life stories of students who were late to mature, had dif-ficulties focusing on their assignments, were fearful about speaking in public, made bad decisions about school attendance, clowned around in class, or simply had different learning styles. With time and effort and with the support of caring parents and teachers, they matured, learned to focus, gained confidence, and learned to make wise life and education decisions that led them to self-fulfillment and career success.

Pedro

I know a student named Pedro, who loved math growing up because he enjoyed the challenge of solving problems in his own creative ways; in tenth-grade geome-try he was fond of playing with proofs. When the high-noon time of algebra (and later algebra II) arrived, he was taught to memorize formulas, something that did not appeal to his unformulaic brain. His high school math grades, except in geometry, ranged between C-minuses and D's.

As a junior, Pedro took the college entrance exams and, to everyone's surprise and the embarrassment of his math teacher, who was in the habit of calling him "dumbbell," got the school's top math test scores, higher than those of straight-A seniors.

Cliff

Another student, Cliff, decided to stop going to school on Fridays during the last quarter of his final year of high school. Bored and alienated by his classes, Cliff preferred to stay home or spend the day playing basketball or riding his bike. Not only did he throw away any chance of contending for a perfect attendance medal (not that he cared), but he also came close to failing two classes, an outcome that would have prevented him from attending the university to which he had been admitted.

In college, Cliff came to value the privilege of taking classes with leading experts in various fields. As a freshman, he was absent only one time (for no good reason) and over the next decade never missed another class until completing his Ph.D.

Lauren

Lauren most probably had the undiagnosed gift of ADHD. She had difficulties focusing on assigned readings, including short books like Hemingway's *The Old Man and the Sea*. Melville's far more voluminous *Moby Dick* was an insurmountable task. Despite these challenges, Lauren did fairly well, generally getting B's in literature classes by reading CliffsNotes, creatively filling in plot blanks and inferring (a nice word for "making up") things about books she had not fully read.

In college, Lauren developed a voracious appetite for books, sometimes reading them in one sitting. At the age of 26 she published a book based on her M.A. thesis, the first of seven she has written so far. Some have earned Lauren state, national and international book awards.

Moby Dick is still on her to-read list.

Jean Pierre

Jean Pierre was a free-spirited, sociable, and gregarious high school student with leadership qualities and a witty, if at times untimely, sense of humor. Those are welcomed attributes in a graduate school seminar and in virtually every profession from sales to public speaking, but in Jean Pierre's school they could, as they did, get him into trouble.

Unbeknownst to Jean Pierre, an admissions recruiter from a North Carolina college came to his school ready to offer him a soccer scholarship. During the Q & A session following the recruiter's presentation, Jean Pierre decided to play class clown. The best question that he could come up with was whether the college's basketball players dunked.

Expensive little joke it turned out to be. The principal requested that the scholarship be rescinded and sentenced him to a three-day suspension.

Eventually, the parts of Jean Pierre's brain that assess risks reached full maturity and he learned to use humor only when and where appropriate. At the age of 26, he received a full-ride scholarship with generous yearly stipends to pursue a Ph.D. at Duke University.

María

Like one in four Americans, María was afraid of public speaking, a condition known as glossophobia. One day in her college sophomore year, her literature professor asked her to read aloud an essay she had written. The request caught her off guard; she was nervous and started to make a barely audible presentation. The professor stopped María, scolded her for her poor performance and asked her to sit down.

Over the years, María gained confidence to the point of being comfortable, and enjoying, speaking in front of audiences as large as a couple thousand. These days, she does not think twice about giving live radio and TV interviews.

Lee

Readers will recognize this scenario. It is a June afternoon, and high school students, parents, teachers, and school administrators are packed into a school auditorium; following a couple of usually unmemorable, hackneyed speeches—"this is not an end, it's a beginning..."—the capped-and-gowned master of ceremony calls up students to receive a wide range of medals. Invariably, two or three of them receive the lion's share of the awards. They walk off proudly, sporting chests full of medals.

But Lee came out empty-handed without even that most coveted of medals, "perfect attendance." He was satisfied with what used to be called "gentleman's C's."

In Lee's old school and schools around the world, attaining high grades and collecting medals has become an unhealthy obsession that oftentimes interferes with—actually, stifles—learning and the development of important skills and aptitudes. I have said in public more than once, to the astonishment of many, that I am suspicious of straight-A students.

With a couple of exceptions, Lee's high school teachers were unwilling or incapable of recognizing or giving him credit for other strengths, such as divergent thinking, creativity (as in coloring outside the lines), intellectual risk-taking, and innovation, all of which are highly cherished in today's employment environment.

Despite (arguably because of) his lackluster high school grades, Lee went on to become a successful scholar. His books have earned him several awards and medals, and his university gave him the highest academic honor it offers its faculty and, somewhat embarrassingly, placed his image in local billboards promoting university excellence.

Well, it is time to come clean. I am Pedro, and Cliff, and Lauren, and Jean Pierre, and María and Lee. I did not write this column to bring attention to my degrees, books, and medals but rather to honor the multitude of students who fail math and other courses, lose interest in school, have difficulties reading, clown their way out of opportunities, are terrified of public speaking and don't get medals at graduation; and to plead with teachers and school administrators to value and reward true and full student diversity.

You never know. One day you may be driving down the road and be surprised to see one of your former C-student's excellence celebrated in an illuminated billboard.

31

The Epidemic That Will Outlive the COVID-19 Pandemic, the Spiraling Mental Health Crisis Among Our College Students

(Creators Syndicate, March 21, 27, 2021)

My Creators Syndicate biography names education among my fields of expertise; yet, since I started my weekly opinion columns in September 2020, I had not written on the subject. I feel compelled to do so this week, addressing what I believe is the most pressing problem in American higher education: the decaying mental health of our college and university students.

As a university professor with over three decades in the classroom and one pandemic year teaching online, I am painfully aware of another raging pandemic: the mental health crisis affecting the nation's university students. It has been decades in the making and sadly will retain its virulence long after we vanquish the ongoing COVID-19 pandemic. We cannot mask or vaccine our way out of it.

Scores of studies document the skyrocketing incidence of anxiety, depression, and other emotional and mental illnesses. A large-sample, longitudinal study of undergraduate students found that the rate of moderate to severe depression increased from 23 percent in 2007 to 41 percent in 2018. Moderate to severe anxiety, meanwhile, jumped from 17.9 percent in 2013 to 34 percent in 2018.

Studies by the American College Health Association from 2018 and 2019 revealed that 6 out of 10 students experienced overwhelming anxiety, while 4 in 10 reported bouts with severe depression.

The COVID-19 pandemic has exacerbated an already dire situation. One study shows that, as early as the first weeks of the pandemic, 85 percent of students endured "moderate to high levels of distress." In January 2021, PBS NewsHour recounted grim statistics from the CDC: three out of four individuals between the ages of 18 and 24 reported poor mental health associated with the pandemic, and 1 in 4 had thoughts of suicide in the previous 30 days.

These and similar studies show the often-hidden nature of the actual day-to-day suffering of millions of young men and women, real students we know personally or hear about. Some show signs of mental distress; others mask—figuratively and, in recent times, literally—their pain with seeming cheerfulness; still others stop attending classes, some incapacitated to the point that they cannot even accomplish the simple task of formally withdrawing from a course, let alone reaching out to their professors for help.

Since the massive shift to remote teaching and learning during the pandemic, it has become harder to tell who among our students is showing emotional problems. For all its merits in terms of access and convenience, distance learning is NOT the same, nor as effective, as what is now called "presential education." This has become increasingly evident since the start of the pandemic. One of the studies cited above identifies among the most at-risk groups those who spend "eight or more hours in front of computer, smartphone or television screens."

While psychology consistently ranks among the most popular undergraduate majors, with few exceptions, faculty members lack formal training in the field. At most higher education institutions, including my own university, however, we receive some instruction and guidelines on how to identify symptoms, approach individual students on the subject and refer them, when deemed necessary, to student health services or other campus offices that provide help.

At the very least, we are there to let them know they are not alone, that we care about their health and that resources are available. The more classes you teach and the more students you have, the harder it is to identify psychological distress. Not even the best clinical eye will allow a psychology professor to spot distress in a student who sits 15 rows up in a class auditorium.

The ravages of the COVID-19 pandemic have severely impacted America's college students, beyond the physical ailments endured by those who have contracted the virus and the psychological suffering wrought on by its virulent spread.

College students, as evidenced by scores of surveys and scientific studies, are facing manifold social, economic, and academic challenges that compound one another, producing further emotional distress. The extant evidence establishes that the poor, women, Asian Americans, and other minority students are particularly vulnerable.

Laptops, iPads, and smartphones, with all their heralded merits, are not adequate replacements for face-to-face interactions. And what we call social media does not foster—but instead actually weakens—social and communal bonds of the sort we are wired to cultivate and enjoy.

A recent Student Voice survey of 2,000 undergraduates revealed that "friends and social life" ranked highest among the aspects of campus life students miss the most since the start of the pandemic. Those who have not yet returned to campus continue to endure high levels of social isolation, but even among those who are back, 38 percent are dissatisfied with their opportunities to "see friends and meet peers." Close to a third express dissatisfaction with chances to connect with professors and university staff. One respondent from a large western state university dramatized the extent of his social disconnection. Two months into the current semester, "The only people I've talked to for more than a minute are staff at doctor's appointments."

Students are also enduring the devastating effects of the economic crisis propelled by the ongoing pandemic. In April 2020, when the general rate of unemployment soared to 14.7 percent, college-age Americans (18–24) endured a rate that was twice as high.

Before the pandemic, around 45 percent of undergraduates held part-time or full-time jobs. College-age students, a substantial proportion of whom work in the restaurant, hospitality, and retail sectors, have been particularly hard hit by the rise in unemployment, many losing their jobs and many others having their work hours significantly reduced.

A July 2020 study by the American College Health Association found that two-thirds of students were feeling more stress due to their financial situation and 17 percent described their financial circumstances as "a lot more stressful."

This semester, two of my students told me they had lost their employment. One, who held two jobs before, lost one and is now the family's only source of income. Another, with tears in her eyes, told me (via Zoom) that she had come close to homelessness not once but twice in the past few months.

A recent OneClass survey revealed that 56 percent of students believed they could no longer afford college. Indeed, enrolments have dropped, albeit not sharply; students are matriculating for fewer credit hours; many are having difficulties affording assigned course books.

Several studies confirm my personal observations that students are facing more academic difficulties. One study reveals that nearly three out of four students were having problems focusing on their academic work. Another study demonstrated that 80 percent experienced lower levels of motivation to complete their work and even show up for class.

This semester, I have had a larger than usual proportion of students withdrawing from my courses and/or stopping attending class. The number who are behind in their assignments is also through the roof.

Students and faculty members are also experiencing Zoom fatigue. A student survey found that nearly one-third of undergraduates "never want to take another class via Zoom." I do not want to teach another one either.

I, for one, am anxiously looking forward to the end of the COVID-19 pandemic, the end of Zoombie education and the return to face-to-face interactions with my students and colleagues, without social distancing and without masks.

32

An Almost Dangerous Occupation? Teaching History in Florida's Public Schools and State Universities

(Creators Syndicate, September 11, 18, 25, 2021)

Last June, the government of Florida enacted two controversial and seemingly contradictory education mandates. On June 10, at the urging of Florida's Governor Ron DeSantis, the state's board of education banned the teaching of "critical race theory" in public schools. Later that month, DeSantis signed into law the "intellectual freedom and viewpoint diversity" bill aimed at Florida's state universities.

As a historian and university professor, the higher education mandate touches me directly; as someone who inherits students that come out of the state's public schools, the K–12 directives impact my work as well.

Those Who Can and Those Who Can't

These state government actions have long roots that date at least to the "culture wars" of the 1980s and 1990s, when American society became increasingly divided and polarized over several cultural issues, including abortion and what some then called "family values," gun ownership, the separation of church and state, and the role of government in general.

Because education is the population's primary socializer, those on either side of these issues pointed their attention to K–12 education, where children are first exposed to social studies, civics, and history courses that address social, cultural, and political subjects; and to university campuses, which some conservatives increasingly viewed as unpatriotic institutions for left-wing indoctrination.

At the time when this country was having bitter debates over national school history standards, historian Arthur Schlesinger Jr. said provocatively: "Being a historian has almost become a dangerous occupation." Twenty-six years later, we can remove the "almost" qualifier from his observation. And for those outside of the extremes, the danger comes from the right and the left.

Originally spearheaded by conservative National Endowment for the Humanities Director Lynne Cheney, the resulting American History Standards were too radical and politically correct for conservatives. Cheney famously tabulated the number of times certain topics and individuals were mentioned in the new standards draft report: the "white males" Paul Revere, Robert E. Lee, J.P. Morgan, Alexander Graham Bell, Thomas Edison, the Wright Brothers, Albert Einstein and Jonas Salk (0 times); Lincoln's Gettysburg Address and Ulysses S. Grant (1 time, each); Harriet Tubman (6 times); the Seneca Falls "Declaration of Sentiments" and American Federation of Labor (9 times, each); the Ku Klux Klan (17 times) and Senator Joseph McCarthy and McCarthyism (19 times).

One thing was true: Those American history standards reflected the progressive views of historian Gary Nash's team at UCLA's National Center for History in the Schools, which in turn reflected the profound transformations in the historical discipline over the previous three decades. "New history," as it was then called, expanded its focus to include women, minorities, workers, and other groups previously "without history," and embraced new methodologies (i.e., quantification) that could answer social history questions about common individuals' quotidian life.

The discipline's transformation brought along a greater degree of professional activism and advocacy as well as left-leaning politicization. It is important to mention, however, that previous generations of historians, short of being politically neutral, generally espoused an uncritical, triumphalist view of American history. Being uncritical is also political.

Historians and other social scientists and humanities scholars, it is no secret, are generally progressive; some are clearly on the left; very few are conservative because, let's face it, universities and the academy have very little tolerance for conservative views. Find me a right-wing university historian and I will trade him for a left-wing member of my local chamber of commerce.

Schlesinger characterized the final revised version of the national history standards as a "sturdy and valuable document, sober, judicious and thoughtful." But at the same time, he recognized that there were extremists at both ends of the spectrum. "Therapists," he called them in derision, who seek to "convert history into cheerleading—each seeking to promote its own values."

Among the culture wars' collateral damage was the teaching profession. Some conservative voices chastised schoolteachers as incompetent, uncaring, and greedy (for goodness' sake!). Someone coined and others repeated the insulting slogan: "Those who can, do; and those who can't, teach." I remember seeing a satirical political cartoon in which an angry taxpayer demanded that teachers' salaries be cut; when asked why he was proposing such a thing, the protester responded that he had no power over the astronomical salaries of athletes and movie stars, but he could do something about the compensation of his school district's teachers.

Years later, teachers and their advocates retorted with a slogan of their own. One can purchase online pins, T-shirts and bumper stickers that read: "Those who can, teach. Those who cannot, pass laws about teaching."

2005/2006

When I joined the faculty of the University of Central Florida in the mid-2000s, debates about the teaching of history in public schools and the social sciences and humanities in state universities had intensified, becoming increasingly partisan and politicized.

The Republican-dominated Florida Legislature considered two bills in 2005/ 2006. One, the Florida Education Omnibus Bill (H.B. 7087e3), which then-Governor Jeb Bush signed into law, mandated the curricular content of K–12 history education. A year earlier, three Republican lawmakers had filed H.B. 0837, An Act Relating to Student and Faculty Academic Freedom in Postsecondary Education, but it did not go up for a vote.

The school law prescribed the content of history curricula. It emphasized the study of America's best known (and least divisive) foundational documents, the Declaration of Independence and the Constitution, with special attention to the Bill of Rights. It also outlined the topics to be covered in history courses, including the standard episodes: "discovery," the colonial era, the Civil War, westward expansion, and the World Wars.

To their credit, lawmakers also made provision for subjects associated with progressive views: the civil rights movement, Holocaust education to encourage "tolerance of diversity in a pluralistic society," African American history, the "contributions" of women and Hispanics and even the "protection of natural resources."

Other curricular prescriptions responded to conservative goals. While the Declaration of Independence and Constitution are widely embraced as bipartisan historical texts, the new provisions included the Federalist Papers, which were originally and continue to be partisan documents.

Other guidelines reflected mostly conservative positions such as sexual abstinence education, "the nature and importance of free enterprise" and the promotion of patriotism through "flag education" and the celebration of veterans.

The most controversial aspects of the law had little to do with what subjects were included and which ones were left out, but rather with the definition of the historical discipline formulated by people who "couldn't teach" (perhaps, "couldn't do") but believed themselves qualified to "pass laws about teaching." As defined by the Florida Legislature, American history "shall be viewed as factual, not as constructed, shall be viewed as knowable, teachable, and testable"—remember that Governor Bush was a fervent promoter of the Florida Comprehension Assessment Test (FCAT) standardized tests that were an integral part of the No Child Left Behind Act, which his brother signed into federal law in 2001.

Well yes, history must be factual; it should not be made up! But most of Florida's lawmakers seemed to ignore the fact that only a tiny proportion of history's facts have been recorded and that the people who recorded them privileged certain facts over others: those they deemed either important or expedient, or both. As one of the bill's critics, state Representative (and schoolteacher) Shelley Vana wondered, "whose facts would they be, Christopher Columbus's or the Indians?"

Because the extant historical record has been created and preserved mostly by those with the power to do so and because invariably, they had biases, agendas and blind spots, history, contrary to the belief of the law's crafters, is indeed constructed.

The same legislators who established provisions for K–12 history education had previously considered the bill named "Relating to Student and Faculty Academic Freedom in Postsecondary Education." Primarily motivated by a desire to protect students' rights to "a learning environment in which they have access to a broad range of serious scholarly opinion," and "to be graded without discrimination on the basis of their political or religious beliefs," the bill also had the stated intent of protecting the academic freedom and "intellectual independence" of professors and researchers and banning the imposition of any ideological orthodoxy on members of the university community. While I had questions about what motivated all these prescriptions, in principle, I saw nothing inherently harmful in that.

But the bill went further. It chastised professors "who persistently introduce controversial matter into the classroom or coursework that has no relation to the subject of study and serves no legitimate pedagogical purpose" and mandated that professors "make their students aware of serious scholarly viewpoints other than their own."

No one can honestly deny that university faculty, particularly in the humanities and social sciences, tend to inhabit the left side of the spectrum—I know; I am one of them. Some, perhaps too many, are intolerant of conservative or heterodox perspectives. I know that too; I have been on the receiving end of their intolerance.

But academic orthodoxy cannot and should not be outlawed. Governor Bush found the bill problematic and saw it as an invitation to waves of lawsuits by students and faculty who were or felt aggravated by ideological intolerance. That is why he opposed it and it did not go up for a vote.

2021

Fast-forward to 2021, a far more polarized and violent political context in which reasonable, honest, and civil debates among individuals on different sides of so many issues have become—it pains me to say it—virtually impossible. The sights and sounds captured in videos taken inside airplane cabins, grocery stores and school-board meeting halls are testimony to our collective descent into forms of barbarism that are simultaneously tribal and selfish.

In this politicized environment, Florida's Governor Ron DeSantis and the state's Republican legislators have revisited some of the education issues their predecessors debated some 15 years earlier. In June, following DeSantis' instructions, the state's Department of Education issued a mandate banning the teaching of "critical race theory" and any other "theories that distort historical events." Later in the month, the state legislature passed, and the governor signed H.B. 233, the

"Intellectual Freedom and Viewpoint Diversity" act, requiring public universities to survey students and faculty about their political beliefs.

And just this month, Republican state legislator Randy Fine filed H.B. 57 (An Act Relating to Racial and Sexual Discrimination), which effectively prohibits all state, county, and municipal agencies, including "public K–20 educational institutions," from offering mandatory trainings, workshops and programs that employ "divisive concepts" and "race or sex scapegoating or race or sex stereotyping."[1] Days later, his colleague Joe Gruters filed the state Senate version of that bill.

Florida, it seems, is fertile ground for such legislative initiatives. This summer, Senator Marco Rubio introduced two complementary bills that parallel and echo state legislation. First, the "Protecting Students from Racial Hostility Act," followed by the "Protect Equality and Civics Education Act."

All these state and federal legislative initiatives use language identical to that of September 2020's presidential executive order, "Combating Race and Sex Stereotyping," issued by transplanted Floridian, now former President Donald Trump.

What's Critical Race Theory?

Until as recently as the spring of 2021, few people had even heard the term "critical race theory," a concept that is misunderstood and/or misrepresented by some of its proponents and most of its detractors.

The concept emerged in the 1980s from within the scholarly field of legal analysis. Promulgated by Black and Latino Ivy League scholars like Derrick Bell, Kimberle Crenshaw (who coined the term) and Richard Delgado, critical race theory rests on the belief that American society is fundamentally racist and, thus, discrimination against nonwhites permeates not only the law and the criminal justice system, but also most institutions and cultural forms. As Delgado and co-author Jean Stefancic explain in their book *Critical Race Theory*, "our social world, with its rules, practices, and assignments of prestige and power, is not fixed; rather, we construct it with words, stories and silence." Those words, the

---

1 The bill was signed into law, becoming effective September 1, 2022. Among other things, it encourages students, including my own UCF students, to report faculty who they feel are attempting to indoctrinate them or are failing to present diverse perspectives.

argument continues, have been historically enunciated by whites who have muffled other voices into virtual silence.

As a decades-long student of slavery and its aftermath in the Americas, some of the central arguments of critical race theory seem reasonable to me. Racism, which is a belief and an attitude, exists, of course—whether it is as omnipresent as some claim, is up for discussion. Forms of discrimination, meanwhile, which are concrete manifestations of racism, are undeniable realities as well.

But other tenets ascribed to critical race theory strike me as dogmatic, contradictory, and even intellectually dishonest. If we use the analogy of critical race theory as a religion, it has spun numerous cults with extreme interpretations (heresies) preached by often-uninformed, self-proclaimed diversity and inclusion coaches and trainers.

Take for example the rejection and characterization of meritocracy as "a vehicle for self-interest, power, and privilege" (UCLA School of Public Affairs, Critical Race Studies Program) imposed by holders of white privilege to exclude and marginalize Black people and other minorities. First, let's not forget that the concept and practice of meritocracy originated in nineteenth-century Great Britain precisely to provide access to education and employment for those at the margins of elite society. It is also true that the application of meritocratic principles has not eliminated discrimination against nonwhites. Believe me, I know.

More recently, other values and concepts have been deemed racist and discriminatory. The list is disturbing: rigor and rational thinking, the Socratic method and linear thinking.

As someone who has tirelessly advocated for diversity and fair inclusion in education and the workplace, I have espoused merit principles and academic rigor but have also argued for broad and creative definitions of merit and rigor. Merit can be accomplished through rigor, and thus educational institutions and employers have the responsibility to provide opportunities for individuals to experience rigor and build their own merit. That some are at a disadvantage, I also know; they must be given all the support possible.

As to critiques of linear thinking, I don't even know where to begin.

33

Rethinking Columbus and 1492 in and out of the Classroom

(Creators Syndicate, October 2, 9, 2021)

Today is the first day of October, a month that is many things. It's National Apple Month (that makes sense, they are in season); it's also National Sausage Month, perhaps because it coincides with German American Heritage Month (aka Oktoberfest), but it is also Italian American Heritage Month (and National Pasta Month)—most likely because Columbus Day falls on the 12th of this month.

What used to be called "discovery" of the New World and is now more commonly referred to as "first encounters" or "initial contacts" is a perennial hot-button topic. Columbus, the historical process' protagonist, is in the eyes of many a greedy, genocidal villain; in short, the cause of most of the calamities that struck the Americas following the fateful year in which he "sailed the ocean blue."

This view of Columbus drew much of its fire from the torrent of conferences, articles, books, lectures, and documentaries produced during the quincentennial commemorations of 1992. I remember attending a lecture by Kirkpatrick Sale, author of *The Conquest of Paradise*, in which he charged Columbus with "eco-terrorism." Later that year, at another university, I witnessed students marching to the chant of "Fuck Columbus; Fuck Columbus;" I kept a copy of the protest's placards as souvenir and historical artifact.

Also in 1992, the City of Berkeley declared October 12 "Day of Solidarity with Indigenous People." Since then, several states and municipalities have either stopped celebrating Columbus Day or have replaced it with Indigenous People's Day.

Statues of the Genovese explorer have been targets of periodic vandalism in the United States and elsewhere in the Americas for quite some time. Back in 1986, upon the flight of Haitian dictator Jean-Claude Duvalier, protesters tore up a statue of Columbus and dumped it, where else?, in the ocean blue. Scores of other statues have been toppled, defaced, and splashed with blood-colored paint. According to CBS News, in the five months after the beginning of the racial protests and riots that followed the 2020 killing of George Floyd, 33 Columbus monuments had been either removed or were in the process of removal in the United States.

I am not here to defend the Admiral, but as someone who has taught Latin American and Caribbean history for over three decades and has written on the subject, I will say this: Columbus was a complex historical figure full of contradictions reflective of his time, a period of profound and interconnected political, intellectual, economic, and social transitions.

Rethinking Teaching About 1492

Debates over how and what to teach in school history courses intensified in the mid-1990s in the context of often-contentious discussions over the National Standards for History. In the past two years, with the spread of "critical race theory," the 1619 Project and the Zinn Education Project into school curricula and legislation that explicitly bans critical race theory in over a dozen states, such disputes have reached a feverish peak. Shouting matches at school board meetings, threats and counter threats, firings of career educators and even episodes of physical violence have become all too common.

Teaching 1492 by focusing on (and expecting students to memorize) the basic facts of Columbus' first voyage, dates, names of vessels and landing sites, and the mutiny he averted by lying to his crew, is bad pedagogy. On the other hand, the politicization of the subject reduces one of world history's most momentous and consequential episodes to a unidimensional narrative of victims and victimizers.

There are far more intellectually stimulating alternatives. We can start by bringing Columbus down to size, reducing him to what he was: just one character, albeit an important one, within a drama with many co-protagonists (co-villains, if you wish), thousands of supporting actors and oceans of red, white, and black extras.

Another useful pedagogical approach is to expand the focus from 1492 to a broader period of circa 1492, that includes the four or so decades before and after those original encounters that forever changed the world, linking Europe, the Americas and Africa and opening the path to what we now call globalization.

Circa 1492 was a context of a Europe in transition from the Middle Ages to the Renaissance; from feudalism to capitalism; from small regional kingdoms to absolute monarchies; and from a worldview dominated by religion and scholasticism to another based on humanism and experimentation.

34

Would You Like to Have Coffee with the Author?

(Creators Syndicate, April 30, May 14, 21, 28, 2022)

I advocate and promote reading. I do it through my columns, in the classroom and every opportunity I have. Of course, not of just any reading material; there is too much junk out there—remember Snooki and The Situation from "Jersey Shore"? They have six books between them—and not just any way of reading either, but deep, contemplative, reflective reading, of the kind where the reader plays an active role, engaging the author in a conversation.

Reading, it is no secret, has been on the decline. People read less; surf, skim, and scan more; comprehend and retain less and are increasingly becoming passive consumers of the written word. The reasons and consequences of these changes are engagingly discussed by Nicholas Carr in his *New York Times* bestselling book *The Shallows: What the Internet Is Doing to Our Brains*. The "ecosystem of interruption technologies," Carr contends, has wired our brains for less attentive reading, producing diminished learning, weakened understanding and blunted imagination.

I also blame the K–12 education system with its obsession with learning facts to be returned undigested in standardized tests; and even graduate programs where students are often advised to only bother with reading the introduction, conclusion, and topic sentences of a few paragraphs here and there. This "CliffsNotes" way of reading invites students to focus on an author's thesis and a few book details, rather than a more intimate, reflective engagement with the author. The result: graduate students who know many authors and books, but superficially so; as superficially as so-called friends on social media.

On Facebook, I just learned celebrities have followers, not friends—not quite sorry to pick on her again, Snooki has 10 million "followers," and "follows" only 25. She has more so-called followers than the entire populations of either Austria, Serbia or Sierra Leone.

Did I choose the right profession? I believe I did. I cherish being an author and college professor. I do not know about followers, but I have friends, real people, of the sort one has coffee with.

I invite students in my Cuban, Puerto Rican, and Caribbean history courses to rewire their brains, to read beyond the facts—I do not test for factual knowledge—to read for interpretation, for style, for voice and tone, for literary value, for beauty and enjoyment.

To get them to think differently about authors and books, I start many book discussions posing questions I often ask myself: "Would you like to have coffee with this author? Why? Why not?"

I ask those questions when discussing assigned books and readings by José Martí, V.S. Naipaul, Jamaica Kinkaid, Fernando Picó, Esmeralda Santiago and other Caribbean writers.

Fernando Picó

When discussing the book *History of Puerto Rico* by the late Fernando Picó, students usually say yes to coffee (even if they have not read his book); some are indifferent ("whatever"); out of courtesy or inertia, nobody says "no."

Would I have coffee with Picó? Well, he was my mentor at the University of Puerto Rico. My classmates and I had coffee with him, many times, and fresh-made passion fruit juice, and pizza, and veal patties (80 percent breadcrumbs) with spaghetti. I distinctly remember the last coffee we had shortly before his passing at a small cafeteria one block from the National Archive in San Juan. They only served café americano, a heresy for Puerto Rico's foremost expert of the history of coffee and a Cuban coffee nationalist.

Having known Fernando (as he like to be called) personally, actually intimately, gives me privileged insights on him as an individual and a historian, some of which I share in class.

We start with the first chapter of *History of Puerto Rico* (geological formation and geography). I remember him telling me, over three decades ago, that he was almost done with the book, except for that part. Rather than expecting students to learn facts about Puerto Rico's geography, I invite them to get to know Fernando. "What geographic aspects does he focus on?" I ask. "Swamp mangroves and mogotes (calcareous hillocks)," someone responds. That is my prompt to go on the offensive with the Socratic method. "And why does he focus on those particular ecosystems?" I push on. Fewer hands go up this time but invariably, a sharp student responds: "Because those were places of refuge for surviving natives and maroon slaves." More Socratic method: "And what does that tell us about Picó and the rest of the book?"

Picó's works reflect the intellectual honesty and humility that characterized him, and his commitment to giving a voice to the poor, the marginal, the so-called people without history (past and present).

Rather than fill the pages of his books with names of Spanish colonial officials and "paper planters," he summons common workers; "thousands of creoles," as he lyrically put it, "who battled day after day with clods and woody vines, and thus forged a nation."

Yes, there is a way to write about those "at the edge of power," as Fernando did, without the preachy, self-righteous tone that has come to characterize so much of the contemporary historical and sociological literature.

Coffee with Fernando Picó? Of course, any day, at any time.

Jamaica Kinkaid

I assign my students well-written books, like Jamaica Kincaid's *A Small Place*, a small book, only 81 pages, about a small island, Antigua. I start my Caribbean history course juxtaposing the first half of Kincaid's book with a video clip from Antigua and Barbuda's Tourism Authority. We notice the similarities: "That water—have you ever seen anything like it? Far out, to the horizon, the colour of the water is navy-blue"; Kincaid continues, "nearer, the water is the colour of the North American sky. From there to the shore, the water is pale, silvery, clear, so clear that you can see its pinkish-white sand bottom. Oh, what beauty!"

Kincaid's poetic prose matches the alluring moving images one sees when visiting visitantiguabarbuda.com. Click on "culture and heritage" and you will see a dance troupe on stage, clad in clownish costumes, a pineapple, a deserted beach, a nicely put together fish plate, a view of Falmouth Bay and three old cannons pointing who knows where.

That type of portrayal is precisely what infuriates Kincaid, the bulk of whose book is an indictment, poetic as it may be (a tirade, one may call it) against Antigua's plantation-and-slavery past and British colonists, those: "bastards," "pitiful lot," "pigs," "human rubbish" and more.

But Antigua and Barbuda became independent in 1981 (seven years before *A Small Place* came out). "True," one can hear Kincaid respond, "Eventually, the masters left, in a kind of way; eventually, the slaves were freed, in a kind of way." That incomplete independence and incomplete emancipation are to blame, Kincaid reminds the reader page after page, for the mosaic of ills afflicting late twentieth-century Antigua and Barbuda: racism and residential segregation, political corruption, underdevelopment and poverty, and widespread ignorance and alienation.

Kincaid is merciless when it comes to run-of-the-mill tourists who dare set foot on her island, whose economy, by the way, depends heavily on foreign tourism: "An ugly thing, that is what you are when you become a tourist, an ugly, empty thing, a stupid thing, a piece of rubbish pausing here and there to gaze at this and taste that, and it will never occur to you that the people who inhabit the place in which you have just paused cannot stand you."

So, would you like to have coffee—tea perhaps—with Jamaica Kincaid? I ask my students. A majority respectfully declines. I do not blame them. We are all potential tourists, of the sort she has chastised page after page.

But I ask them to imagine an over-tea conversation with Kincaid. What topics would she raise? In what tone? What is the sound of her voice like? Will she listen to what you have to say? Would you enjoy it, or not?

Back to the internet: We google J-A-M-A-I-C-A K-I-N-K-A-I-D, then click on video. She sounds nothing like the way she writes. She is poised, soft-spoken, sweetly musical. Sure, I will have coffee (or tea) with her any day, at any time.

V.S. Naipaul

I invite my history students to have coffee with Caribbean authors. Rather than historians, most are literary figures whose careers straddle between fiction and nonfiction (and between poetry and prose); authors like Nobel laureates V.S. Naipaul (Trinidad) and Derek Walcott (Saint Lucia), Carlos Franqui (Cuba), and Luis Muñoz Marín (Puerto Rico).

"Why assign works of literature instead of historical monographs?" you may ask. Reading, I believe, should be pleasurable; but much historical writing is insufferably dry, not to mention preachy and intellectually arrogant. In all honesty, there are fewer and fewer historians with whom I would like to have coffee (metaphorically and literally), or even cross paths with at the annual meeting of the American Historical Association.

In my Caribbean history class, we read V.S. Naipaul, a Trinidadian writer of Indian descent who I consider one of the twentieth century's finest English-language pens. We read and discuss *The Middle Passage: The Caribbean Revisited* (1962), his first work of nonfiction, a travelog based on a visit to Trinidad, British Guyana, Surinam, Martinique, and Jamaica in 1961. It has the critical tone of Kincaid's *A Small Place*, but the wrong politics, of the sort that can kill any author's career. Based on his politics alone, I would have not cared to have coffee with Naipaul—tea as he would have it. But his mastery of the English language, his authentic Caribbean cadence and rhythm, and his poetic prose (bitter and biting as it may be) make me change my mind.

Naipaul orders a cup of tea. "I'll have tea as well," I tell the imaginary waiter with an uncharacteristically meek voice that comes naturally in the company of a living legend. I would have ordered Cuban coffee instead, but I am in the presence of a tea drinker; tea drinker for being West Indian by birth, Indian by ancestry, and British (a knighted one at that) by choice. No sugar in his tea, I suspect. "Sugarcane is an ugly crop," he wrote in *The Middle Passage*, "and it has an ugly history." I take sugar; at least three packets. I am Cuban.

That is the kind of rhetorical twist with which Naipaul regales his readers in *The Loss of El Dorado* (1969), his only book of history where he describes colonial Trinidad as a place that had "dropped out of history," where "nobody came to raid or trade"; and at its lowest point "no one wanted to be governor." It was so sparsely populated that "20 people are a crowd; a hundred make a city"; when a smallpox epidemic struck, "even the monkeys died."

But Naipaul hits his most acerbic notes when talking about the contemporary Caribbean, which he scorns as inhabited by "mimic men;" a region with "no scientists, engineers, explorers, soldiers, or poets" where the cricketer "was our only hero-figure." I disagree and offer his own prolific body of work as exhibit No. 1.

High tea with Naipaul turns out to be enjoyable. Listen to his Nobel Prize acceptance speech and discover the sharp contrast between his severe prose and the way he speaks, in a pleasant, sweet, surprisingly humble voice, sounding like a grandfather reading a bedtime story to his two-year-old grandchild.

Carlos Franqui

Enough with the tea! How about coffee? Black and sweet, the way Cubans have it, often served as *coladas* in thimble-sized plastic cups that remind me of Protestant Communion. Coffee with Carlos Franqui, a Cuban revolutionary who broke with Castro in 1968? Of course. Not an imaginary coffee, as I actually had coffee with him in 2003, during an interview in his San Juan apartment, surrounded by walls full of fine art: a Sandy Candler, a cubist portrait of José Martí, a Joan Miró abstraction scribbled with an equally abstract inscription: "Thinking with my feet is my way of walking."

In my Cuban history class I assign Franqui's brief introduction to *Diary of the Revolution* (1976) not for historical information—as there are a few inaccuracies—but for the quintessentially Cuban way in which he speaks: playfully, musically, with a generous dose of Cuban-brand chauvinism (tongue-in-cheek, with a smile and a wink): "The first rocket was invented by a Cuban," Franqui boasts, but "only on a postage stamp"; we are like Spaniards, "but more graceful."

"Cuba is an adventure without fear of the unexpected, the magical, the impossible or the unknown." Franqui, (frankly) I agree. What other nation would have embarked (*se hubiera embarcado*), wink, on a socialist revolution, as Fidel Castro once said, "under the nose of the United States."

But it is the music in Franqui's prose that makes me want a second, a third cup: "Cuba is not Indian. Cuba is not white. It is neither black nor yellow. It is mulatto, mixed, whitish-black, and tobacco-hued."

Luis Muñoz Marín

He is best known as a statesman and politician, but Puerto Rico's first elected governor, Luis Muñoz Marín, was also a gifted writer (in English and in Spanish). While his poems were, at best, second rate—"Her hair was as the gold on sunset heights," yada, yada—his prose could reach exquisitely poetic notes.

I invite my students to have coffee with the former governor. We read his muckraking essay, "The Sad Case of Porto Rico" published in *The American*

Mercury in 1929. It is an impassioned defense of Puerto Rico's culture and an indictment on U.S. efforts to Americanize the island's economy and its people.

Muñoz Marín uses the transfer of Puerto Rico from Spain to the United States in 1898—incidentally, the year of his birth—as a watershed to juxtapose an idealized world under Spanish colonial rule and what he deemed an assault on the island's recently-acquired autonomy: "Regional autonomy had been granted by Spain, and a native Cabinet with a native Premier [he does not name him, but it was his father] ruled the green fields and polychromatic towns."

The young muckraker held romantic views of the "jíbaros," the predominantly white peasantry of the island's mountainous interior, who "In the old days ... owned a few pigs and chickens, maybe a horse or a cow, some goats, and in some way had the use of a patch of soil." Peasant men, Muñoz Marín nostalgically writes, "tumbled out of hammocks pulling up their trousers for the day, and barefooted women in terribly starched dresses of many colors began preparing strong coffee in iron kettles and serving it steaming in polished cocoanut shells."

Of course, Muñoz Marín drank coffee, patriotically so. He drank it in bohemian cafes in Greenwich Village, in Guayama's Café París, where artists and intellectuals congregated, and in the humble, thatch-roofed homes of peasants during his political campaigns in the most remote corners of the interior. He expressed concern about the Americanization of the island's coffee shops, which increasingly looked "like glittering American beaneries."

In almost every paragraph, Muñoz Marín's prose bursts into flashes of poetry. The island is "a land of beggars and millionaires, of flattering statistics and distressing realities." There are "many more schools," he writes with irony and sorrow, "for their hungry children and many more roads for their bare feet."

Elected governor in 1948, and reelected in 1952, 1956 and 1960, Muñoz Marín led the island's quasi-miraculous processes of modernization, industrialization, and urbanization. When he announced his decision not to run again in 1964, amid shouts of disapproval, he said with his characteristic caudillo firmness, "I am leaving a fortress to return to the trails and *bateyes* of Puerto Rico ... to the mountain sides and the plazas and to the soul of our people." Years later, in his memoir, Muñoz Marín remarked with some regret and a bit of grammatical poetic license: "I have created bourgeoisie. I am lonely of jíbaros."

Derek Walcott

A couple of final cups of literature. Back to tea; back to the English-speaking Caribbean; back to Naipaul's Trinidad. I invite my students to have tea with another literature Nobel laureate, Derek Walcott from the island of Saint Lucia; an island measuring only 238 square miles; "a small place" as Jamaica Kincaid would call it. But in per-capita terms, Saint Lucia has the largest or second-largest rate (pick your source: Wikipedia or the *Guinness Book of World Records*) of Nobel Prize winners (2 out of 180,000).[1]

In class we read "The Antilles: Fragments of Memory," Walcott's 1992 Nobel Prize acceptance speech. Tea with Walcott? Certainly, but it must be of the Darjeeling variety with steamed milk, seasoned with assorted aromatic Indian spices, as we are having it in the predominantly Indian town of Felicity in Trinidad.

"The Antilles" is a poetic, philosophical, descriptive narrative that takes the reader to Ramleela, a dramatization of the Ramayana, a Hindu epic poem, celebrated in Felicity (population under 20,000). The festival's center piece is the burning in effigy of a giant Hindu god, which "like the cane burning harvest," Walcott tells us, "is annually repeated."

Along the way, Walcott showers readers with an unending cascade of metaphors. In his eyes, flames of fire are the color of saffron; the scarlet ibises that fly above him at dusk are "arrowing flocks" and to his ears the sound coming out of the festival loudspeakers is "sinuous drumming."

One day, after a class discussion of Walcott's speech, a student came up to me, a beaming smile painted on her face: "Professor, I am Trinidadian, from Felicity." And to think that she had to migrate 1,800 miles to Central Florida to discover the poetry and universality of her hometown's Hindu festival.

That is precisely why I read and write, and why I invite my students to have coffee (or tea) with the authors we read.

---

1 The other St. Lucian Nobel Prize winner is Sir William Arthur Lewis (1915–1991) who won the prize for his work in the field of economics.

35

I Saw My Entire Life Flash Before My Eyes

(Creators Syndicate, June 11, 18, 25, 2022)

It has long been said that people see their entire lives flash before their eyes at the moment of death. The case of Swiss geologist Albert Heim is well known. One hundred and thirty years ago, following a mountain-climbing accident, which he survived, Heim reported seeing his life replayed as he was falling. Hollywood has often resorted to this intriguing phenomenon as a plot device. Think Bruce Willis in *Armageddon* and Tom Cruise in *Vanilla Sky*.

In case you are concerned: No, I did not have a near-death experience; thank God I am in good health, and you will not see me climbing a mountain anytime soon.

But I did see my life flash before my eyes, in a sort of way, last week at the Library of Congress, where I was conducting research using newspapers spanning the 1960s through the early 2000s. I saw dozens of news stories and op-eds about world events that made me reflect on how much great-power geopolitics have changed during the last six decades—and on the ways in which they haven't changed.

Russia, Then and Now

Given the ongoing Russian invasion of Ukraine and its potential spread into a global conflagration, and my practice as a syndicated columnist, I was particularly drawn to Cold War-era op-eds commenting on military aggressions by what was then known as the Soviet Union.

A June 1976 op-ed by John Chamberlain titled "Do Russians Have the Ultimate Weapon?" reported that the Soviets had aimed microwave beams at the U.S. Embassy in Moscow and that according to the *Boston Globe* those beams "caused or at least aggravated" an ailment affecting U.S. Ambassador Walter J. Stossel Jr. The op-ed quoted from a chilling report by an unnamed, retired, high-ranking army officer on the subject of "psychotronic weapons," which if aimed at a human—this is terrifying—"disarrange the life-sustaining portion of his biological system."

Intrigued about the subject, I searched the internet and found a 2012 NBC News story on psychotronic weapons, which, at the time, Vladimir Putin was touting as the future of warfare. So-called zombie ray guns being developed were, according to researchers, capable of producing "microwave hearing," "a sensation of buzzing, clicking or hissing in the head." The article quoted the British *Daily Mail* saying that those weapons "could be used against Russia's enemies and, perhaps, its own dissidents by the end of the decade."

In 2016, reports began to surface of a mysterious set of symptoms afflicting U.S. and Canadian embassy personnel stationed at Havana, hence the disease's name: Havana syndrome. U.S. officials have since blamed Russia for those attacks and others against U.S. officials and military personnel stationed around the world, even in Washington, D.C.

The *Daily Mail*'s prediction materialized and Chamberlain's question about Russia having the ultimate weapon seems to have been finally answered.

Twenty-two years before the United States invaded and occupied Afghanistan in 2001 with the object of toppling the Taliban regime, Soviet troops crossed into Afghan territory to prop up a pro-U.S.S.R. government. They remained there over nine years.

With the benefit of hindsight, we know that the Soviet-Afghan War ended disastrously for the Soviets, costing them over 14,000 lives and the equivalent of 50 billion dollars. Historians and other observers agree that the war deeply hurt the Soviet Union's international standing and that it was one of the primary factors leading to its implosion in 1991.

But U.S. journalists commenting at the time lacked the benefit of hindsight and, much like those of us who are commenting on the current Russian War in Ukraine, could only speculate about the Afghan conflict's future course and ultimate ramifications.

In February 1980, just weeks into the Afghan War, American journalist Kingsbury Smith wrote columns with alarming titles like "Is War Imminent with Russia?" and "If It Comes to Nuclear War." They reflected contemporary concerns in the Carter White House, the State Department, and the Pentagon about what at the time seemed to be a first step in a new era of aggressive Soviet expansionism.

Just as today's analysts express concern about Putin's intention to further expand into Moldova, Poland and beyond, their 1980 predecessors feared Soviet leader Leonid Brezhnev's expansionist goals of controlling the Persian Gulf oil route and taking over Pakistan.

Smith quoted President Jimmy Carter who said that the Soviet invasion of Afghanistan was "the most serious threat to world peace since World War II" and that his administration was committed to "protect[ing] the security of Pakistan, involving military forces, if necessary." According to another contemporary columnist, Nicholas von Hoffman, the dreadful phrase "World War III" was "on the lips of people making serious prophecy."

Sounds familiar, doesn't it?

My time-travel adventure at the Newspaper and Current Periodical Reading Room of the Library of Congress felt like binge-watching reruns of old newscasts. It brought back memories of stories going back to the 1960s—the man on the moon (1969), recurrent hijackings of passenger airplanes to Cuba (1970s) and the Clintons' failed attempt to pass healthcare legislation (1993–1994); of newsmakers—famous, infamous and everything in between (twice presidential candidate Ross Perot, John Wayne Bobbitt, who starred in the pornographic film *John Wayne Bobbitt: Uncut*, and British pop star Adam Ant); and of companies and brands that no longer exist (Woolworth stores, the Montreal Expos baseball team, Trans World Airlines and Napster).

I also found numerous U.S. political news stories that reminded me of French writer Jean-Baptiste Alphonse Karr's aphorism, "the more things change, the more they stay the same," and made the flashing of my life before my eyes seem to be on a loop.

The Distinguished Gentleman from Ohio

There were mid-1970s stories about Watergate, which appears as a non-moving traffic violation when compared to the political white-collar crime wave we witnessed during the Trump administration. There were stories about political corruption, one titled "Quirky Ohio Congressman on Trial for Corruption." If the image of a polyester-suit-clad, Captain-Kangaroo-coiffured politician popped into your mind, you are right: it's former Congressman James A. Traficant. According to this 2002 AP story, he was "accused of accepting gifts and favors from constituents in exchange for lobbying in Washington." Two decades later, it sounds quaint.

Hillary Clinton in Person and in Effigy

One of the biggest political stories of 1993–1994 was President Bill and Hillary Clinton's push for health care reform, an effort that eventually failed. Remember the "Harry and Louise" multimillion-dollar ad campaign funded by a health insurance lobby group? Okay, but did you know that in 2002, the lovely couple resurfaced in a TV ad, advocating human cloning? That is before they resurfaced again in 2008, this time in support of healthcare reform. Where they the original Harry and Louise or were they clones?

A 1994 story, "Hillary Doll Burned at Stake," informed readers of a Kentucky rally where someone "poured gasoline on (Hillary Clinton's) effigy, which hung like a scarecrow in a dress." "A country band played," the story continues, as the effigy was set ablaze. That was probably the first in-effigy execution or conviction of Hillary Clinton. She was later burned in Pakistan (2011) and India (2014); dressed in stripped prison garb in Pennsylvania (2015); inside a witch's costume in Iowa (2015); in prisoner clothes while flying on a broom in Maine (2015); and hanging from a crane in southern Oregon (2016), wearing a fuchsia-color bra, next to a sign that said "Vote Trump."

KAL Flight 007

I also found headlines that seem to burst out of last week's newspapers. A Nicholas von Hoffman column (1976) that lamented the "Death of Logic" was inspired by statements made by Democratic Congressman Larry McDonald of

Georgia against the National Council of Labor Relations, which he denounced as a Marxist, avowedly pro-Russian entity. Elevated to the presidency of the John Birch Society in 1983, McDonald had a well-earned reputation as champion of anti-communist, anti-abortion, anti-busing and anti-gun control causes.

The life of the anti-Soviet congressman ended like a hybrid of a Tom Clancy novel and *Airport* (the movie): bad weather delayed his August 28, 1983, Atlanta-to-New York flight; hence, he missed his connection to Seoul, South Korea. Rather than take the next Pan Am flight, he opted for cheaper Korean Airlines tickets, scheduled to fly two days later; at a stopover in Anchorage, Senator Jesse Helms of North Carolina (who was attending the same meeting) invited McDonald to join him in another flight, but McDonald refused. A few hours later, Soviet fighters fired on the plane he was flying, killing him along with all crew and passengers.

Donald's Ego and Marla's Shoes

A couple of editorials/stories about future politician Donald Trump caught my eye. A Calvin Trillin 1989 op-ed bore the title: "Donald Trump, the Man with the Skyscraper Ego." It recounted the future president's efforts to inflate his wealth to appear in *Forbes'* wealthiest people lists. Trillin opined on a *New York Observer* poll that revealed Trump had a 94 percent recognition in New York City. The future president's reaction was classic Trump: "Hey, I am very flattered.... But I just wonder who the other people are."

Then there was a 1994 article entitled "Chuck Jones Sentenced up to 4 Years." "Who is Chuck Jones and how was he connected to Trump?" you are entitled to ask. Jones admitted to a "sexual relation" with Trump's second (then current) wife Marla Trump's shoes and boots. Yes, you read it correctly, her shoes and boots, which he had stolen along with assorted pieces of lingerie. Upon his conviction, Jones said outside the courtroom that "the jury was wrong, and we plan to appeal this."

Curiosity Stories

You know the saying: "dog bites man" is not news, but "man bites dog" is. Years ago, I actually came across a true *Miami Herald* man-bites-dog story from 1996.

Such "weird" or "curiosity" news stories have dotted newspapers for a long time, providing respite from news about crime, natural disasters, wars, and politics. Several odd news stories caught my attention as I scanned through reels of microfilmed old newspapers at the Library of Congress.

Florida's a Bridge Too Far

Florida, my home state, is a fountain of odd and strange stories (some of which overlap with political news). That may not surprise you.

Headline: "Florida wants to Annex V(irgin) I(slands)." According to this 1964 story, Democratic congressman from Jacksonville, Florida, Charles E. Bennett proposed the annexation of the U.S. Virgin Islands to be absorbed as Florida's 68th county. He explained his idea's feasibility by saying that some of Alaska's islands were farther away from the mainland than the U.S. Virgin Islands from Florida. Four decades after this story's publication, a Jacksonville bridge was renamed Charles E. Bennett Memorial Bridge, spanning not to Frederiksted, Saint Croix, but across the Intracoastal Waterway.

Barney's Massachusetts Nightmare

As sober and proper as Massachusetts can be, it has generated its fair share of news-story curiosities. Did you know that Puritans banned Christmas celebrations early in the colony's history? Or that in 1919 a wave of hot molasses (an essential ingredient in Boston baked beans) flooded Boston's East End? It is actually not funny; 21 died and hundreds were injured. The disaster has come to be known as the Great Molasses Flood.

Headline: "A Brutal Attack on Barney." It happened in April 1994 in Worcester, Massachusetts, whose official webpage claims it is "the country's most vibrant and livable mid-sized city." At a drugstore opening, a young man beat up Barney; not Congressman Barney Frank, but the "I love you, you love me" Barney. According to the story, the victim was wearing an unauthorized Barney costume, which an official of the Barney Fan Club characterized as "grossly illegal." Vibrant and livable mid-size city, perhaps, but do not visit Worcester in a Barney costume.

Pink Hair Crime in Connecticut

Pink hair has become acceptable, actually fashionable. Think Cyndi Lauper, Rihanna, Nicki Minaj, Katy Perry, even Helen Mirren. But that was not the case three decades ago, when students at New Milford, Connecticut's Schaghticoke Middle School could get into serious trouble for dyeing their hair pink.

Headline: "Student Suspended for Bright Pink Hair." Okay, you are right. It is 2022 and students still get suspended for dyeing their hair pink. But this 1994 AP story is curious because of the pioneering nature of the fourth-grade student's defiance and the consequences she faced.

It is "unnatural and distracting," school authorities claimed; "They are stopping our creativity," a student retorted.

The pink-haired student was suspended and allowed back "only in a class for troubled students." The story quotes the suspended student's mother: "That class is for kids who bring guns to school.... She is just an average kid who experimented with her hair."

If you ever drive through New Milford, you may want to check out the Pink and Blue Salon off Route 1.

U.S. Hispanic Population Forecast

We know that the U.S. Bureau of the Census conducts a population count every 10 years; the Constitution mandates it. Preliminary results are published the following year. The Bureau also offers periodic reports, updated estimates and forecasts of population change.

As a student of Latinos in the United States, I am interested in statistics about the nation's Hispanic population. That is why the following 1986 AP story caught my attention and I found it curious.

Headline: "Hispanic Population in the U.S. to Exceed 36M by 2020." A Bureau of the Census spokesperson interviewed for the story forecasted that the Hispanic population would more than double from 17.3 million in 1986 to 36.5 million in 2020. That turned out to be a gross underestimate. The 2020 census has revealed a Hispanic population of 62.1 million, 25.6 million more than forecasted in 1986.

Out of curiosity, I searched more recent census projections and found one from 2018 prognosticating a growth from 56.1 (2020 estimate) to 94.7 million in

2060. That is the year when I am supposed to turn 100 years old, and according to life span projection tables, I will have already seen my life flash before my eyes.

If you ever want to see your life flash before your eyes, you do not need to wait for the Big Adios. Visit the Library of Congress and spend some time reading through old newspapers. Easier yet, visit https://chroniclingamerica.loc.gov/.

Section V

¡Despierta Latino!

Introduction

There is an expectation that Latino scholars and journalists write on Latino topics, worse yet, that we should only write about such matters. Latino reporters and columnists are pigeonholed—many pigeonhole themselves—into the Latino beat. Curiously, the National Association of Hispanic Journalists presents yearly awards exclusively for works on Latino issues, civil rights and social justice, and investigative reporters who serve as community watchdogs.

I refuse to be limited to the Latino beat and to writing columns only in my primary fields of research, Cuba, Puerto Rico, and Latinos in the United States. Two-thirds of this volume's essays cover broader national and international subjects unrelated to those fields.

That said, as a Latino I care deeply about issues that pertain to our communities. Readers will sense the activist tone and heightened urgency of this section's columns.

This section explores and offers commentary on Latino society, culture, and politics. The essay "Hispanic? Latino? Latinx? What's Nextx?" is bound to be this section's most controversial because it criticizes the unending evolution of identity labels and their imposition by often self-proclaimed Latino leaders. As to the question "what's nextx?" I recently received a communication from a national Hispanic organization—incidentally one I was a member of—that used the anomalous construct "Latina/o/x/s." Soon, someone will come up with something else/x/s.

The section's last two columns address the complex subject of the so-called Latino vote in the 2020 elections.

36

Hispanic? Latino? Latinx? What's Nextx?

(Creators Syndicate, January 30, February 6, 2021)

Three decades ago, when the ethnic/race labels "African American" and "Latino" were gaining traction versus "Black" and "Hispanic," I had a conversation with a fellow historian on the subject. When a corporation is playing too much with its logo, he told me, it is a sign that it is in trouble. Whether that is the case for corporations, I don't know, but over the last few decades, ethnic minority labels have mutated with extraordinary regularity.

There is much confusion, and some controversy, as to which term should be used, "Hispanic" or "Latino." Perhaps "person of color" or the more recently minted "Latinx"?

When I speak in public about Latino history and culture, I am often asked which of those terms is most appropriate? Which ones are offensive, which ones are safe?

A bit of history first. During the Spanish colonial era, inhabitants of Central and South America and the Spanish-speaking Caribbean did not see themselves as either Hispanics or Latinos. They were subjects of the Spanish Crown and identified more with the specific places in which they lived, a city (say Limeños), a region (say Yucatecos), or the ethnic group to which they belonged (say Quechua).

208 | *When the World Turned Upside Down*

Most Latin Americans identify as either Colombian, or Puerto Rican, or whatever their demonym may be; and not a few further clarify—with some chauvinism—that they are, for example, Camagüeyanos (from Camagüey, Cuba) or Arequipeños (from Arequipa, Peru). That is another legacy of Spanish colonialism, a strong identification with the *patriachicas* (localities, literally, little homelands).

When individuals from Latin America resettle in the United States, they are labeled as Hispanic, Latino, or with some other broad pan-ethnic classification. Most continue, however, to self-identify as Chileans, Argentinians, etc.

Those who come from the most culturally nationalistic countries—I was born in one of them—tend to have a stronger aversion to generic, multi-nation labels. The embittered host of an old Miami Cuban call-in TV show used to bite back at any caller who dared utter the word "Latino." In the same vein, some cars circulating in Miami had front license plates that read: "Latino? La tuya," literally: "Latino? Not me, your mother."

Pan-ethnic classifications are particular to the United States, where many embrace and others seek to impose the melting-pot ideology.

Canadians think more along the lines of a national mosaic in which each ethnic group is represented by a particular piece of the mosaic. That is why Canadian census categories include so many ethnic (ancestral roots options). Their 2016 census listed 28 examples (not all the possible options) in the following order: Canadian, English, Chinese, French, East Indian, Italian, German, Scottish, Cree, Mi'kmaq, Salish, Métis, Inuit, Filipino, Irish, Dutch, Ukrainian, Polish, Portuguese, Vietnamese, Korean, Jamaican, Greek, Iranian, Lebanese, Mexican, Somali, and Colombian.

Some comparisons are in order. First, Canadian census categories are not racial as in the United States. Second, they do not consolidate groups into broad pan-ethnic classifications, Hispanics or Asians, for example. Third, they do not "other" some groups and select another as the default. While in the United States we recognize certain groups of people as ethnic, in Canada, people of all cultural ancestries, be they English, Scottish, or Jamaican—even "Canadian," whatever that means—constitute an ethnic group.

Speaking of ethnics, I recall a historians' conference in Oxford, England, many years ago where one of the hosts gave participants advice on nearby restaurant options. There are numerous ethnic alternatives, he said, a Chinese restaurant, a Thai restaurant farther down, and an English ethnic food establishment with a sign on the door that boasts "fresh-cut sandwiches." "The assumption," he said, is that they will be stale.

While they are not completely synonymous, I use "Latino" and "Hispanic" interchangeably and do not find either to be derogatory or offensive.

I first confronted the "Latino" vs. "Hispanic" dilemma in 1992, when I was invited to speak at the residence for Latino students at Colgate University, whose faculty I had just joined. I thought that I had made a good presentation and had connected with the students. But to my surprise, I was sternly scolded for using the term "Hispanic" and lectured robotically by one student on why I should say "Latino" instead.

The litany that I was subjected to that night, included the following arguments: "Hispanic" is reminiscent of Spanish imperialism and its legacy; "Latino" is more inclusive because it comprises Brazilians and Haitians; and as opposed to "Hispanic," "imposed" on us by the U.S. federal government, "Latino" emerged from within the community.

None of the arguments espoused by those students back in 1992 convinced me then, nor do they today, that the term "Latino" is better or less controversial than "Hispanic." This is why: The use of the "Hispanic" label by the federal government beginning in 1976, short of an imposition, actually responded to Hispanic leaders' demands that the government collect information that combined the various Hispanic geographical origins.

"Latino" carries an even heavier imperialist baggage. Few people know that the term was developed and invoked by French imperialists seeking to highlight a common Latin origin in opposition to Anglo-Saxon America. Remember the American drinking holiday Cinco de Mayo? It is actually the day when Mexican troops stopped French invaders in the Battle of Puebla in 1862. Mexicans were defeated the next day but never bought the Latino argument. They are Mexicanos!

What about the broader inclusivity of the term "Latino"? If it is a matter of inclusion, why not include Jamaicans and Barbadians? For linguistic and other reasons, Brazilians are not part of the U.S.'s broader Latino community. They keep to themselves.

What about the "imposition" argument? "Latino" is as much of an imposition as "Hispanic," even if the former was generated by Latino community leaders. It is interesting to note that over several decades, U.S. Latinos have consistently shown a two to one preference for "Hispanic" over "Latino."

After "Latino" came "Latino/a." For a while, some experimented with "Latin@" (which did not gain traction for obvious reasons). Of more recent vintage are "Latine" and "Latinx." We are also often lumped as "people of color" or "brown people," which amounts to the racialization of our diverse ethnicities. The very latest term is the cacophonous "BIPOC," an acronym for "Black, Indigenous and people of color."

Strikingly similar to the offensive term "colored people," "people of color" came into vogue in the 1980s as part of the Rainbow Coalition's unity concept, an idea that never went beyond a concept as courageously explained by Nicolás Vaca in the book *The Presumed Alliance: The Unspoken Conflict Between Latinos and Blacks and What It Means for America.* Anyone familiar with New York City, Miami or Los Angeles politics can attest that, short of collaborative, Latino-Black relations can be tense, even hostile.

It may have been the same Colgate University student group that introduced me to that infelicitous term. "Dear professor of Color," read the salutation in an invitation letter. Most Latinos deem that term inappropriate and perhaps offensive. I did not respond to that letter and still do not respond to that appellative. If you want a response, please never address me as Mr. BIPOC.

"Latinx" began to circulate in 2004, gained traction in the aftermath of the 2016 Pulse Nightclub massacre in Orlando, and has become the preferred terminology in many colleges and universities, as well as in journalism. The term emerged as a critique of "Latino" and "Latina," which some deem reflective of a binary concept of gender. "Latinx," the argument goes, is gender-neutral and more inclusive.

Unlike Spanish pronouns, nouns, and adjectives, which are generally gendered ("maestro" or "maestra," for example), English words are mostly not; "teacher" is used for males and females.

The overwhelming majority of Latinos reject "Latinx," and more than half are offended by it. An August 2020 Pew Research Center poll shows that only 3 percent of Latinos use "Latinx," while 76 percent have not even heard of it. It is more commonly used among younger, liberal, college-educated Latinos/Hispanics. What used to be called Latino studies programs are rapidly changing to Latinx studies programs.

I recognize and respect all individuals' right to self-label as they wish, be it Hispanic, Peruvian, or Brazilian, Brown, Latine or Latinx, even BIPOC. What I reject is the imposition of any ethnic label, whether by the federal government or local activists—or, for that matter, the Royal Spanish Academy, which in 2018 rejected "Latinx" as a Spanish word and the use of the letter "x" as a gender-neutral option to the feminine "a" or masculine "o." It does make for awkward grammar and cacophonous prose: "Ellxs (or elles) son maestrxs expertxs" ("They are expert teachers").

So, what term should you use? It depends on where you are and who is your audience. In the U.S. Northeast, "Latino" is more widely used, while in the South and Texas, "Hispanic" dominates. In colleges and universities, and increasingly so in journalism, "Latinx" has taking the lead.

At the end of the day, no matter which term you use, you are likely to offend someone and be scolded.

The corporation is in trouble. Fixing it will take much more than adopting a new logo or brand name.

37

Hispanic Heritage Month 2020: Some Advice from the Trenches

(Creators Syndicate, September 11, 2020)

Hispanic Heritage Month begins in a few days, on September 15.

I am not a fan of the designation of specific months to celebrate particular ethnic, racial or other identity groups. While the original intentions may have been good, the result is that for most public, corporate and government organizations, Hispanic Heritage Month has become the only time of the year in which any attention is paid to the cultural contributions of the 60 million Latinos that live in the United States.

One of the great sociodemographic paradoxes of the early twenty-first century is that, as the Latino population grows in absolute numbers and proportion (over 18 percent of the total U.S. population), our presence in leadership positions continues to decrease.

I recall a 2006 Florida Orange County Board of Commissioners event at which I was invited to receive and read the Hispanic Heritage Month proclamation (Whereas ... Whereas ... Whereas ...) and to hand out art project awards to Latino schoolchildren. Partly tongue-in-cheek, I told the students that they were the future of Central Florida and that I looked forward to them organizing Anglo Heritage Month events in the future. Some in the audience found that funny; others laughed nervously; pouts and grimaces were sculpted on the faces of a couple of white commissioners.

Hispanic Heritage Month is not only the calendar's equivalent of tokenism; it is generally observed with caricatures of Latin American and Latino cultures, with focus on the four usual suspects: food, music, dance, and folkloric dress.

I have made it a lifetime mission to challenge such reductionist stereotypes. When I founded and ran the Latin American Cultural Festival of Orlando, we made sure to include fine arts exhibitions, chamber music recitals with music by Latin American composers, Latin American arts cinema, and lectures by leading scholars. With the same purpose, I give a multimedia presentation titled "Beyond Tacos, Salsa, and Sombreros: Latin America's Cultural Wealth."

Many years ago, before moving to Central Florida, I was invited to a college cultural event and was asked to appear in ethnic garb. Respectfully, I declined. Standing behind a podium wearing only a Taino loincloth would have been unsightly. At my current university, a buffoonish former provost showed up wearing a Mexican sombrero. Like Bartolomé de las Casas, I did not know whether to laugh or cry.

So how should we celebrate Hispanic Heritage Month? Allow me to fire these six bullets (as in punctuation):

- Celebrate it, but make sure that it's not the only time of the year to recognize the cultural and professional contributions of Latinos.
- Invite the four usual suspects, but also plan events that highlight Latino culture beyond the folkloric. Have the Mexican buffet but bring a Latino poet along.
- Set aside event budgets and human resources that are adequate and commensurate with those of similar monthlong celebrations. (A tropical punch bowl, some tortilla chips, and an off-the-street speaker will not cut it).
- Make sure those events are not just for Latinos but all members of the organization.
- It is not okay for top executives to show up, give a shallow welcome speech and swiftly escape through the side door. When I spoke at the Kennedy Space Center in 2018, its director and the top brass attended and stayed for the duration, something I deeply appreciated.
- A spirit of volunteerism is one of our community's characteristics, but do not exploit it. Many of us give our fair share of pro-bono presentations to schools and non-profits, but organizations with plenty of resources should respect professional work and offer honoraria. I declined a speaking

invitation from a multi-billion company, whose event organizer expected me to do it for free. On top of that, they requested the text beforehand, to run it through their legal department.

Let's celebrate Hispanic Heritage Month the right way. Better yet, let's celebrate with real yearlong inclusion, with respect, with equality of opportunity, and with the recognition that excluding Latinos from leadership positions is wrong and damaging to the effectiveness and bottom line of all types of organizations.

38

Latinos in Florida's 2020 Election

(Creators Syndicate, September 17, 2020)

As a resident of the greater Orlando metropolitan area, every four years around this time of year, I am bombarded with dozens of media requests for comments on the coming elections. The eyes of American political journalists and of some of their colleagues in Europe and Latin America turn to Central Florida for clues as to which candidate will win the state.

Whoever wins the I-4 corridor wins Florida, and whoever wins Florida wins the White House—so goes the maxim, which has held true in every single presidential election going back to 1964, except in 1992, when George H.W. Bush carried the corridor and the state but lost the presidency to Bill Clinton.[1]

In Florida, margins of victory over the past five presidential elections have averaged under 2 percent. In 2012, then-President Barack Obama beat Mitt Romney by a mere 0.88 points. Who can forget the evening of November 7, 2000, and the next day's early hours? Along with millions of Americans glued to their TV screens, I went to bed believing that Al Gore had won the state and thus the presidency but woke up to news that the results were too close to call. It

---

1 In the 2020 elections, Biden won the I-4 corridor but lost Florida.

took a month for George W. Bush to be declared victor in Florida by a margin of only 537 votes.

Which way Florida will go is usually unpredictable. That was the case in 2016, when Donald Trump edged out Hilary Clinton by a much larger-than-anticipated number of votes. The coming elections are similarly unpredictable. Several early September polls show Joe Biden ahead by only 3 points, while the latest NBC News/Marist poll has both candidates tied at 48 percent.

A poll by Bendixen & Amandi International focusing exclusively on heavily Democratic Miami-Dade County found that among likely voters, Biden is ahead but only by 17 points, a much narrower margin than Clinton's 30-point advantage four years ago.

A recent GQR poll points to significant changes among the state's Latino registered voters, particularly Cubans. In that group, Trump holds an 18-point lead over Biden, while preferences are inverted among non-Cuban Hispanics, with Biden leading by 17 points. In Florida, Cuban and Puerto Rican voters cancel each other out.

A Bit of History

Back in 1970, 9 out of 10 Hispanics residing in Florida were Cuban. While they (we) are still the largest Hispanic group in the state, we are down to around 25 percent, largely the result of mass migrations from Nicaragua and Puerto Rico since the 1980s and a more recent flow of exiles and immigrants from socialist Venezuela.

Since the 1990s, the sharper relative demographic growth of second- and third-generation Cubans and post-1980 exiles vis-à-vis earlier, older, and more conservative exiles reduced the rate of Cuban support for Republican candidates. In 2002, nearly two-thirds of registered Cuban voters were or leaned Republican. By 2013, the percentage had dropped below 50. The trend was clear, but no one, me included, anticipated a tipping point as early as 2012, when Barack Obama edged Mitt Romney 49 to 47 percent.

While in 2016, Trump received a lower percentage of the Latino vote in Florida than Romney in 2012 (35 to 39 percent, respectively), he attracted a higher percentage of Cuban votes than Romney (54 to 47), a reflection of a reversal of the "leftward" trend among Cuban voters. Clinton, meanwhile, received a whopping 72 percent of the state's Puerto Rican vote.

What Should We Expect in November?

The contest between Republican-leaning Cubans and Democratic-leaning Puerto Ricans will likely determine which presidential candidate carries Florida's coveted 29 electoral votes.

While Cubans still outnumber Puerto Ricans in the state, the latter have a 100 percent voter eligibility rate because they are U.S. citizens by birth. Cubans, however, have much higher rates of registration and voter participation.

Roughly 50 days before the elections, Trump's campaign has done a far better job courting Cuban Floridians than Biden's campaign has with the state's Puerto Rican electorate.

It's likely, almost assured, that on November 3, we will go to bed not knowing who won Florida and the presidency, and that vote counting will go on for weeks. In 2000, the nation and the world witnessed the state's vote recount spectacle—the wide-eyed guy with a magnifying glass looking for hanging chads and the invasion of out-of-state, preppy-dressed young Republicans storming ballot-count centers.

We can anticipate greater problems than figuring out hanging chads, and larger, angrier mobilizations of partisans during any recount. This time, they will not be in preppy clothes. Some will be armed.

39

A Second Opinion: The Democratic Party Needs a Battery of Tests and Biopsies to Figure Out Why Its Support among Latino Voters Slipped in 2020

(Creators Syndicate, November 7, 2020)

I am about to hit the send button of an email with this column. It is 4:30 p.m. on the Friday of election week. And what a week it has been! CNN and MSNBC have Joe Biden ahead in four of six yet-to-be-called states (Arizona, Pennsylvania, Georgia, Nevada). Victory is imminent for the Biden/Harris ticket, but over-cautious news organizations want to avoid "DEWEY DEFEATS TRUMAN" headlines.

Unlike the 2016 presidential election, when Donald Trump's victory surprised almost everyone, even his own campaign, this week's electoral results have been mostly in line with pre-election polls. The most notable exception is the fact that Latino support for Biden's candidacy was weaker than anticipated and proportionately slimmer than it had been for Hillary Clinton four years earlier.

In the aftermath of Republican presidential candidate Mitt Romney's 2012 defeat, the Republican National Committee conducted a thorough self-evaluation, an autopsy of sorts. "We need to campaign among Hispanic, Black, Asian, and gay Americans," concluded the coroner's report, "and demonstrate we care about them, too."

The imminently victorious Democratic Party needs no national autopsy—it is neither dead nor agonizing—but the disappointing level of Latino support calls for a battery of tests, including regularly scheduled X-rays, and second and third opinions. But some patients do not follow through with their treatments.

The party needs to demonstrate that it cares about Latinos, not as what party activists and many progressives want us to be, but as who we are: a 61 million-strong, diverse group (in class, ideology, race, gender, age, religion, language, and national origin) whose individual members are entitled to hold varied points of view and vote the way we see fit.

Largely responsible for the misunderstanding and mischaracterization of America's Latinos are some of our own activists and intellectual leaders who have their own classist and elitist version of "deplorables": "los deplorables" who do not conform to the stereotype nor embrace the full premanufactured blue-hair-Democrat progressive package.

As for this week's electoral results, this is what we know so far. A larger number of Latinos voted for Trump than four years ago; Trump's percentage of the Latino vote increased from 28 to 32; Biden has commanded the majority of the group's votes, but at a substantially lower rate than Hillary Clinton in 2016.

This is particularly evident in the two quasi-battleground states that remained red, Florida and Texas, where Latinos constitute 20 and 30 percent of the electorate, respectively.

Most political analysts and pundits have taken the easiest route to explain Trump's increasing electoral support among Florida Latinos. Trump's anti-Cuban regime rhetoric and policies, the simplistic argument goes, lured tens of thousands of Cuban voters in his direction. Miami-Dade exit polls reported by NBC News, show that was not the case. Fifty-five percent of the county's Cuban American electorate cast votes for Trump, only one percent more than state-wide Cubans in 2016.

We must look for explanations elsewhere: in the famous Interstate 4 corridor. Osceola County, south of Orlando, is a heavily Puerto Rican enclave. In 2016, Clinton carried Osceola by 25 points, but Biden's victory margin is under 14. This suggests that Puerto Rican turnout was lower than expected and, as a group, Puerto Ricans were unenthusiastic about Biden, Trump's paper-towel-tossing spectacle in Puerto Rico notwithstanding.

In Texas, CNN exit polls tell us, 40 percent of Hispanics voted for Trump, 6 points higher than four years ago. Particularly striking was Trump's robust performance in several Rio Grande Valley counties. Shockingly enough, he won

Zapata County, where 85 percent of the population is Hispanic, grabbing 52 percent of the vote, hundreds of immigrant children in cages notwithstanding.

The Democratic Party could have done much better among Latinos. May the election results be a "*despierta* Biden" message. Latinos were part of the Democratic Party winning coalition. We deserve a fair slice of the celebration cake and seats at the grown-ups table—figuratively and literally (i.e., the Cabinet table).[1]

The Democratic Party and its allies need to hear second and third opinions as to who Latinos are and what we want; to go beyond the usual activist and progressive interlocutors; to learn that not all Latinos listen to NPR; that only 3 percent self-describe as Latinx; that most go to church on Sunday (Catholic or Evangelical); that most do not drink Patrón-brand tequila; that except for AOC and a few other cool Latinos, most do not attend the Met Gala in extravagant garb; that some have the right to be anti-communist; and above all, that voting Republican does not mean that they are alienated—to use Marxist lingo—nor dropped from outer space.

---

1 During his presidency, Biden has named several Latinos to Cabinet positions: Alejandro Mayorkas (Homeland Security), Miguel Cardona (Education), and Xavier Becerra (Health and Human Services).

Section VI

Puerto Rico, the World's Oldest Colony

Introduction

I started my career as a historian in Puerto Rico in the mid-1980s, where I researched and published on various topics of the island's history. I also wrote occasional columns for two local dailies on social, cultural, and political subjects. One of those early columns addressed the escalating brain drain; and turned out to be prophetically autobiographical as I joined that exodus a few months later, leaving Puerto Rico to pursue a doctorate at Duke University. At the time, it was a temporary move that became permanent, my third migration in 25 years.

My first foray into the study of Puerto Rico was in political history, specifically a study of the New Progressive Party, a party that champions statehood for the island and whose 1968 surprising electoral victory opened the doors to five decades of bipartidism. The island's political status question—whether it becomes independent, joins the fifty states of the Union, or retains some sort of autonomous association with the United States—continues to divide Puerto Ricans with no end in sight.

Two of the columns in this section address the perennial status question, tracing its evolution from the early twentieth century through recent plebiscites. The commonwealth political status has remained virtually untouched since 1952, but Puerto Rico's autonomy has eroded since the explosion of the island's fiscal crisis in 2015, most notably through the imposition by the U.S. Congress of the Puerto Rico Oversight, Management and Economic Stability Act (with the ironic acronym PROMESA).

This section also traces the evolution of Puerto Rico's economy over the twentieth century and first two decades of the twenty-first, with special attention to the effects of its process of deindustrialization, including widespread unemployment and mass exodus to the United States.

I happened to be visiting Puerto Rico in late July 2019 when the island had its own "unimaginable," a massive, spontaneous popular mobilization that forced the resignation of the island's governor Ricardo Rosselló. In situ, I wrote this section's column "Puerto Rico's Democratic Revolt Result of Decades of Mounting Tectonic Pressure."

40

Crisis in Paradise

(*The Puerto Ricans*, November 2020)[1]

The first two decades of the twenty-first century have been disastrous for Puerto Rico, a compounding series of developments that have brought the island to a seemingly insurmountable economic, social, and political crisis: the termination of Section 936 of the U.S. Internal Revenue Service Code; the erosion of political autonomy and sovereignty under the commonwealth status; the debt crisis that exploded in 2015; the deadly and destructive impact of Hurricane María in 2017; and the political crisis and mass popular mobilization culminating in the disgraceful resignation of Governor Ricardo Rosselló in the summer of 2019.

In 1996, President Bill Clinton signed into law a bill that began the 10-year phase out of Section 936, which since 1976 had provided tax exemptions or reductions for U.S. corporate profits as long as they were reinvested in Puerto Rico. This began a decade-long countdown that ended in 2006. In 2005, the government ran out of operating funds and temporarily furloughed all nonessential

1 Kal Wagenheim, Olga Wagenheim and Luis Martínez-Fernández, eds., *The Puerto Ricans: A Documentary History* (Princeton, NJ: Markus Wiener Publishers, 2020).

public employees. That year, Puerto Rico entered a prolonged—still running—streak of consecutive years of falling (or stagnant) GDP growth rates.

While some scholars and observers of Puerto Rican reality question the extent of the impact of the demise of Section 936, it is a fact that Puerto Rico's manufacturing sector fell sharply from around 150,000 jobs in 1997 to around 100,000 in 2007. The crisis was compounded by the U.S. and worldwide recessions that erupted in 2008.

From the moment the United States established colonial domination over Puerto Rico in 1899, the island's economy has depended on—and has been limited by—federal legislation. The resulting balance, producing some beneficial provisions like including Puerto Rico's exports within the U.S. tariffs system but also harmful restrictions such as mandating that transportation of goods between the island and the United States be in U.S. Merchant Marine vessels, the most expensive in the world.

The commonwealth status in place since 1952, seemed to offer, as pro-commonwealth 1996 Resident Commissioner candidate Celeste Benítez repeatedly said, "the best of both worlds": the benefits of association with the United States (i.e., Section 936) without the federal personal income tax burdens levied upon residents of the 50 states.

In recent decades, the political status debate has become more complex and intense. Pro-statehood Governor Pedro Rosselló (Ricardo's father) pushed through a referendum in 1993 in which none of the three traditional formulas (commonwealth, statehood, independence) received a majority of the votes, but a substantial percentage of the electorate (46.3) came out in support of statehood. Re-elected in 1996, Rosselló advanced another referendum in 1998. This time, the consultation included two additional options: "Free Association" (a sort of commonwealth with expanded autonomy) and "None of the Above," the latter of which received 50.3 percent of the votes; 46.5 percent voted for statehood.

Since its creation in 2000, the President's Task Force on Puerto Rico's Status produced reports in 2005, 2007, and 2011. The first and second reports outlined the three traditional options; differentiated the "territorial" commonwealth status from the nonterritorial (sovereign) options of statehood and independence; and recommended a two-phase consultation: first, for voters to express their preference for either remaining under the status quo or changing it; and second, if they favored a change of status, to select one of the two nonterritorial options.

More recently in 2016, the U.S. Supreme Court, while opining on a Double Jeopardy Clause case, maintained that Puerto Rico and the United States were not separate sovereignties, that the Commonwealth's sovereignty was subordinate to federal sovereignty, where it has its origins, and that someone prosecuted in a federal court cannot be prosecuted for the same crime in a Commonwealth court.

After 10 years of uncontained economic bleeding, the island's long-mounting public debt reached a critical point in the summer of 2015, when Governor Alejandro García Padilla declared the obvious, that the Commonwealth's 73-billion-dollar debt was unrepayable. Because it is not a state of the Union, more-over, Puerto Rico could not benefit from Chapter 9 bankruptcy protection.[2]

Short of giving the Commonwealth the right to declare bankruptcy, in April 2016, Congress delivered a bill to create an oversight board composed of seven presidential appointees to "achieve fiscal responsibility and access to the capi-tal markets." The resulting Puerto Rico Oversight, Management and Economic Stability Act (PROMESA) created the Financial Oversight and Management Board of Puerto Rico, tasked with working with the insular government toward balancing its budget and creating a fiscal plan with the primary goal of paying off the public debt.

The law that created PROMESA exposes the inadequacy of the common-wealth status and makes evident the fact that Puerto Ricans are second-class citizens who are not protected by some federal laws such as the minimum wage and are not entitled to the same levels of Medicare, food stamps, and other fed-eral social programs. Could it be that the commonwealth status now offers "the worst of both worlds"?

The economic crisis perfect storm was exacerbated by an actual perfect storm: Hurricane María. On September 20, 2017, just two weeks after the rav-aging Hurricane Irma passed close to the island's northeastern coast, Hurricane María struck as a category 4 hurricane with 155 mph winds. With an estimated 90 billion dollars-worth of damages, it is the most destructive hurricane to ever hit Puerto Rico.

For several months following María's destructive path, the government of Puerto Rico maintained an official death toll of only 64. Widely regarded as a gross undercount, concerned Puerto Ricans called for an honest and scientific recount. Studies conducted in the next few months concluded that the death toll surpassed 3,000.

Hurricane María prompted a wave of emigration to the United States that expanded the already massive exodus that had been growing for decades. The

2 In mid-March 2022, Puerto Rico successfully renegotiated part of its debt, cutting down $22 billion worth of bonds debt to $7 billion.

ongoing wave had begun in the early 1980s during the world recession stemming from the period's severe oil crisis. The U.S. census estimated in 2000 that 3.4 million Puerto Ricans lived in the United States, a number that grew to 4.7 million in 2010. Around 2005, the Puerto Rican population residing in the 50 states surpassed the island's population. The latest census estimates (2018) include 5.68 million nationwide, 1.19 million of them in the state of Florida.

41

Puerto Rico's Democratic Revolt Result of Decades of Mounting Tectonic Pressure

(The Globe Post, July 26, 2019)

Puerto Rico is undergoing its most dramatic political transformation since it became a U.S. territory in 1898–1899. Late Wednesday night, after two weeks of unprecedented popular mobilization and massive protests, Governor Ricardo Rosselló reluctantly and unapologetically announced his resignation effective August 2.

During the first half of the twentieth century, Puerto Rico experienced a gradual expansion of self-rule and civil rights that culminated in the creation of a democratic commonwealth in 1952, neither independent nor a state of the Union but freely associated with the United States.

Under the leadership of progressive politician Luis Muñoz Marín and his dedicated think tank and loyal followers, and with the support of the Franklin D. Roosevelt administrations and others that followed, Puerto Rico experienced miraculous economic and social development. Measuring only 3,515 square miles, the island became America's "showcase of democracy" and model for successful capitalist economic prosperity.

Tax Benefits and Recession

These extraordinary developments, however, were underpinned by structural dependency on the United States and special concessions by the insular government to U.S. corporations and investors. Among them stands out Section 936 of the U.S. Internal Revenue Service Code (established in 1976) that freed corporations from profit tax payments if they reinvested those funds on the island.

For decades, leaders of the pro-commonwealth Popular Democratic Party claimed that their status preference was the best guarantee for economic prosperity because it allowed the continuation of Section 936, a provision that states of the Union did not enjoy. To kill the anti-statehood 936 argument, then Governor Pedro Rosselló did not raise a finger to defend that provision, arguing instead for its elimination. The result was a 10-year gradual phase out that ended in 2006. That year, the economy entered a deep recession from which it has not yet recovered.

The crisis that exploded in the middle of the century's first decade is complex, with multiple reverberations that feed off of each other. Many factories that enjoyed tax exemptions closed, eliminating some of the best paying jobs; mass emigration of Puerto Ricans to the United States (largely to Central Florida) increased sharply, ridding the island of thousands of Puerto Ricans in productive ages; house prices plummeted and the tax base shrank.

Attempts to Save Puerto Rico's Economy

Beginning in 1973, Puerto Rico, its municipalities, and the Commonwealth's public corporations issued millions of dollars' worth of bonds to balance their budgets. In 2014, many of those bonds were downgraded to "junk" status, and a few months later, the unpopular pro-commonwealth Governor Alejandro García Padilla declared that the 73-billion-dollar debt was unrepayable.

The U.S. government, in defense of U.S. bondholders, established in Puerto Rico the PROMESA Board, endowing it with broad powers that impinged on the island's traditional fiscal and political autonomy, including gaining final say on insular budgets.

Governor Ricardo Rosselló, a promoter of statehood, has proven supine. He has imposed austerity measures with detrimental effects on the masses: higher taxes, public utility fee hikes, reduction of public services, and the systematic defunding of the state university system. More alarming yet, are plans to slash retiree pensions, eliminate federal minimum wage protections for younger workers, and sell off, wholesale, public lands and other state properties.

Hurricane María and Endemic Corruption

In the wee hours of September 20, 2017, Hurricane María struck the island, causing unprecedented damage and the death of over 3,000 residents. The Rosselló administration stubbornly maintained for months that the actual death toll was under 100. To add insult to injury, President Donald Trump visited the island and tossed rolls of paper towels at a gathering of friendly Puerto Ricans. Since then, the Trump administration has withheld the bulk of fund transfers allotted for disaster relief and reconstruction.

In the meantime, members of the island's governing party have engaged in horrendous acts of corruption that include not distributing food and water to hurricane victims because keeping those provisions in truck containers generates enormous profits to well-connected contractors. Two weeks ago, federal authorities arrested several high-ranking administration officials on corruption charges, including the former secretary of education.[1]

Popular indignation with the insular government had already reached a feverish peak when in July 2019 the Center for Investigative Journalism released 900 pages of chats exchanged between the governor and several of his cabinet members and closest political associates. Long familiar with the government's ineptitude, abuse of power, and corruption, the people of Puerto Rico read those atrocious chat statements laden with misogynistic, homophobic, and other insulting comments.

Chat group members bragged about their own corrupt acts, applauded the fact that they had successfully pushed thousands of Puerto Ricans out of the island, denigrated political opponents, and worse yet, made sick jokes about those killed by the hurricane. The publication of those infamous chats was the crisis' let-them-eat-cake moment. The masses mobilized like never before and charged against the island's tropical bastille.

---

1 On August 4, 2022, federal authorities arrested former governor Wanda Vásquez on bribery charges connected with her unsuccessful 2020 gubernatorial campaign.

Social and Political Earthquake

The ongoing protests are the "Big One": a social and political earthquake result-ing from decades of mounting tectonic pressure along the manifold fissures that divide society: rich versus poor, men versus women, light-skinned versus darker-hued, the old versus the young, and those in favor and against gay rights.

The island will continue to shake after Rosselló steps down. We can expect thunderous aftershocks for months and years: pressures to clean up all govern-ment institutions, fights against the indignities perpetrated by PROMESA, the auditing of the public debt, and the abolition, for once and for all, of the fraud of the island's status-preference-based party system. The Commonwealth is a cadaver, statehood is not an option—now less than ever—and independence will continue to be but a unicorn in the horizon.

This 100 × 35-miles island, in a peaceful way, has lectured the world on the meaning of true democracy.

42

Puerto Rico, Its Expanding Diaspora and the 2020 Elections

(Creators Syndicate, September 26, 2020)

Puerto Rico is in the throes of a prolonged, seemingly unsolvable, multi-layered crisis. The catalog of insular plagues is extensive: a $70 billion-plus unrepayable debt; periodic hurricane strikes (like María, on September 20, 2017) and scores of earthquakes (almost unheard of before 2020); the loss of tens of thousands of manufacturing jobs in the last two decades; a concomitant mass exodus to the United States and contraction of the island's tax base; rising crime; and endemic political corruption. And let's not forget COVID-19.

The island has been losing population since the start of the century. Three million, two-hundred thousand Puerto Ricans reside on the island, over 5.6 million on the mainland. Both populations travel back and forth and maintain tight transnational bonds.

Recent Florida polls showing a smaller-than-expected margin in Latino voter preference between Donald Trump and Joe Biden, coinciding with the start of Hispanic Heritage Month, have shifted the eyes of both campaigns to the Sunshine State. Much of the attention targets the over one million Puerto Ricans who reside there (417,000 registered to vote), mostly along the I-4 corridor.

Happy Día Hispánico, Amigous!

On the first day of Hispanic Heritage Month (September 15), Democratic nominee Joe Biden made his first visit to the state since his presidential nomination and gave speeches in Tampa and the Puerto Rican enclave of Kissimmee in the Orlando Metropolitan area. Biden spoke on numerous issues of interest to Latinos and specifically targeted Puerto Rican voters, announcing the launch of his campaign's Puerto Rican agenda.

He took a few jibes at Trump's response to Hurricane María, vowing that he would never throw paper towels at hurricane victims, sell or trade Puerto Rico, or nuke incoming hurricanes, possibilities the president had seriously explored.

Three days later, 46 days before the elections and 1,094 days after Hurricane María struck the island, Trump surprised most observers with the promise of $13 billion worth of FEMA grants to rebuild the island's infrastructure—infrastructure week again? He promised over $9 billion for rebuilding the electric grid and the balance for school infrastructure. Lastly, he vowed to facilitate the return of U.S. pharmaceutical companies to the island, whose flight he unfairly blamed on Biden.

Whether Trump will deliver those goodies, or whether he will be in power long enough to do so, is unclear. Whatever the case, thus far, FEMA and HUD disaster relief funds have been purposely delayed. The corrupt and inept administrations of disgraced former Governor Ricardo Rosselló and his unpopular designated successor, Wanda Vázquez, are also to blame, having spent (as of March 2020) only 0.1 percent of $1.5 billion disbursed for emergency housing reconstruction.

It is not surprising that Trump is promising tax cuts for pharmaceutical and medical equipment manufacturing corporations to incentivize their return to Puerto Rico. I do find suspicious, however, his campaign promise of multibillion-dollar allocations to rebuild an electrical grid owned and operated by a public corporation and the reconstruction of public schools.

Trump is ideologically inclined to privatization and reducing the size of government, and the island's pro-statehood party, which has been in power since 2016, encourages the privatization of utility companies and the transformation of public schools into for-profit charter schools. Will American taxpayers be paying to refurbish infrastructures that will end up in the hands of corporations and private investors?

Biden's Puerto Rican agenda, while equally opportunistic is more coherent and comprehensive. Like Trump, he promises federal disaster funding for electric and school infrastructures and facilitating the return of good-paying pharmaceutical companies. Biden's plan goes further, including the reconstruction of roads, bridges, ports, utilities, and implementation of clean energy projects. He also promises some debt relief.

In line with his penchant for self-congratulation, Trump claims that his response to Hurricane María has been "an incredible, unsung success," that he is "the best thing that ever happened to Puerto Rico" and that his recently announced funding constitutes the "largest emergency relief award in history."

The president is entitled to his self-opinion, but his 11th-hour relief package pales in comparison with the New Deal's comprehensive Puerto Rico Emergency Relief Administration and Puerto Rico Reconstruction Administration. I spoke about this in an interview with Salon.com and was immediately Breitbarted—I owe the verb to a UCF colleague.

Trump is no Roosevelt—neither is Biden, for that matter—and the current insular political leadership bears no resemblance to the people who joined efforts with former Governor Luis Muñoz Marín to rid the island of its misery, pull it out of the Great Depression and turn it into a prosperous modern nation.

43

The 20 Plagues of Contemporary Puerto Rico

(The Globe Post, July 16, 2020)[1]

Ten plagues struck Old-Testament Egypt; much smaller contemporary Puerto Rico has suffered at least twice as many.

Since 2005, Puerto Rico has endured a profound crisis, arguably deeper and harder to solve than the Great Depression. Most local politicians lack the imagination and moral rectitude to confront current challenges, and Donald Trump, to put it in the kindest terms possible, is not Franklin D. Roosevelt.

The deepest and longest-lasting plagues are endemic and date back over 500 years: (1) colonialism and (2) dependency. Not only is Puerto Rico still a colony, but over the past decade, congressional legislation and Supreme Court decisions have actually reversed the movement toward expanded autonomy. The island government can no longer implement annual budgets without the approval of PROMESA, an oversight body imposed by Congress.

Long dependent on food imports for its survival, in the last three decades, Puerto Rico has undergone a sustained deindustrialization process (plague No.

---

1 This is an abbreviated and updated version of the column published on July 16, 2020. The original version included 16 plagues.

3). Virtually everything must be imported; there is not much external trade except of people: temporary imports of U.S. tourists and permanent or semi-permanent exports of Puerto Ricans to U.S. cities, from Boston to Miami and all the way to California. The island's economy has been in recession (plague No. 4) since 2006.

A concomitant plague (No. 5) is the island's depopulation. According to the U.S. census, population peaked around 2000 at 3.8 million; it has fallen ever since to an estimated 3.2 in 2020, a reduction that has severely eroded the tax base and reduced home values. Polls and surveys attest to the fact that those who leave are escaping the plagues of unemployment (No. 6), frozen wages (No. 7), and rising crime (No. 8), largely fueled by drug trafficking (No. 9). Another rapidly spreading plague is gender and homophobic violence (No. 10).

A seemingly unbeatable plague is the island's $73 billion debt (No. 11), deemed unrepayable by hapless Governor Alejandro García Padilla in July 2015. Widely considered the worst Puerto Rican governor ever, he seemed to concur, when he did not seek re-election in 2016. That was a short-lived distinction. His successor, baby-faced and self-absorbed Governor Ricardo Rosselló was forced to resign in disgrace in August 2019. Government corruption, ineptitude, and nepotism are plagues Nos. 12, 13 and 14.

Even nature has conspired to sink the island deeper into poverty and despair. María, one of the island's most devastating and deadliest hurricanes ever (No. 15), left in its wake 3,369 dead and $90 billion in damages. Earthquakes (No. 16) are not common in Puerto Rico, but since December 2019, the island has been rocked continuously by tremors and earthquakes, the strongest of which reached a magnitude of 6.4. In June, Puerto Rico was covered by Sahara dust (No. 17), the worst storm of its kind in 50 years.

Half-man made and half natural disaster, recurrent droughts (No. 18) have plagued the island for decades. The drought of 2015 was the worst in 20 years. This summer's drought has forced authorities to ration water service (24 hours with and 24 without).

Did I forget to mention No. 19, COVID-19?

Expect No. 20, any time soon.[2]

---

2 The plague of darkness: In June 2021 the government of Puerto Rico signed an agreement with the Canadian American LUMA Energy company to transmit and distribute electricity on the island. LUMA has hiked rates several times and blackouts have become nearly daily occurrences. The electric grid failed when the island was struck by Hurricane Fiona five years after Hurricane María.

44

Can't We Just Sell Multi-Plagued Puerto Rico and Solve the Political Status of the World's Oldest Colony?

(The Globe Post, July 16, 2020)[1]

This past weekend, the *New York Times* reported that Donald Trump had suggested to then-Homeland Security Secretary Elaine Duke that the United States sell Puerto Rico after it was struck and severely damaged by Hurricane María in September 2017.

Months later, according to other news reports, the real estate-mogul-turned-reality TV personality-turned-president wanted to purchase Greenland from Denmark and possibly swap it for Puerto Rico. Perhaps not a bad deal: 836,330 square miles with only 56,081 inhabitants in exchange for 3,515 square miles overflowing with 3.2 million people.

There is precedent for such lopsided territorial trades. Back in 1763, at the end of the French and Indian War, a defeated France agreed to yield sovereignty over French Canada in exchange for Britain's devolution of the Caribbean colonies of Guadeloupe and Martinique.

In 1867, Secretary of State William H. Seward purchased Alaska from Russia at two cents an acre. A parallel attempt to obtain the Danish Virgin Islands failed

---

1 This is an abbreviated version of the column published on July 16, 2020.

that year, but 50 years later, the United States acquired all three of them at $292 per acre.

But we are not in the 1700s, 1800s, or even 1900s. Colonies are no longer bought, sold, or traded.

André Breton, not even in his worst surrealist trance, could have conceived a Puerto Rico-for-Greenland swap in what seems like a madcap game, a crossbreed of Monopoly and Risk.

World's Oldest Colony

In 1997, the eve of the centennial of the so-called Spanish-American War, former Puerto Rico Supreme Court Justice José Trías Monge published *Puerto Rico: The Trials of the Oldest Colony in the World*.

Spanish adventurers led by Juan Ponce de León conquered the island beginning in 1508; it remained a Spanish colony long after all other American Spanish territories (except Cuba) gained independence in the 1820s and 1830s. On July 25, 1898, U.S. military forces disembarked in Puerto Rico and after a few skirmishes with Spanish soldiers took control of the island, absorbing it a few months later as a formal colonial domain.

When Trías Monge's book came out, Puerto Rico had endured 489 years of colonial rule. Nearly a quarter of a century later, it is still the world's oldest colony, only older.

Even before 1898, Puerto Rican politicians were divided along the lines of political status preference: independence, complete integration to the Metropolis (Spain, later the United States), or a hybrid accommodation, securing a degree of self-rule while remaining under the sovereignty of another nation.

In 2020, the island's politicians and their partisans are still split along the same lines, with each of the three main political parties anchored around a particular status option: the pro-U.S. statehood New Progressive Party, the Popular Democratic Party which advocates for the continuation and/or enhancement of the current commonwealth status, and the Puerto Rican Independence Party.

From Sad Case to Economic Miracle

Having grown and lived in a suburban middle-class family during what many consider Puerto Rico's best years ever (1970s through mid-1980s), I still find it difficult to write and teach about the island's history during the first four decades of the twentieth century, when it was as neglected and impoverished as most of the rest of the Caribbean.

In a 1928 article titled "The Sad Case of Porto Rico," future Puerto Rican governor Luis Muñoz Marín wrote lyrically about an island that languished under U.S. colonial rule: "a sweatshop that has a company store—the United States," with "many more schools for their hungry children and many more roads for their bare feet."

Another insular governor, New Dealer Rexford Guy Tugwell, gave a similarly somber title to his Puerto Rico years memoir, *The Stricken Land*, a catalog of squalor and pestilence, bitter realities he worked to combat in alliance with Muñoz Marín, then president of the island's Senate.

Under the leadership of progressive insular and continental elected and administrative officials, and with generous funding for the island's New Deal letter soup—PRERA (Puerto Rico Emergency Relief Administration), PRRA (Puerto Rico Recovery Administration), WPA (Works Progress Administration), among other programs—the island gradually convalesced out of its severe depression.

Insular authorities took bold steps to improve and transform the economy, breaking up large estates measuring more than 500 acres to distribute small plots among landless peasants; establishing and running factories to produce carton, glass, ceramic tiles, cement, and shoes; clearing slums; electrifying rural areas; luring U.S. corporate capital; and building adequate public housing for the tens of thousands who were migrating to urban centers.

Statistics can lie but can also tell the truth. Between 1940 and 1970, life expectancy increased from 40 to 70 years; the rate of deaths attributable to parasites and infectious diseases dropped from 60 percent in 1940 to a little over 12 percent in 1966; and enrolment at the University of Puerto Rico's main campus (Río Piedras) skyrocketed from just over 5,000 in 1940 to almost 27,000 in 1970.

Politically, the decade and a half that followed 1940 expanded the electorate, drastically reduced political corruption, and saw a considerable increase in insular self-rule through the provisions of the Commonwealth Constitution of 1952.

To be fair, it was not a complete paradise: more Puerto Ricans died of cardiovascular diseases, the abuse of drugs proliferated, hundreds of thousands were pushed out to the U.S. mainland, and radical separatists endured persecution at the hands of the state.

Sell or Swap?

As a colony Puerto Rico does not govern itself. Ultimate decisions about the island's present and future are in the hands of the U.S. Congress which retains the authority to incorporate the island as a co-sovereign state of the Union, as it did with Alaska and Hawaii in 1959; renouncing sovereignty by granting it independence as Portugal did with Angola, reluctantly so, in 1975; or transferring it to another nation, as Great Britain did with Hong Kong in 1997.

My list of "never evers" is shrinking daily, but for the time being, I feel comfortable saying that the United States will not sell or swap its beleaguered colony, and its citizens will retain the dubious honor of being the world's oldest colonial subjects.

45

Should We Get Married or Continue Living Together? Puerto Rico's Never-Ending Status Question

(Creators Syndicate, November 21, 2020)

Allow me to use the analogy of a human couple. Puerto Rico's Independence Party advocates separation and, eventually, divorce—with alimony, of course. The New Progressive Party (PNP) has consistently courted Congress with hopes of everlasting marriage. The other major party, the Popular Democratic Party (PPD), prefers a reformulation of the current domestic arrangement: sort of living together but sleeping in different rooms, perhaps seeing others.

Two matters make the status-centric nature of the island's main parties misleading—actually, dishonest. First, Puerto Rico cannot singlehandedly determine its final political status. Congress has the last word. Thus, insular politicians continue to promise something they cannot deliver. They have been spinning their wheels for decades on what is essentially a non-issue.

Second, the Puerto Rican electorate is far from making up its mind about a final status option. Unlike Alaska, where 83.5 percent of voters approved of statehood in 1958, and Hawaii, where over 93 percent cast ballots to become the 50th state in 1959, Puerto Rican support for statehood has hovered under 47 percent. If Puerto Rico wants to propose, it needs to convince itself first.

Congress is equally of two minds, split along strict partisan lines. Democrats enthusiastically support statehood for Puerto Rico because it would translate into two additional Democratic senators and five Democratic U.S. representatives. For that reason, Republicans vigorously oppose its admission to the Union.

If at least one member of the couple made up its mind, it could woo the other into permanent union. As it stands, neither side is ready to pop the question, or answer yes if proposed to.

This month's referendum was the PNP's sixth attempt since 1967 to demonstrate majority support for statehood, the apparent logic being that if you play the lottery long enough, you are bound to win eventually.

Pro-statehood politicians have worded plebiscites and referenda in diverse ways, like a lawyer in court who asks a witness different versions of the same question until she elicits the answer she wants. The first and second time (1967 and 1993), voters had three options: commonwealth, independence, and statehood. On both occasions, the commonwealth formula won, and statehood came in second. Independence trailed a distant third.

In 1998, the menu included two additional options: free association (a sort of enhanced commonwealth) and "none of the above." Rejecting the PNP-crafted plebiscite's official definition of commonwealth, the PPD advised its members to vote "none of the above." That alternative received a slim majority of 50.3 percent. Statehood got 46.5 percent.

In 2012, Puerto Ricans were asked the question in yet another way. It was a two-part consultation: first, "Do you agree that Puerto Rico should continue to have its present form of territorial status?" Fifty-four percent voted no.

Voters were also given the opportunity to select among statehood, free association, and independence. With statehood receiving 61 percent of the vote, the PNP spun the results as a resounding victory. But closer examination paints a different picture. Forty-six percent of voters supported the Commonwealth, roughly the same number of votes cast for statehood in the second question. It was a virtual tie.

Five years later, the PNP pursued a different strategy, forcing voters to select between only two options, statehood and independence. Facing scrutiny from the U.S. Department of Justice, the plebiscite had to be reworded to include three alternatives: statehood, a consolidated option of free association/independence, and commonwealth.

The PPD called for a boycott, likewise the Independence Party. Consequently, voter turnout was under 23 percent. Only 517,216 Puerto Ricans participated in the 2017 plebiscite, roughly one-third of the total who had voted in the previous year's general elections. As a result, statehood received 97.2 percent of the votes, but of less than a quarter of the electorate.

Tellingly, in this month's elections, tens of thousands of Puerto Rican voters demonstrated that they have caught on to the status fraud by breaking ranks with the traditional status-centric parties. Gubernatorial candidates of two new parties (Alexandra Lúgaro, Citizen Victory Movement and César Augusto Vázquez Muñiz, Project Dignity), neither of which presented a defined status preference, receiving 21 percent of the vote, combined.

The District of Columbia is 86 percent serious about marriage. If it achieves that dream, when it hurls the floral bouquet (or garter belt), Puerto Rico's pro-statehood politicians will dive to catch it.

In the meantime, both would be wise to hold off on the deposit for the reception hall, the DJ, and the star-shaped table flower arrangements.

Exercises in Cuban Historiographical Maroonage

Introduction

This section includes seven essays in my primary fields of expertise in Cuban history and culture. They constitute a small portion of this work, the first of my books that is neither solely nor primarily focused on Cuba.

My transition away from Cuba-focused research and publishing is largely the result of having recently completed the ambitious research agenda I had set for myself years ago, including a trilogy on nineteenth-century Cuba and Puerto Rico and what I conceived to be my historiographical bookends: comprehensive histories of early colonial Cuba (*Key to the New World*, 2018) and the Revolution (*Revolutionary Cuba*, 2014).

But I have also witnessed the sustained intellectual decay in the field which, on the one hand, is still marked by stale 1960s and 1970s leftist politicization and, on the other, is bogged down by superimposed twenty-first century U.S. identity politics. It is not a pretty combination.

Unfortunately, Cuban studies have also taken on the plantation model, with its masters, overseers, and a multitude of laborers waiting for scraps to fall off the planters' mahogany tables, I am, and have been for a while, a maroon Cuban scholar.

Viva Castro!

Cuban studies, and more broadly Latin American studies, expanded dramatically during the 1960s in the United States and elsewhere because of the Cuban Revolution. "What happened in Cuba?" and "what could be done to avoid it happening again elsewhere?" were the driving forces behind the Alliance for Progress, generous Ford Foundation and Rockefeller Foundation grants for the study of Latin America and the establishment of dozens of Latin American Studies centers at U.S. and European universities.

Nineteen-sixty-six saw the founding of the Latin American Studies Association (LASA). One of its founders, historian Howard F. Cline, ironically referred to Fidel Castro as the "remote godfather" of Latin American studies and suggested—tongue-in-cheek—that in the future, practitioners erect a statue in his honor.

The field of Latin American studies from its inception has been marked by a romantic fascination with the Cuban Revolution and its bearded leaders. It is as if comfortable (clean-shaven) middle- and upper-middle class American intellectuals have lived revolution vicariously through the Castros, El Che and other rebels, the same way millions of sheltered (preppy-sweatered and bobby-socked) youths lived rebellion through Marlon Brando and James Dean, without the risk of falling off a speeding motorcycle or having their teeth knocked out in a street fist fight. It was so easy to be a revolutionary while drinking soda milk shakes at the local air-conditioned diner (or French wine at the faculty club).

Seven Maroon Essays

This section's first essay examines Fidel Castro's youth and how his experiences at Colegio Dolores shaped his character and influenced policies and actions he implemented once in power decades later. In his early teens, he wrote a letter to FDR offering to show him around the mines of Mayarí whose iron he suggested could be used to build U.S. ships.

The next essays look at far more recent developments and how individuals who hold romantic views of the Revolution, with varying degrees of intellectual honesty, produce and diffuse distorted images of my homeland. In one essay I offer unsolicited advice for candidate Bernie Sanders at the start of the 2020 primary season: "stay away from the Cuba trap" (in case you are curious, I supported Sanders, attended a couple of his rallies, and have voted for him twice); in another essay, I criticize a series of factual distortions and misrepresentations offered by Cuba expert Medea Benjamin in a June 2021 *AlterNet* article.

Other individual pieces denounce the rising tide of authoritarianism and repression, beginning with the state's renewed attempts to censure and control artistic creation through the provisions of Decreto 349, its heavy-handed militarized response to the July 11–14, 2021 protests and the government's successful in-the-bud nipping of protests scheduled for November 15 of the same year.

Two of the section's essays connect and compare developments on the island with attempts to weaken democracy in Washington, D.C., and Tallahassee, Florida.

The section's closing column "Sixtieth Anniversary of the Cuban Missile Crisis Finds Communist Island in Deepest Crisis Ever" discusses circumstances leading to a wave of massive popular protests exploding spontaneously throughout Cuba since August 2022 and what these protests may mean for the survival of the 63-year-old dictatorship.

46

"My Good Friend Roosevelt": Fidel Castro to FDR, November 6, 1940

(*History Today*, February 2019)

Historians and other social scientists have long examined Cuba's relations with the United States and Fidel Castro's enmity toward its government. During his 55-year rule over Cuba, Castro contended with—and arguably outsmarted—10 U.S. presidents, from Dwight D. Eisenhower to George W. Bush. Perhaps better than anyone else, Castro was keenly aware of the fact that the histories and destinies of Cuba and the United States are fatefully intertwined.

A little known 1940 document housed in the U.S. National Archives and Records Administration suggests that Castro's hostility toward the United States may have roots that go deeper than previously thought, perhaps back to when, as an eighth grader, he felt snubbed by U.S. President Franklin D. Roosevelt.

"My good friend Roosevelt," opens a letter from a young Castro to Roosevelt, dated November 6, 1940, the day following the president's second landslide re-election. As a student at the Jesuit-run Colegio Dolores in Santiago, Castro heard the news on the radio and sat down to write a letter of congratulation, three pages long, on school stationary, in neat cursive but broken English.

Although Fidel told Roosevelt that he was 12 years old, according to his official birth date, August 13, 1926, he would have been 14. It's very unlikely that he made a mistake about his own age; and there would have been no logical advantage to present himself as younger than he was. In fact, his letter conveyed that he was mature and knowledgeable beyond his age: "I think very much," he told the president.

For decades, Castro's birth date has been shrouded in mystery, the source of much speculation; it is possible that his father, Ángel Castro, bought a forged birth certificate with the object of presenting Fidel as a 10-year-old, the minimum age required for admission to fifth grade at Colegio Dolores.

The all-boy Colegio Dolores was one of Cuba's most prestigious schools; certainly, the most respected in Santiago, Cuba's second city. Its student rosters included the sons of some of eastern Cuba's wealthiest and most prominent families: the Bacardís, Casas, and Cubeñas, among others.

Fidel and his two brothers, Ramón and Raúl, were social outcasts. They had a wealthy father but carried the stigma of illegitimacy. While married to María Argota, Ángel Castro sired Fidel and six other illegitimate children with Lina Ruz González, a maid at the Castro household, 30 years younger than him.

Thus, the Castro boys grew up in an uncomfortable, and often humiliating, social limbo. Because of their low social status and rural origins, many of their classmates looked down on them. Fidel resented this and sought recognition and admiration by excelling in academics and sports.

Such humiliations probably explain Fidel's often-violent behavior toward other children. The painstakingly researched book, *The Boys from Dolores* by Patrick Symmes, recounts several instances of wrath and violence. One day, Castro struck out when playing baseball with a makeshift ball made of taped-together bottle caps. The crowd of students jeered at him. Publicly shamed, Fidel threw the bat at his scoffers, striking a classmate and dislocating his shoulder. One of Fidel's staunchest rivals, José Antonio Cubeñas, chastened the struck-out player: "Animal!" "Beast!" then pinned Castro to the floor. Symmes referred to that episode as a turning point in Fidel's life: "Everyone had seen him knocked down."

On the missive's second page, the precociously savvy Castro gets to his main point: "If you like, give me a ten dollar bill green American"—not for chocolate or movie tickets; it was a matter of curiosity, because he had never seen such a bill, he said.

At the end of the letter, most likely as an afterthought, is a postscript obviously crafted to increase his chances of getting Roosevelt's attention and that ten-dollar bill. "If you want iron to make your sheaps," he wrote, then crossing out the error and writing "ships," "I will show to you the biggest [sic] (minas) of the land. They are in Mayarí. Oriente Cuba." The American-owned Spanish-American Iron Co. had been extracting and processing iron ore there since the first decade of the century.

Fidel's offer possibly reflected his precocious intuition. Was he anticipating the eventual need for United States involvement in World War II, at a time when that was not under open consideration? Just a few days earlier, FDR had made a campaign promise that he would not send "our boys" to war; the Lend-Lease Act would not be signed into law until March 1941, almost four months after Fidel's letter. On December 8 and 11, 1941, Cuba declared war on Japan, Germany, and Italy, just a few hours after the United States had issued its declarations of war.

To his surprise, Fidel received an official response on White House stationary. He showed it off to his schoolmates and got it posted on the school bulletin board. According to historian Luis Aguilar, who attended Colegio Dolores at the time, Roosevelt's letter was the trophy that catapulted Fidel to popularity and admiration. Aguilar also reminisced about Castro's anger at the fact that FDR had not sent the ten-dollar bill and being snubbed by the president's rejection of his offer to show him around the iron mines of Mayarí. Americans are "assholes," Aguilar remembered Castro saying on that occasion.

Without claiming that the letter exchange with the U.S. president was the genesis of Castro's unremitting decades-long anti-Americanism, the experience certainly did not boost any admiration he may have had toward the United States. His experiences at Colegio Dolores did, however, shape his character and world view. He strove to excel in and out of the classroom and sought attention through daring acts, be it leading fellow students to the top of Pico Turquino, Cuba's highest mountain, writing to FDR, or engaging in fist fights with his rich classmates.

Years later, his electoral political ambitions thwarted by Fulgencio Batista's 1952 coup, Castro formed and led a guerrilla movement to bring down Batista by force; his 1953 attack on the Moncada Army garrison failed; following a brief prison stay and exile in Mexico he launched yet another attack in 1956, whose survivors sought refuge in the Sierra Maestra, whose peaks Fidel had climbed with fellow classmates from Colegio Dolores

Castro approached former classmate Cubeñas, requesting funding and the use of his family's farm to support the armed struggle. Cubeñas, once again snubbed Castro, not even acknowledging those requests.

In 1959 when he traveled to Washington to meet with President Eisenhower, Castro likely remembered what transpired 19 years before. His delegation's main objective was to secure financial support from the U.S. government; but tellingly,

Castro told his finance minister Rufo López-Fresquet that he did not want "this trip to be like that of other Latin American leaders who always come to the United States to ask for money." The ten-dollar "snub" may have influenced his decision to avoid the humiliation of asking another U.S. president for money only to be rebuffed again.

Eisenhower did not extend the courtesy of meeting with Castro; he opted to play golf that day leaving Vice President Richard Nixon in charge of the meeting. Castro did not ask for financial support and Nixon did not offer it. Whatever prospects may have existed for a friendly coexistence between revolutionary Cuba and the United States were destroyed that fateful April day. Castro felt he had been treated like a child. He came out of the meeting visibly angry, complaining "this man has spent the whole time scolding me."

Back in Cuba, Castro acted on his deep-seated rancor against Cuba's elites. Among the targets of property confiscation were the families of several of his rival classmates, most of whom went into exile. The Cubeñas left Cuba in 1960, settling in New York City, where José Antonio pursued a literary career. Likewise, with the Bacardís, the Casas, and most wealthy Cuban families. Castro's regime also nationalized U.S. properties on the island, including the iron mines of Mayarí: no Cuban iron for U.S. warships.

In 1961, Castro ordered the closing of all private schools, including Colegio Dolores and the also Jesuit-run Colegio Belén, where he finished high school. Later that year, both schools merged in exile in Miami, with the founding of Belén Jesuit Preparatory School.

When Castro died in November 2016, he had outlived perhaps all his Dolores and Belén classmates, including José Antonio Cubeñas and Luis Aguilar.

Whether the absence of a ten-dollar bill in FDR's letter had any impact on a 14-year-old Fidel's future actions may be speculative. But there is no doubt that the Eisenhower administration's failure to offer a 33-year-old Castro a few million dollars' worth of support resulted in perpetual headaches to the next nine U.S. presidents and cost billions of dollars over the next six decades.

Unsolicited Advice for Bernie Sanders: Stay Away from the Cuba Trap

(The Globe Post, February 26, 2020)

Bernie Sanders' recent statements about Fidel Castro and the Cuban Revolution have fired up major controversy and given plenty of ammunition to his mainstream Democratic primary opponents.

During Sunday night's "60 Minutes" interview, anchor Anderson Cooper raised the topic of Cuba and, like a magician who pulls a rabbit out of a hat, presented 35-year-old footage of an interview in which Sanders had spoken praisefully about the Cuban and Nicaraguan revolutions.

The presidential candidate was heard saying that the Cuban people did not rise because Castro "educated the kids [and] gave them healthcare." While the revolution did expand free healthcare to all Cubans, Sanders left out a critical part of the equation: Cuba became a police state that effectively crushed all opposition and continued to repress Cubans for decades.

Sanders gave honest responses to Cooper, saying what he now believes. He stated that he was "very opposed to the authoritarian nature of Cuba." He should have left it at that but added that "the Cuban revolution wasn't entirely bad." Then he went on to say, "You know, when Fidel Castro came into office, you know what he did? He had a massive literacy program. Is that a bad thing?"

Cooper pressed on, commenting, "there are a lot of dissidents imprisoned in Cuba." "That's right," Sanders responded. "And we condemn it."

As a historian trained to critically analyze sources and information, be they written, visual or spoken, I find no fault in most of what Sanders said; these were refreshingly candid answers from a man, who like many of his generation, was attracted to radical ideas and had sympathies for anti-imperialist movements like the Cuban Revolution.

Was everything about the Cuban Revolution negative? Of course not. Did Castro lead a massive education campaign to eradicate illiteracy? Yes, that happened, and it was internationally recognized as a major social accomplishment. It was also, I must add, a campaign used to indoctrinate tens of thousands, who learned to read reciting sentences such as "The young and the old, united, pledge with Fidel: to defend Cuba. We will never be defeated."

Cuba's Repressive Regime

After decades of international pressures to free its dissidents, the Cuban strategy changed from long term-imprisonment to intimidation, systematic harassment (sometimes violent), and temporary incarceration.

For anyone who still holds on to the fantasy of a benign revolution that can do no wrong, these words from Amnesty International's 2017/2018 Cuba Report should suffice: "A family of four human rights defenders were detained … for allegedly leaving their house during the period of state mourning for Fidel Castro in 2016. The three siblings were given one-year prison sentences for 'defamation of institutions, organizations and heroes and martyrs of the Republic of Cuba' and 'public disorder.' Their mother was sentenced to house arrest."

It may surprise some readers to learn that most U.S.-based Cuba experts are uncritical apologists of the Cuban regime. How can otherwise progressive academics who are so jealous of their own freedoms be so blind to the sordid realities of Cuba's repressive regime? The late Cuban author Guillermo Cabrera Infante likened them to "the three monkeys": they do not see, do not hear, and do not speak. Cabrera Infante was onto something when seeking explanations to such behavior through the lenses of zoology.

The Cuba Trap

As front-runner in the Democratic primaries, Sanders will continue to take flak for his seemingly radical views, statements, and policies, including his obsolescent romantic perspective on the Cuban Revolution.

Having written what I, and numerous critics, believe to be an honest and fair book on the revolution, *Revolutionary Cuba: A History*, I can attest to the fact that most people hold black-and-white views on the revolution. This ranges from the willfully uninformed to the over-informed (academics like me) and from the extreme right to what passes for left. Pseudo-leftist reviewers had a field day with my book. The right does not have scholars who review academic books but has operatives who engage in dirty tricks of their own.

As for Sanders, I have some unsolicited advice: continue to be honest but stay away from the Cuba trap. Remember that over the past 60 years, several U.S. presidents and presidential candidates have run aground or sunk in the treacherous waters of the Florida Straits.

Painting Republican presidential candidate Richard Nixon as soft on communism was part of John F. Kennedy's successful campaign arsenal in 1960. One year later, Kennedy endured the pain and embarrassment of the Bay of Pigs fiasco, which he referred to as the worst experience of his life.

Two decades later, Jimmy Carter suffered the consequences of mismanaging the Mariel boatlift crisis, which he encouraged when he said, "We'll continue to provide an open heart and open arms to refugees seeking freedom from Communist domination."

In 2000, presidential candidate Al Gore lost Florida, and thus the general election. It is widely acknowledged that Bill Clinton's conciliatory policies toward Cuba and his handling of the Elián González affair, the fierce custody battle between the United States and Cuba over the young Elián, eventually cost Gore enough Cuban American votes to swing the Florida results toward George W. Bush.

Another political casualty was Janet Reno, U.S. Attorney General at the time of the Elián González affair. When she tried to run for Florida governor in 2002 she was stopped in her tracks during the primaries. Cuban American voters paid her back.

Again, Sanders should stay away from the Cuba trap lest his opponents summon the spirit of a dead Castro as Sanders' Jeremiah Wright (candidate Obama's controversial pastor who in a sermon uttered "God Damn America"), or worse yet, in the case of earning the Democratic nomination, replay the narrative of Elián González, costing him thousands of votes in Florida and by extension the presidency.

48

"Are We Not Your Fellow Artists?": The Solitude of Cuba's San Isidro Movement

(Creators Syndicate, December 5, 2020)

Liberty, equality, fraternity. So goes the French Revolutionary motto to which the abolitionist society Les Amis de Noirs responded with the iconic image of a kneeling, shackled Black slave who asks, "Am I not your brother?"

The motto and the image have been circling my mind since I first learned, around two weeks ago, about the systematic harassment and repression of young Cuban artists of the San Isidro Movement. "Are we not artists?" I envision them asking their colleagues and artsy types around the world. Most, however, have no response.

The San Isidro Movement is composed of a few hundred Cuban artists and intellectuals who have been protesting the 2018 Decreto 349, a decree that severely restricts artistic expression and the commercialization of artists' creations, be they rap concerts, theatrical productions in private homes or paintings sold in city parks.

In September 2020, a group of artists and intellectuals, among them Luis Manuel Otero Alcántara, Yanelys Núñez Leyva, and Tania Bruguera signed the San Isidro Manifesto. The document proclaimed their right to creative independence, freedom from dogmatic dictates by government entities and the free pursuit of non-traditional aesthetics.

The signatories rejected the appointment of "supervisor-inspectors" (arts komissars) tasked with censoring artistic creation and warned with NATO firmness that "an attack on one of us, is an attack against the collective."

On November 9, police agents arrested San Isidro Movement rapper and performance artist Denis Solís. Two days later, he was judged and sentenced to eight months in prison for contempt of a police officer whom he claimed had illegally entered his home. The rapper's crime: calling him "an animal inside of a uniform."

On November 18, 18 young artists including Otero Alcántara quartered inside the movement's art gallery; some began a hunger and thirst strike demanding the release of Solís. A few days later, state security agents burst into the gallery and arrested most of them.

When Otero Alcántara was re-arrested on the 27th, around 200 San Isidro activists and their supporters did something unprecedented. They staged a street protest in front of a government agency building, the Ministry of Culture, forcing the vice minister to meet with them.

In response, the Cuban state has unfurled a four-pronged offensive: mobilizing SWAT and other repressive forces—is the nightstick mightier than the rapper's microphone?—unleashing thuggish counter protesters—Fidel! Fidel! Fidel!—deploying *oficialista* artists such as members of the state's Cuban Rap Agency—such a thing exists—and mounting an Orwellian all-media propaganda campaign. Let's not forget that Castro coined the term "fake media" back in 1959 when Donald Trump was playing boy soldier at the New York Military Academy.

Protesters, the Cuban government claims, are mediocre artists who are subsidized by and respond to Miami mafiosi and Trump's "imperialist" administration. In an hourlong Cuban TV special on the subject, a parade of "state experts" referred to the protests as a "soft coup" and a "deflated theatre" and linked movement leaders to "exiled terrorists".

Several leading non-dissident Cuban artists have, in fact, spoken out against the restrictions. These include singer-songwriter Silvio Rodríguez, graphic artist José Ángel Toirac, film director Carlos Lechuga, and actor Luis Alberto García.

While some international organizations such as Amnesty International and the International Society for Human Rights have brought attention to art censorship and the ongoing wave of repression, international artists and intellectuals, with minimal exceptions, neither see nor hear, much less speak.

Earlier this week, Cuban American interdisciplinary artist Coco Fusco boldly called on American foundations (i.e., the John Simon Guggenheim Foundation), museums (i.e., MoMA) and the progressive media (i.e., *The New York Times*) to speak out.

Why This Silence?

It may sound silly, but it is a matter of popularity and coolness. Supporting Cuban dissidents has never been cool. Fusco was, until recently, as cool as they come. Now she is not. After writing *Revolutionary Cuba*, I became more uncool than ever.

"Don't you dare censor that painting of the Virgin Mary made out of elephant dung!" the cool ones say. "What about my performances?" I can hear Bruguera ask. "And don't you dare remove that book from my local library!" they say. "Why are my books and those of fellow Cuban exiles absent from Cuban libraries?" I respond. "Defund the police," they demand. "What about the Policía Nacional Revolucionaria?" my oppressed compatriots ask.

Those who remain silent about Cuba are, above all else, kindred spirits of those tormented souls whom a fourteenth-century Florentine writer described as "Pacing around with weary steps and slow.... Who's haggard looks express fatigue and woe" (*Inferno*, Canto XXIII, The Hypocrites).

49

A Tale of Two Other Cities: Rising Authoritarianism out of Washington, D.C., and Havana

(Creators Syndicate, December 26, 2020)

"It was the best of times; it was the worst of times." Thus begins Charles Dickens' historical novel *A Tale of Two Cities*.

In Washington, D.C., and Havana, the final months of 2020 have undeniably been among the worst of times: "Foolishness" (lack of wisdom), "incredulity" (no belief), "darkness" (absence of light); it is a Dickensian "Autumn of despair."

Deceivingly yet successfully, Donald Trump's presidential campaign made anti-communism one of its key political weapons. Trump presents himself as protector against a Cuban-style socialist/communist agenda hidden inside the Democratic Party's Trojan horse.

But the United States has perhaps the world's least fertile soil for the cultivation of socialism. For goodness' sake! Tens of millions of citizens, many of them poor and uninsured, even oppose the idea that all Americans should have access to medical care, whether they can afford it or not.

Besides, communism is dead, even in China and Cuba; and in Europe, democratic socialism has been in retreat for decades. A handful of countries may still be ruled by communist parties but have fully embraced perverted versions of capitalism—state capitalism in the case of Cuba. What remains stubbornly alive are the authoritarian and repressive traits characteristic of communist regimes.

To the surprise of most observers, in recent years, the world's oldest and most successful democratic republic has become fertile ground for authoritarian undemocratic rule, abuse of power and generalized political corruption. And to think that this country not too long ago sacrificed 405,399 lives to defeat Nazi Germany, Mussolini's Italy, and Imperial Japan.

Leftists (real and phony ones), it is true, have been crying wolf (fascism) for a long time, but the sharp-fanged beast is finally at the doorstep. Some of the wolf's most blatantly authoritarian actions thus far are the dispatch of military units to the streets of Washington, D.C., in June, and the following month's deployment of assorted armed and masked federal agents to Portland, where they beat and arrested peaceful protesters without cause and shoved them into unmarked vehicles headed for undisclosed detention centers.

Those are the kinds of things that happened in unabashedly repressive regimes—Chile's Pinochet; Batista's and the Castros' Cuba; and Mugabe's Zimbabwe—and continue to happen in North Korea, Russia and Saudi Arabia, whose strongmen President Trump holds in high regard. And then, there is China.

This November, Cuba's political police and other repressive forces launched an offensive against the peaceful demonstrators of Havana's San Isidro artists movement, several of whom were arrested Portland style, albeit in clearly marked police vehicles. Havana's streets were militarized Washington style, by SWAT forces. Cuba observers recognize the unprecedented nature of those protests.

Even before his electoral defeat, Trump and his loyalists sabotaged and delegitimized the American electoral process. Since then, they have continuously claimed that Democrats, in alliance with the Nicolás Maduro regime, stole the 2020 elections. This week alone, Trump uttered with a straight face that he won by a landslide, met with his closest associates to discuss a military option to overturn the election results, and granted pardons to a roster of corrupt and lawless associates including three convicted former Republican congresspeople, four mercenaries convicted of war crimes and a traitor.

We are beyond the unimaginable, and there is no telling how far Trump will go to retain power and sabotage President-elect Joe Biden's incoming administration. My list of never-in-America continues to shrink.

Those of us who know dictatorship first-hand recognize foreboding signs of growing authoritarianism. My family fled dictatorial Cuba as exiles in 1962 (I was two at the time); eight years later, we left Peru, where we had resettled, in the aftermath of a leftist military coup. I retain vivid TV images of Peru's democratically-elected President Fernando Belaúnde Terry being dragged out of the presidential palace in his pajamas, his eyeglasses dangling precariously from one ear.

Decades of study of dictatorship in Latin America contribute to my apprehension. As a graduate student, I studied the collapse of other democracies: Brazil (1964), Argentina (1966), Chile and Uruguay (1973). The latter two had long and robust democratic traditions. I also spent an entire decade researching Cuba's socialist revolution.

And just this week, I finished an article on Dominican dictator Rafael L. Trujillo, a narcissistic, megalomaniac multimillionaire who demanded absolute loyalty and adulation, who treated opponents vengefully and loved all things military, especially parades and rallies; a racist who hated Black immigrants from Haiti (one of Trump's "shit-hole countries").

Americans, wake up! Let's turn the future into a Dickensian "Spring of hope" flowing in "wisdom," "belief" and "light." MADA, let's (make America democratic again).

50

An Honest Response to a Colleague's Views on Cuba and U.S. Policy Toward That "Immiserated" Island

(Creators Syndicate, June 5, 12, 2021)

For this week's column, I planned—actually, started writing—the fourth and final installment of my column "The Strange Etymologies of 'the Left,' 'Liberals,' and 'Progressives.'" But I just received a link from a dear colleague to Medea Benjamin's June 3 article on *AlterNet*, "Biden Has Refused to Move an Inch on Cuba Policy—Despite His Promises." The author's name rang a bell, and upon googling it, I recognized her as co-author of an important book, published in 1989, *No Free Lunch: Food and Revolution in Cuba*. Thus, I decided to write on Cuba instead.

Wikipedia outlines Benjamin's lifelong commitment to numerous social and political causes including anti-war movements, universal health care and living wages for all workers—all of which, by the way, I support wholeheartedly. As I continued to read on her, I learned that while living in Cuba in the early 1980s, she wrote a piece against Cuban government censorship, which earned her deportation from the island. Thus, it appeared we also share an abhorrence of censorship.

Benjamin starts by praising the humanitarian work of Carlos Lazo, "an energetic Cuban American high school teacher in Seattle." Lazo formed the Bridges of Love organization, whose goal, Benjamin explains, is "to lift the searing U.S. blockade that is immiserating their loved ones on the island." Lazo has also joined efforts with the Syringes to Cuba initiative.

But what Benjamin calls a "blockade" is not such but rather a trade embargo, and a partial one at that, which, since 2000, excludes food, medicines, and humanitarian supplies, including syringes. Even if the embargo banned the export of U.S.-made syringes to the island, which it does not, Cuba could still purchase them from other nations. The problem is that Cuba does not have the funds to purchase syringes and many other essentials.

The Cuban government, I should add, nonetheless manages to acquire all the necessary armored vehicles, equipment, and weapons to repress its own people, as was recently displayed in efforts to crush protests led by Cuban artists of the San Isidro Movement.

Moreover, syringes are quite simple manufactured goods that can be produced in virtually any country, much more in Cuba, which, for a poor country, has a well-earned reputation as a leader in the invention, production, and export of complex biomedical and pharmaceutical products. Visit the BioCubaFarma webpage and you will find that it has 78 manufacturing facilities that produce over 100 products including vaccines, medications, and advanced biotechnology equipment that Cuba exports to 50 countries.

The reason for Cuba's scarcity of syringes to vaccinate its citizens against COVID-19 is certainly not the U.S. embargo. The Cuban ruling elite holds on to an anachronistic and failed political and economic system that has turned what used to be (in the 1950s) one of the top three wealthiest and most advanced Latin American countries into the hemisphere's beggar. In Honduras, one of Latin America's poorest nations, a Cuba solidarity group is raising money to purchase one million syringes to send to Cuba.

I thank them, as I do Lazo, for these humanitarian initiatives. But as a Cuban, I also feel embarrassed by my homeland's largely self-inflicted poverty.

Blaming the U.S. embargo for the island's misfortunes has a long history dating back to when it was imposed in 1960 (and expanded in 1962). But the following quote from none other than Che Guevara is revelatory. Diminishing the importance of the impact of the embargo, he stated in 1963: "Our difficulties stem principally from our errors."

Benjamin also affirms that Cuba's current economic crisis (more accurately, another valley in its perpetual crisis) is "largely a result of the COVID-induced shutdown of the tourist industry and a tightening of the embargo under Trump." To her credit, here she uses the term "embargo," but the current crisis results from systemic problems that have been aggravated by the island's dependence on the tourist industry, which is vulnerable to disasters such as 9/11 and the current pandemic.

One-third of the way into her article, Benjamin lays out her criticism of the Biden administration's policy toward the island. She starts by quoting his presidential campaign promise to "promptly reverse the failed Trump policies that have inflicted harm on the Cuban people and done nothing to advance democracy and human rights."

The claim that the president "has not moved an inch" while true, is unfair and premature, especially if we consider other major national and international crises: the ongoing global pandemic, the aftermath of January 6, a bloody flare-up in the Israel-Palestine/Lebanon conflict; Russians hacking U.S. businesses and critical infrastructure; and the Chinese being up to no good. Need I say more?

I believe we should cut the Biden administration some slack; it has been in power fewer than six months. And compared with much larger fish to fry, Cuba is but a mere luminous sardine. And let's not forget that, traditionally, Latin America has been on the State Department's back burner, minded only whenever the boiling pan overflows.

Speaking of moving inches, the Obama administration gave Cuba an entire yard of concessions, including diplomatic recognition, removal of the unfair designation as "state sponsor of terrorism" and relaxation of trade and travel restrictions. President Barack Obama even traveled to Havana to meet Raúl Castro, the first presidential visit since Calvin Coolidge's in 1928. It is Cuba that has refused to move an inch toward democracy or respect for human rights.

Obama was clearly duped, and President Joe Biden should avoid the same mistakes, demanding instead concrete improvements in human rights and democracy, especially considering a heightened wave of repression since November 2020, months after Biden made the campaign promise quoted above.

One of Benjamin's, let's call it "weakest claims" for the sake of civil conversation, is her contention that "a push for action has also come from the grassroots." She uses the example of anti-blockade caravans in Miami, the largest of which included 200 people. I would call that a "mini-Miami caravan." Miami-Dade has 2.7 million inhabitants; any person dressed as a pirate with a parrot perched on his shoulder in an empty Miami parking lot is bound to attract a larger crowd.

What about the grassroots movement for freedom and democracy in Cuba? It is easy and safe to ride in a caravan of airconditioned vehicles in Miami or for me to write this column at my desk. But hundreds of brave Cubans are risking detention, imprisonment, and state-organized mob violence for their plight for the basic freedoms that Benjamin and I enjoy.

Benjamin mentions a recent report by Oxfam demanding the end of the U.S. trade embargo—they also call it "blockade"—which also gently encourages the Cuban government to "continue implementing the transformations enshrined in the new Constitution, approved in 2019, in order to guarantee human rights, social justice, and the enjoyment of freedom, solidarity, wellbeing, and individual and collective prosperity as described therein." Come on, Oxfam!

Readers interested in a fuller picture may want to read Freedom House's "Cuba: Government Must Cease Repression of Critics": "The international community must demand accountability from the Cuban government for its actions and to immediately stop unlawful arbitrary detentions, house arrests, forced exile, and smear campaigns against dissenting voices"; as well as Amnesty International's latest report on the island: "Authorities continued to clamp down on all forms of dissent, imprisoning political leaders, independent journalists and artists."

Benjamin's article ends on an odd note: "Biden ignores the crisis in Cuba at his own peril. The dire food and medicine shortages may well spark a migration crisis." She also quotes cubanologist William LeoGrande's prediction of "a mass exodus of desperate people."

I wish to end with two closing questions for these two experts: Are Cubans less deserving of democracy and human rights than citizens of Honduras or Guatemala? And why is their immigration to the United States more of a problem than the massive inflow of their brethren from Mexico and Central America?

51

The Shattered Mirror: Democracy and Anti-Democracy on Both Sides of the Florida Straits, 2021

(Creators Syndicate, July 17, 24, 31, 2021)

I was not even born when Fidel and Raúl Castro's rebel army defeated strongman Fulgencio Batista's forces on New Year's Day 1959. And here I am, at the age of 61, writing once again about yet another economic and political crisis tearing through my tyrannized homeland. *¡Ay, Cuba!*

July 11

Last Sunday, July 11, 2021, the unimaginable happened in Havana and 60-odd other cities and towns. Thousands took to the streets in a spontaneous and seemingly uncoordinated fashion to protest the communist government's failure to provide food, medicines, COVID-19 vaccines—not even the subpar Chinese and Russian brands are readily available—and other necessities. Protesters, the vast majority of whom were young, marched peacefully through city streets and boulevards demanding food and medicines while chanting calls for the resignation of President Miguel Díaz-Canel, the end of communist dictatorship, and freedom: "Libertad! Libertad! Libertad!" Street protests continued over the next three days.

This is unprecedented. Since 1960, only once before had Cuban citizens staged mass street demonstrations, actions suppressed by the communist state, whose constitution almost comically recognizes "the rights of assembly, demonstration, and association for legal and peaceful purposes" (Title V, Art. 56). It happened on another sizzling summer day, on August 5, 1994, when hundreds marched down Havana's streets, most visibly along El Malecón (seawall). The protest turned into a riot which police forces and the so-called Rapid Response Brigades quickly quashed. Despite their somewhat dignified name, those brigades are simply state-organized bands of civilian thugs who revel in beating up dissenters and egging their homes.

This Sunday's protests were far larger and more widespread, from the western town of San Antonio de los Baños, where they began, all the way east to the city of Palma Soriano.

Word about the protests spread on the internet and through various social media. Back in 2007, the ruthless head of the Ministry of the Interior, Ramiro Valdez, had warned against the internet which he dubbed "the wild colt of technologies [that] can and must be controlled." Since last Sunday, the world has witnessed a veritable technological stampede and the state's violent efforts to lasso, break and push protesters back into the stable.

The Cuban government, as I have been saying for years, is a failed state, unable to provide for the basic needs of the population, including adequate supplies of food—70 percent of which must be imported—medicines, which are sorely lacking despite the government's claims that it is an international medical power, and housing, much of which is in disrepair. Havana, once called the city of columns, has become a city of scaffoldings, permanent ones at that.

Among the few things that work well on the island is the complex system of internal espionage and repression housed under the Ministry of the Interior, which is charged with security and public order. The system begins at the block level with neighborhood watch organizations called Committees for the Defense of the Revolution, or CDRs.

It includes the National Revolutionary Police, NRP. What about defunding them too? Amazon, it turns out, sells NRP shirts for $23.99. Come on, Jeff Bezos, your father Miguel had to flee Castro's Cuba at the age of 16. You may want to respond to Pitbull's personal plea for you to help the Cuban people. And stop peddling those offensive t-shirts!

It is puzzling that Cuba's repressive apparatus was seemingly caught off guard, allowing the protests to go on for several hours and several days thereafter. When it came, the government's response was brutal, effectively so. Rapid response brigades clubbed, punched, and dragged protesters, including women and children; police officers and Black Wasp special forces that seem to have stepped out of a Star Wars movie beat and arrested several hundred protesters. Over 100 demonstrators have disappeared for days, and the U.N., the Organization of American States and numerous international organizations are demanding their immediate release.

There are reports of a handful of deaths, but Cuban authorities have only confirmed one fatality, that of a 36-year-old man shot by police on Monday. In an information release, the Ministry of the Interior said that it mourns his death. Whether they meant it or not, the anti-government movement has a martyr, Diubis Laurencio Tejeda, whose life mattered and so will his death.

Mirror Shards

Historically, the United States and Cuba have shared, as President William McKinley once said, "ties of singular intimacy"; ties ranging from amity and hardy alliance—think World War II (Cuba declared war on Japan two days after Pearl Harbor)—to spasms of deep hostility that peaked during the Bay of Pigs invasion in 1961 and the Cuban Missile Crisis the following year.

Cuba and the United States are bound by an intractable geographic reality, the proverbial 90 miles; and since the start of the Cuban Revolution both have tensely coexisted like a couple forced to live under the same roof after a nasty divorce.

As a Cuban-born author who lives in Florida and writes about Cuba, my heart, brain, and pen are split along both sides of the Florida Straits. And as a defender of freedom and democracy, I wholeheartedly support pro-democracy movements on the island and, by the same token, am concerned about efforts to weaken democracy and civil rights in Florida and the other 49 states.

Despite its utter failure in Cuba and imperfect success in the United States, the pursuit of freedom and democracy are foundational values shared by both peoples. The father of the Cuban "patria" (homeland) José Martí ranks among the hemisphere's most important and influential freedom fighters and proponents of democratic rule and racial equality. Everyone should read his works. I recommend starting with the "I Cultivate a White Rose" poem and his book-length essay *Our America*.

Capitals and Capitols

In many ways, the United States and Cuba are mirror images. Take the U.S. Capitol and its younger counterpart in Havana; while not identical, they are remarkably similar. Guess which one is larger. It is Havana's—one meter longer, one meter wider, and one meter taller.

In the past six months, both capitols have been scenes of the global conflict between democracy and despotism. What happened in and around the U.S. Capitol on January 6 should be evident to all who watched the carnage on TV; there are, nonetheless, insurrection deniers who claim the rioters were antifa militants and who liken the Capitol's violent capture to a routine tourist excursion.

As soon as Washington police forces removed the pro-Trump mob from the Capitol premises, barricades went up to defend America's most iconic democratic symbol from further attacks. Six months later, all the fences and barricades came down; on the same weekend, Cuban police forces erected barricades of their own around their slightly taller capitol, where several hundred Cuban citizens had gathered to peacefully protest the 62-year-old dictatorial regime.

Instead of demanding the end of the violent assault, which he incited, Trump praised the mob as patriotic. He had harangued his supporters—or were they antifa forces in pro-Trump costumes?—to disrupt the democratic process and obstruct the peaceful transition of power.

When on July 11 and over the next few days, thousands of Cubans took to the streets, Trump's tropical counterpart President Miguel Díaz-Canel did something similar. He ordered state-organized bands of civilian thugs to harass, beat and help arrest demonstrators. Díaz-Canel, mark my words, will regret his infamous July 12 televised harangue: "The order to fight has been given—into the street, revolutionaries!" This was an unprecedented call for civil war.

Curiously, none other than Che Guevara's daughter, Aleida, dismissed protesters as "low-class people" and blamed the unrest on the U.S. embargo. Wait a minute Ms. Guevara, I thought Cuba was a classless society. Whether one admires, hates or is neutral about El Che, it is a fact that he worked (even manual labor) shoulder-to-shoulder with the humblest of Cubans. And regarding the embargo, in 1963, he rejected it as a valid excuse: "Our difficulties spring principally from our errors."

52

Sixtieth Anniversary of the Cuban Missile Crisis Finds Communist Island in Deepest Crisis Ever

(Creators Syndicate, October 8, 14, 29, November 11, 2022)

Sixty years ago, on October 22, President John F. Kennedy addressed the nation on TV with dire warnings about the build-up of Soviet nuclear missiles in Cuba, weapons capable of causing massive casualties and destruction within a 1,000-mile radius—striking distance to Washington, D.C., and the entire Southeast of the United States. That night, JFK announced several military measures, including an offensive weapons quarantine around Cuba.

The world stood on the brink of nuclear war for 13 long days until the United States and the Soviet Union negotiated a peaceful end to the crisis that included, much to Fidel Castro's chagrin, the removal of all Soviet missiles from the socialist island.

Fast forward 60 years and 11 U.S. presidents. With Vladimir Putin hurling threats that he will use nuclear weapons against Ukraine ("This is not a bluff," he insisted), this week President Joe Biden stated: "We have not faced the prospect of Armageddon since Kennedy and the Cuban Missile Crisis." There is no such thing, Biden reiterated, "as the ability to easily use a tactical weapon and not end up with Armageddon."

There are several parallels between the 1962 Missile Crisis and the current situation. Both conflicts brought the United States and Russia (the bulk of the former Soviet Union) close to war. On both occasions, Cuba was dragged into the confrontation between two global powers and was pulled closer to Russia which dangled the carrot of heavily subsidized oil shipments. There is no such thing as free oil, then nor today. Havana must side with Moscow in the U.N. and other international bodies.[1]

Some major differences stand out, however. In 1962, under Fidel Castro, the Cuban regime was politically stable and the economy, while not prosperous, was also stable. And Soviet Premier Nikita Khrushchev remained a rational player throughout the crisis. Today, in contrast, Cuba is ruled by an increasingly unpopular leadership headed by President Miguel Díaz-Canel and faces a seemingly unsurmountable economic and political crisis. And Khrushchev, with all his eccentricities, did not behave erratically; neither did he show signs of mental instability, megalomania, and paranoia, like Putin does.

Putin's Cuban allies appear to face imminent regime implosion. Cuba's coffers are empty, and the communist regime is unable to provide the population with its basic needs including food, medicine, electricity, public transportation, and even trash removal. Long neglected, the infrastructure is in disrepair and the collapse of buildings has become an almost daily occurrence.

Popular Mass Protests Began in 2020 and 2021

Since the spontaneous and unprecedented Havana Malecón (seawall) riot of August 1994, Cuba had not witnessed large anti-government manifestations until November 2020, when around 200 artists and intellectuals of the San Isidro Movement staged a protest in front of the Ministry of Culture. The government immediately suppressed the movement and its supporters.

Even more unprecedented were the mass street protests of July 11–14, 2021, when several thousand engaged in peaceful demonstrations in over 60 cities and towns. While the regime's shortcomings during the COVID-19 pandemic

---

1 Cheap oil has its price. On March 2, in the U.N., Cuba refused to vote to condemn the Russian invasion of Ukraine; on September 21, Cuba was one of only six nations (all dictatorships) voting against allowing Ukrainian President Zelenskyy to address the U.N. via video; and on October 12, Cuba abstained from condemning the attempt to illegally annex Russian-occupied regions of Ukraine.

sparked that round of protests, citizens also protested shortages of food and basic necessities. They openly challenged the government chanting "¡Libertad! ¡Libertad! ¡Libertad!" and Díaz-Canel's newly minted nickname, homophone to the Chinese beer brand Tsingtao.

The army of repressors included members of the National Revolutionary Police, Black Beret brigades of the Ministry of the Interior, bands of club-toting civilians sanctioned by the state and even—the unprecedented—military units commanded by Minister of the Revolutionary Armed Forces General Álvaro López Miera. Cubans have historically held the armed forces in high esteem precisely because they had never raised a finger against the civilian population. That changed on that fateful week in July 2021.

Not a few members of Cuba's high-ranking military elite opposed this new role. I shy away, as much as possible, from conspiracy theories, but would be remiss if I failed to mention that between July 11 and 26, a total of five active or retired generals died, without explanation. By July of the following year, another nine generals had perished, including 62-year-old General Luis Alberto Rodríguez López-Calleja. Because of his family ties with Raúl Castro (the general was formerly married to Castro's daughter), his key role in the Communist Party's Politburo, and his position as executive president of the Business Administration Group (GAESA), Rodríguez López-Calleja was considered Cuba's second most powerful man.

Cuban generals, of course, are not immortal. They die like everyone else, but five within sixteen days, and another nine in the following twelve months, is a statistical anomaly, particularly because the military brass has access to the best hospitals and medical care as well as imported vaccines and the finest anti-COVID-19 treatments and medications.

During and in the aftermath of the historic mass protests of July 11–14, 2021, the Cuban regime unleashed a wave of brutal repression. The Cuban human rights organization Cubalex documented a total of 1,124 arrests (566 of the arrested remained in custody) as of October 19.[2] As reported by Agence France-Presse, in mid-February 2022 nearly 900 individuals had been charged, including 55 under the age of 18. Prison terms have ranged between 2 and 30 years.

---

2 In August 2022, Cuba led the world in number of political prisoners with 1,002, followed by Iran (634) and Russia (420).

Human Rights Watch, Amnesty International, and the international media reported on arbitrary arrests, abuse of detainees and "jiffy justice," often without the presence of defense lawyers.

An October 19, 2021, *Washington Post* article shed light on specific cases of abuse. Twenty-year-old Michel Parra was arrested for marching peacefully in Matanzas and taken to a state security interrogation facility, where he was slapped, kicked while on the floor, and hit repeatedly with a baton. Independent journalist Orelvys Cabrera, *The Washington Post* reported, was detained and "forced to strip naked in front of military officials," and was placed in a small, crowded cell for 33 days and fed "rice with dirt." Another dissident, 39-year-old María Cristina Garrido, was thrown into a cell whose floor was covered with feces for refusing to yell "Viva Fidel!"

Speaking of Fidel, after being convicted of leading an armed attack on the Moncada Army garrison in 1953, he was sent to the Isle of Pines Model Prison. While there on April 14, 1954, he wrote a letter to a friend, boasting about that day's meal: "I am going to dine on spaghetti with squid [he was allowed to cook his own food], Italian bonbons and fresh coffee and then smoke a four-inch H. Upman cigar." "They look after me; they take good care of me," he continued.

Attempting to Put the Wild Colt of Technologies Back into Its Stable

Back in 2007, then-Minister of Communications Ramiro Valdez denounced the dangers of the internet and announced his intention to limit the population's access to it. "The wild colt of new technologies," he said, "can and must be controlled." He feared that internet communications could be used to spread dangerous ideas such as freedom and democracy.

Through the internet and social media, Cubans learned about the mass protests of July 11 that broke out seemingly spontaneously in the western town of San Antonio de los Baños, spreading soon thereafter to dozens of cities and towns. Incidentally, 89-year-old Ramiro Valdez showed up to the site of the San Antonio demonstrations in an attempt to calm down protesters but was shouted away with chants of "Asesino! Asesino!" and "Libertad! Libertad!"—a previously unimaginable turn of events.

Only five weeks after the July protests, Cuban authorities passed Decree 35 as an attempt to put the "wild colt" back into its stable. The decree demanded that internet providers interrupt, suspend or cancel services of any user that publishes false information against "public morality" and "respect for public order." The Ministry of the Interior and the military were, thus, charged with preventing and eradicating what Decree 35 dubbed "cybersecurity" threats.

The November 15 Protest That Never Was

In September 2021, Cuban playwright Yunior García Aguilera, one of the leaders of the San Isidro Movement, began organizing a protest through the Archipelago Group Facebook page. It was scheduled for November 15, but the government unleashed civilian pro-government mobs to harass García Aguilera and other organizers. The government banned the protests and kept García Aguilera from embarking on a solo march on the 14th. He had intended to march carrying a white rose, an allusion to Cuban martyred patriot José Martí's poem "I Cultivate a White Rose." He had to settle for waving the rose through his window next to a handwritten sign that read "My house is being blockaded."

Fearing for his safety, García Aguilera left Cuba a few days later bound for Madrid, where Martí had been deported in 1871 by colonial authorities after his release from a prison in the Isle of Pines.

"And for the cruel one whose blows / Break the heart by which I live / Thistle nor thorn I give / For him, too, I have a white rose" (J. Martí).

Martí knew that there was a time for poetry and a time for war. He died in battle in 1896, while charging a Spanish battalion armed only with a small handgun. He was shot dead, riding a white horse, dressed in a three-piece suit.

Cuba's Worsening Economic Crisis

Twenty twenty-one was one of Cuba's worst economic years since the start of the revolution. With a 70 percent-plus rate of inflation, the island's "misery index" (inflation and unemployment combined) was the world's highest at 1,278, followed by Venezuela (774) and Sudan (397). Unable to pay its foreign debt of over 20 billion U.S. dollars, Cuba reached an agreement with the Paris Club creditor nations to postpone payments for a year and in February 2022 (two days before invading Ukraine), Russia deferred $2.3 billion worth of debt repayments until 2027. There is no such thing as free U.N. votes.

The waning of the COVID-19 pandemic and the resulting reopening of Cuba to international tourism in November 2021 were expected to bring economic stability, if not recovery; but other developments—skyrocketing oil and grain prices stemming from the war in Ukraine, a crumbling infrastructure, and the destructive effects of hurricanes Fiona and Ian in September 2022—have caused further economic damage, inflicting additional suffering on the population.

The Cuban government lacks the cash and credit to purchase essential goods to cover the population's most basic needs: food, medicine, electricity, transportation, and safe housing.

Cuba is suffering food scarcities reminiscent of the worst times of the so-called Special Period in 1993 and 1994. Shortages of wheat flour have moved the government to resort to producing cassava bread, the staple of the pre-Columbian indigenous diet: *"A falta de pan, casabe."* Independent vendors of pizzas and sandwiches are no longer allowed to sell those foods. Encouraged by liberation-theologian-turned-nutritionist-of-misery Frei Betto, the Cuban government is promoting recipes that include fried potato and carrot skins (just the skins) and chunks of trunks of banana plants, which are sold neatly wrapped in cellophane in government stores.

Cubans are going hungry; a steady stream of videos uploaded to social media shows emaciated citizens foraging for scraps in trash containers and heaps of assorted rubbish piling up on city sidewalks. Other videos document the dilapidated and filthy state of hospital facilities, which are increasingly devoid of functioning equipment. And to think that many around the world, including many fellow Cuba experts, continue to perpetuate the myth that Cuba is a global medical power.

Medicine, as in the exportation of Cuba-trained doctors, has been for decades a source of hard currency. *The Economist* reported in 2020 that 28,000 Cuban doctors were being rented to foreign countries. This August, despite suffering a scarcity of doctors, Cuba announced that it would send 500 physicians to the Calabria region of Italy in return for $3,500 per doctor, per month (with each doctor receiving only $700 of that amount).

A Crumbling Infrastructure

The Cuban regime has neglected the island's infrastructure by deferring maintenance for decades. As a result, streets and roads are scarred with potholes and buildings are collapsing by the dozen. The energy infrastructure has suffered serious damage, most notably the August 5 explosion and fire of eight large oil tanks on the island's only supertanker port in Matanzas. Badly needed millions of barrels of oil burned for four days. Venezuela offered to help reconstruct the facilities and Russia dispatched a tanker with $70 million worth of oil.

Even more vulnerable is Cuba's electric grid. Hurricane Ian, which hit Cuba with winds of over 125 mph on September 27, produced an island-wide blackout. Parts of western Cuba endured several days without electricity and long periods of blackout have plagued the island since.

"Qu'ils mangent de la brioche"

There is no evidence that French Queen Marie Antoinette ever said: "Let them eat cake." And according to most sources, the original misattributed phrase, mentions brioche instead of cake. But who's counting calories; be it cake or brioche (or cassava bread as in Cuba), the phrase has survived to mean a privileged person or group that harbors condescending, unsympathetic attitudes toward the poor and powerless.

In the face of Cuba's generalized squalor, President Díaz-Canel and the communist ruling elite are exhibiting a let-them-eat-whatever-they-can-find stance. They are, to be sure, very well-fed, judging by pictures and videos circulating on Twitter and other social media, starting with Prime Minister Manuel Marrero Cruz. This September, while tens of thousands of regular Cubans were going to bed hungry, the stout functionary proudly presided over the 12th Varadero Gourmet Festival. You can listen to his speech on YouTube: "What is it that we do best? Our creole cuisine"; "eating pork, tamales, *congrí*, beans, all those things that characterize us." I can't vouch for its authenticity, but a Twitter video is circulating of a party where his purported "family and cronies" appear dancing while a delicious-looking pig roasts in the background.

Scores of photographs and videos are also circulating with images of the excesses of Cuba's—to borrow a Marxist term—lumpen bureaucracy; a tropical *deuxième état*: profusely bejeweled, designer clothes-clad, limo-chauffeured, and mansion-roofed. Other media uploads denounce abuses committed by repressors (*esbirros*), snitches (*chivatos*), and some Committee for the Defense of the Revolution leaders. The Cuban state has responded with a new law, effective December 1, 2022, that penalizes with up to eight years in prison the act of uploading offenses against communist leaders and the "revolutionary process."

Flight

As in previous crises, thousands of Cubans are fleeing their homeland. Attempts to escape and seek asylum in the United States have shot through the roof since 2021, breaking all previous records. Between October 2021 and September of this year, the U.S. Coast Guard intercepted 6,000 at sea; another 38,000 (fiscal year 2021). In fiscal year 2022, 224,647 Cubans crossed into the United States by land, and another 3,000 managed to touch American soil by sailing on rafts, a whopping 2 percent of the population (4 percent of the economically active population).

Previously Unimaginable Domestic Challenges

A new wave of Cuban protests, larger, more widespread, and more militant and violent than ever before, began cresting this August, sparked by (and under the cover of) prolonged, daily blackouts aggravated by the explosion of eight large oil tanks in the province of Matanzas and damage to the electric grid caused by hurricanes in September. By October 12, a total of 92 protests had been tallied. One of the largest protests took place in Nuevitas, Camagüey Province, on the evenings of August 19 and 20, when thousands of Cubans took to the streets, banging pots and pans, chanting anti-government slogans, and pelting special police units' vehicles. Government forces repressed the protesters brutally, beating dozens and arresting 40, including 11-year-old Beatriz Aracelia Rodríguez Frejioo, who had been beaten by a policeman, was detained and interrogated for 12 hours. What kind of revolution is this?

Another unprecedented aspect of this wave of protests is the recourse to arson and sabotage, again under the cover of darkness. Since August, protesters have shouted "Candela! Candela!" (fire, fire). Among the targets of suspected arson caught on tape are a fast-food establishment in Holguín, a camping facility in Las Tunas, a large, thatched hut in Boyeros, agricultural equipment in Niquero, and truck tires and trash containers in different towns.

Of all the protest chants the most resonant and significant is "No tenemos miedo!" (we are not afraid). Indeed, Cubans are challenging the state in previously unthinkable ways: raising barricades in streets and roads, turning police vehicles upside down, insulting functionaries and members of the police in their faces.

Can the Genie Be Put Back in the Bottle?

In 1989, when the communist world began to disintegrate, I believed that the demise of the Castro regime was around the corner. I recall a conversation with a Cuban relative who was visiting the United States. I think the regime will collapse within one year, I told her. Her response took me by surprise. Visibly and audibly angry, she retorted: "No! Don't say that! We cannot withstand one more year of this." A year passed; a decade passed; 33 years have passed, and Cubans still suffer communist dictatorial rule.

I learned the lesson and have never again ventured into such prognostications, not even in casual conversation.

But I will say this: Cuba's economic situation will not improve; Cubans will continue to live in misery; many have lost all fear and will continue to protest.

Not Boring at All: Globalization and World Affairs

Introduction

As a historian I find it irresistible to take a jab at Political Scientist Francis Fukuyama for his audacious 1989 announcement of the end "of history" and his anticipation of "centuries of boredom" thereafter. But if I am to be true to this book's philosophical argument that "all history is contemporary history," I must recognize that Fukuyama's analysis and prognostications reflected the world as it was (and as where he saw it going) when he published his article "The End of History?" which to be fair, is punctuated with a question mark.

Fukuyama also seasoned his essay with a generous sprinkling of qualifiers, "we may be witnessing," "seems to," "it may be possible," "virtually," "potentially." And he left the door open to two major sources of challenge to the triumphant formula of capitalist liberal democracy: religious fundamentalism and nationalism.

This section consists of 11 opinion columns on global issues and international affairs. I wrote the first of them in March 2020, shortly after the World Health Organization declared COVID-19 a pandemic. There was no telling then how long and far the pandemic would go but I felt compelled to reflect on its potential ramifications by looking at past pandemics and how they related to other world crises.

Most of this section's other essays and columns cover international politics and conflicts. In some, I trace the historical and etymological evolution of political/economic ideologies such as monarchism, liberalism, socialism, communism, and fascism.

During the first quarter of 2022, my attention shifted almost exclusively to global tensions, rumors of war, and one of this book's most unimaginable unimaginables: the brutal Russian invasion of Ukraine.

The column "Wars and Rumors of Wars in Times of TikTok," seeks to answer the question "Is America ready for a major conflagration?" Two other columns explore connections between international conflicts and Olympic games. In one of them I wrote that I felt "safe saying that Russia will observe an Olympic truce until at least the end of the games." Four days later, Russian president Vladimir Putin announced the start of a "special military operation" aimed at, as he put it, de-nazifying Ukraine.

A final column is a lowercase "r" republican criticism of the unabashedly monarchist responses of the American people and media to the death of Queen Elizabeth II and the ascension of Charles III to the British throne.

53

What History Tells Us About COVID-19's Future Impact

(The Globe Post, March 31, 2020)

Earlier this month, I had a conversation with a friend and esteemed fellow historian about the exploding coronavirus crisis. "The disruptions that we will face," I gloomily told him, "will be greater and deeper than anything we have seen since World War II and the Great Depression." "Tell me more," he said.

Days later, on March 18, newscasters, TV analysts, and editorial writers began to draw parallels between the rapidly unfolding health crisis and the deadliest war ever and biggest economic meltdown in modern history.

History offers the best tools to understand the present and even prepare for future outcomes because historians look at human and social developments with a long-term perspective and in their complex interconnectedness, multi-camera videos rather than isolated snapshots.

Unprecedented Global Catastrophe

We are witnessing an unprecedented global catastrophe that originated from Wuhan, China, sometime in November 2019. Within a few days, it became a provincial viral epidemic. Then it crossed China's borders, spreading to and paralyzing several world economies: South Korea, Iran, Italy and beyond. Within three months, it had created health and economic havoc in virtually every nation.

Massive epidemics, catastrophic disasters, and prolonged deadly conflagrations are pivotal moments that often alter the course of history. This is particularly true in contexts of deep pre-existing tensions between nations, ethnic groups, castes and classes, economic sectors, and socioeconomic ideologies.

These are often moments or periods of transition that spin other catastrophes and produce historical watersheds: from one distinct historical era to another; from political autonomy to colonialism or vice versa; political swings from right to left or left to right; dictatorships; one class losing power to another; and sometimes, the world turning completely upside down.

The Black Death and Smallpox Pandemics

Let's begin with the fourteenth century. The Black Death pandemic that peaked in Europe between 1348 and 1350 had widespread, profound, and long-lasting economic, social, and political consequences. The death of roughly one-third of Europe's inhabitants proved advantageous to surviving peasants and laborers, who were now able to acquire land at lower prices and earn higher income.

The Black Death, historians agree, eroded the power of manorial lords over the peasantry. This led to the demise of serfdom in Western Europe and created the circumstances for the emergence of absolutist national monarchies. The Middle Ages convalesced into what historians call the Early Modern Period (1500–1800).

In 1519, on the other side of the Atlantic, smallpox made its lethal debut in Mexico, among an Indigenous population that lacked immunities to the virus. The ensuing high rate of death among Mexico's inhabitants (over 90 percent), along with more advanced weaponry, allowed Spanish conquistador Hernán Cortés and a couple hundred Spanish adventurers to bring the mighty Aztec Empire to its knees in little over two years.

Spain established the world's first global empire. It would be three centuries before Mexico could free itself from the Spanish colonial yoke.

Between 1770 and 1773, a colossal famine exterminated approximately one-third of the population of the Bengal region of India and modern-day Bangladesh. This was a perfect-storm scenario, a lethal cocktail of climatological disasters, plagues, British commercial greed and imperial ineptitude.

The Four Horsemen of the Apocalypse galloped over India. Conquest, bolted on a white horse, the consolidation of British commercial and fiscal control over vast expanses of Indian territory. The other horsemen followed: War on a red horse from the Battle of Plassey (1757) to the Battle of Buxar (1764); then came Famine atop a black stallion, the severe droughts of 1768–1769 that destroyed the region's rice crops; and finally, Death, on an ashen horse trampling over a pile of 10 million likewise ashen corpses.

Back to Europe. It's France, 1788; and an extraordinarily harsh winter destroys that year's grain harvest. The price of bread nearly doubles, and widespread famine ensues. Particularly hard hit is the City of Paris, where angry hungry mobs storm the Bastille on July 14, 1789. Elegantly wigged and coiffured heads roll by the dozen, the roused bourgeoisie demolishes the Ancien Régime and establishes a republican government of equal *citoyens*.

The Revolution echoes throughout Europe and in the French colony of St. Domingue (Haiti) where slaves rise up in arms in alliance with a yellow fever epidemic; they route Napoleon's mighty army, abolish slavery, and declare independence.

The So-Called Spanish Flu Pandemic

Pandemics like revolutions are not the rule but rather historical exceptions. The 1918–1920 global influenza pandemic, better known as the Spanish flu, stands as the second deadliest ever with 20–50 million victims. Rather than in Spain as its name suggests, it is widely believed to have originated in a military base in Kansas, thence spread by U.S. troops deployed to France during WWI. The mass movement of returning soldiers and the miseries of war (poor nutrition and hygiene) facilitated and accelerated the pandemic's global spread. Another WWI epidemic, typhus, ravaged Poland, Russia, and Romania with a death toll of 2–3 million.

Depression Virus

Fast forward to 1929. Following several weeks of volatility in the New York Stock Exchange, on October 28, the Dow Jones fell by 12.82 percent, and the next day, on Black Tuesday, it plunged by another 11.73 percent. It hit rock bottom on

July 8, 1932. Investors jumped out their office windows—if only in the morbid imagination of sensationalist journalists.

Unemployment shot up to 25 percent, salaries tumbled, and soup kitchens and shantytowns now dotted the landscape. Beginning in 1930, choking clouds of dust rolled eastward from Colorado to New York City and from Nevada to the nation's capital, destroying crops, killing cattle and farm animals, and displacing 2.5 million malnourished farmers.

Because of the interconnectedness of most of the world's economies, the meltdowns in the United States and Great Britain sprung a domino effect. The depression became a global crisis.

When the American, British, and other European markets collapsed, they brought down scores of national economies that had come to depend on the purchasing power of industrial nations. Cuba's sugar-exporting economy buckled; the same thing happened in coffee-exporting Brazil and tin-rich Bolivia. Africa's Ivory and Gold Coasts, whose economies depended on exporting cocoa and palm kernels to Europe, fell into severe depressions. Similar outcomes ravaged vast regions of Asia.

The Depression virus spread to other vulnerable organs of society, shaking the social order, and producing feverish political change. In Latin America, for example, nearly every nation saw profound social and political transformations: crumpling oligarchical regimes, labor unrest, the ascendance of militarism, populist revolts, and coups of diverse political coloration.

Economic bankruptcy and generalized misery energized fascist movements and governments in Italy, Germany, Japan, Spain, and elsewhere where nationalist leaders promised to restore economic prosperity and national pride. We know how that went.

The United States, Canada, Great Britain, and France endured profound social, economic, and political changes of their own: laissez-faire capitalism disintegrated to be replaced by the modern capitalist welfare state. Franklin D. Roosevelt's New Deal is a textbook example.

The 1930s generated a new formula of increased government intervention and regulation, marked by massive injections of state capital to combat unemployment and widespread deprivation, to foster a semblance of social equality, and to jump-start virtually every sector of the economy.

Meanwhile, the Soviet Union, at the time the only communist country, was largely disconnected from the world economy. Under Joseph Stalin's iron fist, the U.S.S.R. embarked on an accelerated, somewhat successful, process of industrialization, while the aggressive and violent collectivization of farmlands resulted in massive famine during the 1930s, with an estimated 5 million deaths, three-quarters of them in Ukraine.

September 11, 2001

Back in New York City. It's one year, nine months and eleven days into the New Millennium (no one remembers Y2K, the catastrophe that never happened). At 8:45 a.m., a hijacked American Airlines Boing 767 crashes into the North Tower of Manhattan's iconic World Trade Center. It was the first of four commercial jets hijacked by terrorists affiliated with Al-Qaeda that day. Chaos breaks loose. The death toll reaches 2,977, the Dow Jones mirrors the collapse of the Twin Towers, and stock markets around the world plummet as well. A mild recession already underway deepens in the United States and other regions of the world. Hardest hit are the property insurance, travel, and tourism industries, and the poor around the globe.

In retaliation for the 9/11 attacks, the United States and Great Britain bomb Afghanistan and invade it soon after that. In March 2003, the United States went to war against Iraq. Since then, the Horseman of Death gallops roughshod throughout the Middle East, from Kabul to the shores of Tripoli.

One of the legacies of 9/11 was the passage of the Patriot Act that granted federal authorities expanded powers to detain immigrants indefinitely, search homes and offices, and expand citizen surveillance. While originally meant to be temporary, most Patriot Act provisions are still in place.

Unfolding Catastrophe and Potential Consequences

According to World Health Organization statistics, as of today (March 24) there are 375,498 confirmed cases of Novel coronavirus worldwide; this is, of course, the proverbial tip of the iceberg. The same organization reports 16,362 deaths to date. The United States' own CDC has modeled terrifying worst-case projections: 214 million Americans infected, 1.7 million dead. The economic costs of the pandemic will be in the tens of trillions.

The coronavirus is rapidly spreading in a world rife with social, political, and geopolitical tensions. If history is of any value, many of these are likely to build up and perhaps explode, producing social restructuring, firing up domestic conflicts, further eroding civil rights, and igniting wars.

Growing Inequality

In the past three decades, most of the world has experienced an obscene increase in wealth and income inequality. According to 2015 U.N. statistics, 62 of the world's wealthiest individuals had as much wealth as 50 percent of the global population, which is 3.7 billion people. The wealth gap in the United States is likewise staggering. In 2017, the Washington D.C.-based Institute for Policy Studies estimated that the three richest Americans (Bill Gates, Warren Buffett, Jeff Bezos) had more wealth than the bottom half.

The economic disruptions of the present crisis are likely to expand income and wealth inequality and accelerate the squeezing of the middle class, particularly small business owners and the legions of contract workers of the gig economy.

Economist Thomas Piketty, one of the world's leading experts on wealth inequality, has sounded the alarm about the dire social and political consequences of inequality, which he describes as "incompatible with the meritocratic values and principles of social justice fundamental to modern democratic societies." Piketty expressed concern about the rise of oligarchy and pessimism about the direction of the United States.

U.S. Democratic Foundations

It is no secret that Donald Trump's administration has worked diligently to erode the nation's democratic foundations, the civil rights of citizens, and human rights of undocumented immigrants, while expanding the power of the Executive at the expense of the other two branches of government.

Historically, times of war and crisis have limited rather than expanded individual rights. Even Abraham Lincoln, during the Civil War, suspended the writ of habeas corpus, the requirement for arrested people to be brought before a judge before being confined. Another great wartime president, Roosevelt, while expanding civil rights for African Americans, ordered the internment of 120,000 Japanese and Japanese American citizens. Trump has begun referring to himself as a "wartime president," but to paraphrase Lloyd Bentsen: "President, you're no FDR."

Just a few hours ago, Betsy Woodruff of *Politico* revealed disturbing information about requests by Trump's Department of Justice to Republican lawmakers to draw legislation permitting federal authorities to detain individuals without trial for indefinite periods, extend the statute of limitations provisions, and further limit asylum claims in the name of the current emergency but also applicable in the case of natural disaster or civil disobedience.

Economic stagnation and lack of wage growth have, indeed, aggravated social tensions in the United States. Trump and other demagogues on the right are inciting racial hate and even violence. Social and political scientists recognize that the nation and its political leadership are as polarized as they have been since the Era of Reconstruction (1865–1877) and serious commentators increasingly raise the terrifying specter of a second Civil War.

The paralysis of the economy, the rise of unemployment, and uncertainty about the course of the 2020 presidential campaigns and scheduled elections bring us closer to such dreadful scenario. While thousands of consumers line up outside Walmarts and COSTCOs to buy bread and toilet paper, hundreds are doing the same outside gun and ammo shops, which are reporting soaring sales, especially in states most affected by the pandemic.

If a second Civil War happens, and I hope it will not, it will not be like the first time around: clashing phalanxes of gray- and blued-clad armies from different geographic regions; but rather as in the Spanish Civil War of 1936–1939, between red and blue neighbors and cousins shooting at one another.

End of History?

In 1989, political scientist Francis Fukuyama published "The End of History and the Last Man," a provocative essay in which he argued that the great conflicts of the twentieth century, capitalism vs. communism and democracy vs. totalitarianism, were over. The undisputed victors, Fukuyama declared, were capitalism and liberal democracy. The last three decades have proven him wrong.

Liberal democracy has been the target of unremitting attacks even in the long-time bastions of the United States, Great Britain, and France. The unholy alliance of nationalist and white supremacist masses, populist leaders, and proponents of crony capitalism is on the offensive and likely to gain ground in a context of a prolonged pandemic accompanied by months, if not years, of economic decline.

Historically, natural disasters and severe economic crises increase competition for food and other natural resources. They also make some countries vulnerable to foreign attacks and may push some nations into war out of fear and desperation.

Before the coronavirus crisis there were several global hot spots of tension with the potential of escalating into armed conflict, among them the most explosive are Israel and Iran; Turkey and the United States; India and Pakistan; North Korea and the U.S. allies South Korea and Japan; and the United States and China. It does not help to have a cast of world leaders that include megalomaniacs, expansionists, bullies, and at least three confirmed assassins.

And to think that Fukuyama anticipated a "powerful nostalgia for the time when history existed" and feared the "prospect of centuries of boredom." What is unfolding before our eyes is neither new nor normal; and not at all boring.

54

1989, History's Stubborn Twists and the Commencement Speaker Who Warned Us to Remain Vigilant

(Creators Syndicate, October 3, 2020)

Thirty-one years ago, in 1989, the Soviet Empire—the "Evil Empire," as Ronald Reagan liked to call it—began to unravel. And two years later, the once-mighty U.S.S.R. voted itself into dissolution.

Not to claim any prophetic powers, but when I read and saw news in May 1987 that an inexperienced teenage German pilot crossed into Soviet airspace and managed to land a Cessna near Moscow's Red Square, I smelled the land of Lenin rotting from within.

The United States won the Cold War. Then President George H.W. Bush declared the advent of a New World Order. We were promised an enormous so-called peace dividend, but it lasted less time than a pizza in a college dorm—more accurately, less than a $130 billion government funds piñata at a retreat for greedy bankrupt bankers. Remember the Savings and Loan debacle of 1989 and the early 1990s? Remember that no one remembered it, and thus, we fell into the Great Recession in 2008? Remember that since then, Republican legislators and President Donald Trump have forgotten to remember yet again?

The end of the 1980s and dawn of the 1990s was an exciting time. As a Duke University history Ph.D. student, I found the evening news exhilarating, particularly the revolutionary events of 1989. One of our fellow students, a young German, left suddenly, returning to Europe to witness, participate in, and chronicle the unfolding collapse of the Eastern bloc. He changed his thesis subject and had the rare privilege among historians to live through one's dissertation.

None other than Tom Brokaw gave our commencement speech on Mother's Day 1990. Anthologized among the best commencement speeches ever, it overflowed with the wisdom of a truly engaged intellectual, one of those rare three-eyed beasts: one eye on the present, another on the past, the third telescoped into the future.

"Your time, 1990," Brokaw told us in his unassuming Midwestern voice, is "a time of explosive, dizzying, exhilarating, cataclysmic change." He reviewed the headlines of the previous year beginning with the protests and bloody massacre at Tiananmen Square—remember the Goddess of Democracy statue and the unknown Tank Man? Then came Poland's Solidarity Movement that ignited a pandemic of freedom that spread throughout Central and Eastern Europe: East Germany, Czechoslovakia …. Even Romania's Draculesque communist dictator, Nicolae Ceausescu, fell from power, the stake of democracy rammed through his chest by seas of torch-bearing Romanians craving freedom and democracy.

Winds of democratic change swept far beyond Europe. "You can feel the Earth moving now," continued Brokaw, "as freedom and independence erupt with volcanic force from the tip of South Africa to the northern Baltics, from the remote reaches of Mongolia to the rarefied heights of Nepal."

Not that I would have left for Havana and abandoned my nineteenth-century Cuba dissertation, but I was envious of the liberation of so many other countries, while in my homeland, freedom came only in the form of an emotive song by Miami's Willy Chirino. Thirty years later, the song's catchy refrain ("Our day is coming soon … is coming soon … is coming soon") rings in my ears like a cruel joke.

"You are privileged," Brokaw told our graduating class, reminding us also of our responsibility to remain vigilant against bigotry and racism, against those who "use the weapons of democracy to tyrannize those who do not completely embrace their own narrowly cast beliefs" and those politicians who "see reelection as their only obligation to the common welfare."

And here we are in the fall of 2020. Three decades after the end of the Cold War, Russia, the losing side, has successfully meddled in the U.S. elections not once but twice, helping erode our democratic system and institutions. Meanwhile, Trump, from the winning side, has come under the spell of former KGB agent and Russian dictator Vladimir Putin. If Trump could get away with shooting a man in the middle of Fifth Avenue, Putin has indeed gotten away with poisoning former Russian spies and political opponents abroad and offering bounties for the heads of dead American soldiers.

By now we should all have been disabused of the Cold War-era belief that capitalism and democracy go hand in hand in opposition to communism and authoritarianism; and of Francis Fukuyama's contention that the former triumphed over the latter.

55

The Right, the Left and Everything at the Other End

(Creators Syndicate, October 10, 17, 2020)

We are accustomed to placing political and economic ideologies along a spectrum that runs from extreme left to extreme right. At one pole, we find communists; socialists are to their right; fascists inhabit the other end. Most people also hold on to the Cold War-era belief that capitalism and democracy are partners, and that communism and authoritarianism go hand in hand.

There are other ways, however, of examining the relation between political ideologies and economic systems, which make clear that rather than extreme opposites along a spectrum, communism and fascism closely connect like the two ends of a horseshoe. Likewise, the relation between democracy and capitalism has been historically tenuous, and in the past two decades, it has become an increasingly uncommon pairing.

Socialism and Communism

Some definitions are in order. Let's start with socialism. President Donald Trump and his partisans for several years have hurled the S-word at the Bernie Sanders/

Alexandria Ocasio-Cortez wing of the Democratic Party; Joe Biden did the same during the primaries.

Fair enough. The septuagenarian senator from New Hampshire and the 30-year-old freshman congresswoman proudly self-describe as socialists. That they add the adjective "democratic" before the socialist label is significant.

Both accept the socialist tag because they define it the Scandinavian way, advocating capitalist, free market economies where the state has a robust role providing social services, reducing inequality, and limiting capitalist excesses through progressive taxation and regulations that protect workers, consumers, and the environment.

When Trump spoke at the United Nations on September 24, 2019, he declared that socialism is "one of the most serious challenges" the world faces; Reaganesque words but in bad prose, insincerely stated and decades past their expiration date. When Trump speaks about socialism, however, he is not thinking about comfortably middle-class Norwegians munching smoked salmon and sipping aquavit but rather impoverished Cubans and Venezuelans chafing under dictatorial rule.

Will the true communists take a step forward? No one moves because they are all but extinct, a few surviving in preserves (i.e., universities). The left left!

What about China, Cuba, and Vietnam? Are they not communist? They are communist only because they are ruled by repressive communist parties, but their economies are capitalistic, especially in China, home to over 800 billionaires. Cuba, the Caribbean's little China, officially has no billionaires, but its state capitalist economy is run by a privileged, high-ranking political and military caste—the worst of both worlds, if you want my opinion.

After Bernie Sanders' primary defeat, Trump and Co. redirected the S-word against centrist Biden and the Democratic Party. At his September 27 characteristically rambling press conference Trump raised the specter of socialism. The Democratic Party "has been taken over by socialists, extremists and probably communists," he said.

Two days later, Trump and Biden had their first presidential debate. Had it been a pay-per-view boxing match, I would have changed channels and demanded a refund. To find an event that had been so overhyped and turned out so disastrously, one must go back to 1986—Ronald Reagan was president—when 30 million viewers watched Geraldo Rivera's live TV special "The Mystery of Al Capone's Vaults" (I fell for that too). After two suspenseful but uneventful hours, Rivera opened Capone's safe to the sight of a few empty bottles and debris. The presidential debate turned out to be debris as well.

Seven minutes and 25 seconds into the fight's first round, a cornered Trump struck a socialism jab at Biden. "Your party wants to go socialist.... And they're gonna dominate you, Joe," he said. Proving that his reflexes are still sharp, Biden punched back with a response that momentarily transported me to Louis XIV's France: "I am the Democratic Party...." Biden has continued to counterpunch, most notably in his recent NBC News Town Hall in Miami, where he delivered a formidable one-two. "Do I look like a socialist?" he said. "Look, I'm the guy that ran against a socialist."

Just past Thursday, Trump derided Democratic vice-presidential nominee Kamala Harris as a "communist." "She's not a socialist. She's well beyond a socialist," he said. He also called her a "monster."

Will America ever go communist, or even socialist? Not likely, because those formulas place the collective above the individual, a value that runs counter to America's entrenched individualism.

And as to right-wing ideologies being at the opposing pole of communism, think twice. As my fellow Cubans living in the United States should acknowledge, Soviet-style socialism infected the island precisely because the right-wing dictatorship of Fulgencio Batista opened the way for continued tyranny, the next time around under the guise of Marxist liberation.

A vote for Trump is not a vote against communism; nor does voting for the Joe Biden-Kamala Harris ticket translate into support for socialism, let alone communism.

Not even Obamacare, the Republican Party's primary target of the "socialist agenda," comes close to socialized medicine. The besieged health care legislation does not even offer a public option in which government-run plans compete with private insurance companies.

Democracy and Authoritarian Rule

That I or anyone else must spend time making such clarifications is testimony to widespread ignorance surrounding the meaning of socialism and related terms, and worse yet, the increasing susceptibility of the American public to demagoguery and manipulation.

"The ignorance of one voter in a democracy impairs the security of all," said former President John F. Kennedy. Six months later, his own martyrdom proved that the hatred of one gunman could impair the entire democratic system. Think of the potential lethality of millions of ignorant, manipulated, armed-to-their-teeth Americans.

Ignorance, not communism, is the greatest threat to democracy; and democracy, despite Republican Senator Mike Lee's recent hair-raising tweets, is a foundational objective of this nation. Perhaps counting on our ignorance, the senior senator from Utah made the claim that the word "democracy" does not even appear in the U.S. Constitution. For that matter, neither does the word "prospefity" ("prosperity"), which he touts among the Founding Fathers' three primary objectives. And by the same unlogic, the right to hug people without wearing a mask at a so-called super spreader event does not appear in the Bill of Rights. Do we need to read any further than "We the people ..." to understand what the founders meant?

Polarized political environments like the one in which we live generate polarized language, black-and-white categories in which economic systems and governments are either/or—capitalist or socialist, democratic or authoritarian—and in which individuals are classified as patriots or traitors. This is not new. Eleanor Roosevelt criticized "having everyone who is a liberal called communist, or everyone who is conservative called fascist."

Different nations and individuals define democracy differently. Sometimes the word means the opposite. Before the reunification of Germany in 1990, dictatorial East Germany was called the German Democratic Republic. At present, out of 193 U.N. member nations, several include the word "democratic" in their official names, yet some of them are anything but. *The Economist*'s 2019 Democracy Index ranks North Korea, officially the Democratic People's Republic of Korea, least democratic, followed by the Democratic Republic of Congo.

In case you are wondering how the United States fares, we are not even ranked in the top, 22-nation "full democracy" category headed by three democratic socialist nations, Norway, Iceland, and Sweden. We stand at No. 25, near the top of the next category, "flawed democracy." The first such index, in 2006, in contrast, ranked the United States 17th, solidly within the "full democracy" category.

Reasonable, informed individuals generally agree on the definition of modern democracy: that power stems from the people who, through free and competitive elections, select their representatives and leaders; that government must protect the dignity and individual rights of the entire population; that everyone is entitled to equal protection under the law; and that nobody is above the law.

And what about the relationship between capitalism and democracy, and between that economic system and authoritarian rule?

Although it thawed into extinction over 30 years ago, the Cold War's legacy is eminently present in the way we look at the world and even in the vocabulary of geopolitics and political economy. Because international power politics were played out for so long along a spectrum with a democratic, capitalist United States and its Western allies at one pole, and the communist Soviet Union and the Eastern Bloc at the other pole, we hold on to the idea that capitalism and democracy go together.

Worldwide, the connection between democracy and capitalism began to erode sharply during the 1960s and 1970s when, for example, some of Latin America's most modern capitalist nations took a turn toward dictatorship: Brazil, Argentina, Chile and even Uruguay (theretofore considered the Switzerland of South America). For some time, authoritarian capitalism also flourished in Asian countries like Taiwan, Singapore, the Third Republic of South Korea and, more recently, the People's Republic of China.

If anything, under the currently dominant form of capitalism, whether we call it "super capitalism," "illiberal capitalism," "crony capitalism" or "oligarchic capitalism," "prospefity," to use Senator Lee's term, seems to flourish better under authoritarianism than democracy.

56

The Strange Etymologies of "the Left," "Liberals," and "Progressives"

(Creators Syndicate, May 15, 22, 29, June 19, 2021)

Languages, especially vocabularies, are in constant flux. Like living organisms, they are born and evolve. And although some, such as English, seem immortal, they also die.

New, updated editions of dictionaries include neologisms. This year, for example, Merriam-Webster added 520 new words ranging from BIPOC, abbreviation of "Black, Indigenous, People of Color" to—news to me—"hygge," "a cozy quality that makes a person feel content and comfortable." Even more common is the addition of new meanings for words that already exist: "tweet" or "mouse," to name but two.

Political terminology is no exception. Take the words "the left," "liberal" and "progressive," which, in the United States, are often used interchangeably.

The word "left," which Republicans so liberally (as in often) hurled at Democrats during the 2020 electoral campaign, has had an interesting trajectory, from exclusively signifying location and direction (as in "to one's left") to a political and ideological term often used derogatorily, referring to something evil or sinister. The Latin word for left is "sinister."

Long before "left" and its counterpart words in many other languages had any political meaning or connotation, it was associated with misfortune and the unfavorable. In ancient Greek augury rituals, omens appearing on the left side or direction—flying birds, for example—were portents of calamity and harm. Thus, sinister also came to mean inauspicious, adverse, and improper. By the dawn of the Early Modern Age, the concept of "the left" had taken on even graver connotations of evil and immorality.

The gospel narrations of the crucifixion tell us that two thieves were crucified along with Christ—"one on the right hand, and another on the left"—and that one rejected Christ's offer of salvation and the other repented. While the Bible does not say which one was on what side, tradition places the unrepentant thief squarely on the left.

As seen in many cultures around the world, not just in the West, the words for "left" are also associated with weakness, lack of skill and awkwardness. Since only around 10 percent of the world's population is left-handed, the left hand and leftness were connected to difficulty and lack of skill, in contraposition to the right hand and those who are right-handed. The adjective "dextrous" (or "dexterous") comes from the Latin word "dexter," which, since ancient times, has had three different meanings: "located on the right," "skillful" and "south." In the United States, left-handed baseball pitchers are commonly referred to as "southpaws," but that has nothing to do with politics or ancient Rome.

The French word for "left" ("gauche") also means "awkwardness." Curiously, "gauche" is also an English word, but when it crossed the English Channel—or is it the French Channel?—it only retained the awkward part of its definition. The word "adroit," meanwhile, from the French "droit" ("on or of the right") means "physically skillful and smart."

So, when, where, and how did words for "left" acquire their current political meaning? The year was 1789. Paris was ablaze with revolutionary fervor, and a new government formed around a powerful legislative body called National Assembly.

While the crown, the nobility and the church hierarchy deemed revolutionaries forbearers of calamity, agents of evil and perhaps even awkward, the new meaning of "left" was the result of a historical accident. When the assembly convened, radical anti-monarchists sat on the left (from the perspective of the assembly president), while monarchists sat on the right. That is when "gauche" also came to mean political radicalism defined as revolutionary, anti-monarchical and somewhat egalitarian positions—a new meaning that spread in French and later in English newspapers and magazines.

It took much longer for the political definition of "left" to cross the Atlantic. The first edition of *Webster's Dictionary*, published in 1828, includes the location definition ("as the left hand, arm or side") and attributions such as weak, deficient, sinister, and unfortunate, but there is no mention of political orientation.

It would take another century for "the left" to reach the United States, both as a common political term and actual political practice, during the 1930s amid the Great Depression.

Despite the increased use of political attack labels like "leftist" and "right-wing" in contemporary American politics, throughout most of the twentieth century, in terminology and practice, the dominant political scale was "liberal to conservative." This in contrast with Europe, where the political spectrum is wider, and rather than insults, such labels are proudly embraced by those at or close to either pole of the political spectrum.

The words "liberal" and "liberalism" have undergone their own trans-mutations since the last quarter of the eighteenth century when they were origi-nally tied to Adam Smith's free trade ideas, which he and others believed would benefit both capitalists and workers. These terms acquired social and political connotations, as in advocating freedom and democracy, in the first decades of the nineteenth century.

Both strains of liberalism (the economic and the social/political) were har-monized in the late 1830s and early 1840s through the creation of the British Liberal Party, which advocated social reform, the expansion of individual liber-ties, limits on royal authority and, most importantly, free trade.

The United States, meanwhile, while built on liberal, republican principles, harbored the gross incongruity of slavery, which is now popularly referred to as "America's original sin." But as a good friend and fellow historian reminds me, the sin of Native American forceful displacement and exploitation preceded the importation of the first 20 African slaves to Jamestown, Virginia, in 1619. But somehow, the foundational national love story of John Rolfe and Pocahontas (also in Jamestown) and the fictionalized celebration of Thanksgiving Day seem-ingly absolve America of that other original sin.

The other great American foundational paradox was the fact that the South, the region most amiable to free trade (and low tariffs), was less egalitarian and more undemocratic than the North. This may very well explain why the political label "liberal" did not catch on in the United States until the 1920s.

In postcolonial Latin America, the great political divide was between liberals and conservatives; the former embracing an ideological package influenced by the French Revolution, British parliamentarism and the liberal Spanish Constitution of Cadiz of 1812. It amalgamated the ideas of popular sovereignty, equality under the law, republicanism, abolition of slavery, anti-clericalism, and individual civil liberties.

After decades researching, writing and teaching Latin American history, I have not found a better source on the Latin American liberal versus conservative divide than Gabriel García Márquez's masterpiece *One Hundred Years of Solitude*, where readers discover that differences between liberalism and conservatism are fluid and that blood—and other social solidarities—is thicker than ideological coherence; thus, the tongue-in-cheek maxim that in nineteenth-century Latin America liberals drank in public and prayed at home while conservatives prayed in public and drank at home.

By the 1920s, in Great Britain, it had become evident to trade unionists and left-leaning politicians that free trade did not deliver the promised prosperity and, if anything, increased worker exploitation and accentuated class disparities between capitalists and workers. Thus, a new more ideologically socialist party, the Labor Party, emerged in the 1920s as Britain's opposition to the Conservative Party, which took on the mantle of "laissez-faire" economics.

Not as far to the left, stood America's late 1800s and early 1900s liberal formulations known as "progressivism." The progressive package responded against the excesses and ills of the Gilded Age, including labor exploitation, the formation of trusts, political corruption, and pollution (environmental as well as moral). What we call the American left has always had a puritanical strain from prohibitionist progressivism to present-day political correctness.

Democratic presidents Franklin D. Roosevelt, Harry S Truman, John F. Kennedy, Lyndon B. Johnson, and Jimmy Carter wore the "liberal" label with pride; while their Republican counterparts Dwight D. Eisenhower and Richard Nixon pushed liberal programs that today's conservatives would deem left wing and anti-American.

The 1970s saw the explosion of an anti-liberal backlash that catapulted Conservative Margaret Thatcher to 10 Downing Street (1979–1990) and Republican Ronald Reagan to 1600 NW Pennsylvania Avenue (1981–1989). Both campaigned and governed on conservative economic principles of deregulation, budget austerity, low taxes, and privatization, principles originally associated with laissez-faire liberalism but are now the hallmarks of conservatism.

This was not Adam Smith's original well-intended economic liberalism but rather an updated, take-no-hostages attempt to destroy the social, economic, and political advances of liberalism (in its various incarnations: classical nineteenth-century liberalism, laborism, progressivism and social democracy). Christened "neoliberalism," this new package rested on economic principles espoused by British economist Friedrich von Hayek and American economist Milton Friedman.

Four decades after Reagan and Thatcher's ascent to power, neoliberal thinkers shamefully hold on to a perverted version of Smith's promise of shared prosperity; they affectionally call it "trickle down."

Since its origins in revolutionary France, the definition of "the left" has continuously evolved in time and space, from anti-monarchical egalitarianism, through various industrial-age socioeconomic formulations, such as socialism, communism, and anarchism, through Depression-era statism to the present, when it means sharply different things in different places.

Not only are there deep contrasts in what people call "the left" in Paris, Chicago, and Lima; domestically, the term is understood and used differently in Berkeley, California, Batton Rouge, Louisiana, and Atlanta, Georgia. I can hop on a plane in Madison, Wisconsin, or London as a right-winger and disembark a communist in Little Rock, Arkansas, or Miami. Is it the altitude? The bad airplane food?

In the middle decades of the nineteenth century, "the left" and "the right" became matters of social class. On the left hand were the working classes, particularly the urban proletariat in increasingly industrialized nations like Great Britain and France, and on the other hand were the owners of what Karl Marx called the means of production (factories, land, warehouses, and the like). According to Marxists—it makes perfect sense to me—members of the working classes and capitalists often have diametrically opposed interests and thus are in continuous tension, "class struggle," in Marxist parlance.

Thus, the period's leftists formed labor unions and political parties advocating for the improvement of working conditions, higher salaries and, in its most radical iterations, gaining control of the means of production and even abolishing private property altogether. Political scientists call such goals "materialistic"; the public refers to them as bread and butter issues.

There were, to be sure, other ideological aspects to the industrial-age left—anticlericalism and internationalism, for example.

Despite its foundational anti-monarchism—more like taxophobia (come on, Merriam-Webster)—and liberal democratic political system, America, neither in the nineteenth nor twentieth centuries, has been fertile ground for leftist ideologies, the one salient exception being the era of the Great Depression and the New Deal.

While dubbed everything from "commie" and "pinko" to "fascist," Franklin D. Roosevelt does not quite fit the materialistic definition of the left and certainly did not advocate for government ownership of banks, businesses, and other enterprises. For goodness' sake! Capitalism had imploded; banks failed wholesale; Wall Street tanked; and hundreds of thousands, perhaps millions, went hungry and became homeless. If anything, New Dealers and their Keynesian counterparts in Great Britain saved, and thus preserved, a system that had failed miserably. Roosevelt did more to uphold capitalism than former President Herbert Hoover did to destroy it.

More than the two world wars, the greatest global conflict of the past century was the seemingly unending Cold War that partitioned the world in two, as did Pope Alexander VI in 1493, but this time into a U.S.-led capitalist, democratic half, and a Soviet-led socialist/communist half. This is, of course, an oversimplification: the partition was not as clear-cut; not every country took sides; and in different locations (Greece, Korea, Guatemala, Cuba, Vietnam, Angola), it went from cold to boiling hot.

The sixties and seventies brought new definitions of the left in Europe and the United States and around the world. Gradually, leftist parties and movements incorporated a broad catalog of new isms: pacifism, feminism, environmentalism, and other "nonmaterialist" issues only tangentially linked to class, such as abortion and gay rights.

The United States, except for two moderate leftist outbursts (New Deal and Great Society), has sat historically on the center right. And by Western European standards, what passes for left in the United States is, at best, centrist.

The British wrote the book on individualism, but we expanded, perfected, and published it in oversized luxury editions. Individualism does not mix well with community-centered, let alone collectivist, ideas. That is why even self-professed American lefties prefer to talk about race, gender, and ethnicity than about class.

Fast-forward to the era since former President Donald Trump's election. Political polarization has reached explosive levels, its biggest eruption thus far being the January 6 bloody Trumpist assault on the Capitol. I look back on U.S. history to find a period of radical conservatism approximating the current situation and come up empty-handed. Likewise, a segment of the traditionally centrist Democratic Party, the Bernie Sanders-Elizabeth Warren wing, has gained considerable strength and influence.

But increasingly, I find myself agreeing with philosopher of nothingness Jean-Paul Sartre, who once said that the left and the right were empty vessels.

Activists, politicians, pundits, and academics are filling those vessels with whatever is expedient or purely fashionable, coherence not required.

After peaking during the mid-1960s, the "liberal" political brand entered a prolonged crisis from which it has never recovered. Many blue-collar Democrats and increasing portions of the middle class rejected what they perceived to be the unpatriotic nature of the anti-Vietnam War movement and countercultural attacks on traditional morality and family values. Likewise, working-class Catholics, one of the pillars of the Democratic Party, once opposed its current pro-choice stance. And substantial numbers of white Southern voters who resisted the expansion of civil rights switched to the Republican Party.

As a political category and as an ideological package, American liberalism hit rock bottom in the 1972 elections, when incumbent Republican president Richard Nixon defeated Democratic challenger George McGovern. It was the second-largest electoral landslide in U.S. history: 520 electoral votes for Nixon, only 17 for McGovern. The Republican message that Democrats had become the party of "Amnesty, Acid, and Abortion" (the amnesty being for draft-dodgers) was successful.

It did not help that the last Democratic president to embrace the "liberal" label, Jimmy Carter (1977–1981), had a lackluster, and in the eyes of many, failed presidency.

According to University of California, Berkeley linguist George Lakoff, the Republican attack on the term "liberal" originated during Nixon's 1967–1968 campaign, when Republicans coined the term "liberal elite" to decry their opponents' lack of touch with common men and women. Other derogatory terms such as "Volvo liberals" and "chardonnay liberals" followed.

By the time Reagan reached the White House, "liberal" had become a political insult. As Reagan famously put it in a 1988 speech, "it's time to use … the dreaded 'L' word, to say the policies of our opposition … are liberal, liberal, liberal."

The biggest proof of the success of the attack on liberalism is that liberals gradually stopped identifying themselves as such, preferring "progressive" instead, a vaguer term with less negative historical baggage. Rather than neutral, the word "progressive" has a positive ring and more widely welcomed connotations.

Reagan and his British counterpart, then-Prime Minister Margaret Thatcher, not only succeeded at denigrating liberals and defeating them at the ballot box, but also undermined the socio-political structures built during decades of liberal rule. This included tax cuts, liberalization of international trade, weakening labor unions and cutting social spending and welfare.

While their respective parties eventually lost power in 1993 and 1990, their agendas and legislation have survived them, opening the doors to the acceleration of globalization since the 1990s. In fact, rather than a full swing back to liberalism, former President Bill Clinton and former Prime Minister Tony Blair's governments were characterized by what some call "new politics" and others "the third way": a hybrid, centrist model that reconciles center-right economics (i.e., NAFTA) with center-left social positions such as maintaining a somewhat weakened social safety net (i.e., workfare).

It was the other Clinton, Hillary, who most forcefully wrote the "liberal" label's epitaph, beginning in 2007, when in a primary debate she refused to describe herself as "liberal" but rather as "a modern progressive." During her second run for president in 2016, she explained that "liberal" "has been turned up on its head and it's been made to seem as though it is a word that describes big government, totally contrary to what its meaning was in the 19th and early 20th century." "I prefer the word 'progressive,'" she continued, "which has a real American meaning, going back to the Progressive Era at the beginning of the 20th century."

The importance of ideology in general has declined during the first two decades of the twenty-first century, culminating in the election of former Democrat, now-Republican, Donald Trump, known for his ideological opportunism—much of it in contradiction to traditional conservative values such as fiscal conservatism, foreign policy hawkishness and free trade. His brand of right-wing populism is more about the cult of personality than any coherent ideological package. It is the political echo of globalization which, like in Europe, feeds off the discontent of millions who feel victimized by the seemingly irreversible processes of corporate outsourcing and deindustrialization, and a concomitant rise in unemployment, lower wages, and mass migration.

The year 2016 marked the start of the third crisis of liberalism in the last 50 years, regardless of what its leaders called themselves. The first pushed millions of Democrats to support Nixon in 1968 and 1972; the second gave rise to the so-called Reagan Democrats of the 1980s; and the third to Trumpism.

57

Wars and Rumors of Wars in Times of TikTok: Is America Ready for a Major Conflagration?

(Creators Syndicate, January 15, 22, 2022)

The British won their World War I battles, the aphorism goes, on the polo fields of Eton and Harrow (elite boarding schools for boys). As poetic as that may sound, those battles were actually won—some lost—in the farmlands of Devon and factories of Manchester and Liverpool.

But one thing is true: Throughout history, sports and games have served as preparation for war. Think of pankration, the bloody Greek martial art routinely practiced by Spartan boys, and the English medieval game Prisoner's Base in which the team that captured the most prisoners won.

And where were the U.S. military forces that bombarded and invaded Panama, Bosnia, Somalia, Afghanistan, and Iraq trained? I propose it happened, to some extent, in video game arcades at Chuck E. Cheese and suburban bedrooms, where teenage boys played air combat and first-person shooter video games for endless hours.

What some historians consider the earliest video game, "Spacewar!" was created in 1962 (year of the Cuban Missile Crisis) by Massachusetts Institute of Technology computer scientists funded by the Pentagon. Since then, the U.S. military has employed war video games not only for training but also for pre-training and as recruitment tools. The names of some popular war video games are suggestive, "Tactical Iraqi" and "Afghanistan '11."

TikTok GIs

But where will America win or lose its battles in future, some believe looming, wars? I fear it is happening in front of smartphones, swiping endless successions of TikTok videos.

TikTok was developed by a Chinese company in 2016 and transmitted—I use the verb deliberately—to the rest of the world in 2017. It consists of millions of short video clips, most of which last 15 seconds, some of lip syncing, others of people doing viral dances, even some participating in dangerous challenges like filing their teeth. No, this is not a typo—filing with one "l," as in sharpening them with a file.

In 2021, TikTok surpassed Google as the most visited webpage; the app has been downloaded more than three billion times. TikTok is particularly appealing to members of Generation Z (roughly those born between the mid-to-late 1990s and the early 2010s). Nearly half of all males and 70 percent of females between the ages of 13 and 19 use the app daily an average of almost 70 minutes.

Mental health professionals and scientists around the world have recognized and warned the public about the addictive nature of TikTok, which some have dubbed a "viral form of societal poison," "mass social media-induced illness" and "digital crack cocaine." Watching TikTok videos releases doses of dopamine, which can lead to addiction. Side effects include shortened attention spans, anxiety, depression, and tics (without a "k"—you must spend time outdoors to get those).

It would be difficult to argue that the app is good preparation for war, as was the case with pankration for Spartan warriors, Prisoner's Base for medieval English crusaders and the video game "Doom" for American ground troops in Afghanistan and Iraq.

But this three-part column is not about TikTok, which I see as a symbol not just for Gen Zers but for American society in general. It is about the potential for a major conflagration in the near future and how well a divided, self-indulgent, out-of-shape and increasingly emotionally unstable citizenry is prepared for the challenges of war, on the battlefields and the home front.

Wars and Rumors of Wars

In the book of Matthew, Jesus prophesized "wars and rumors of wars," and numerous catastrophes in the end times: famines, earthquakes, increased wickedness, and false prophets. And then come the Four Horsemen of the Apocalypse: pestilence, war, famine, and death. Twenty twenty-two has begun with increasingly loud rumors of war and the four horsemen galloping roughshod across the planet.

Government officials, serious students of geopolitics and international relations, and the serious media (those who call apples, apples) have been, for some time, sounding the alarm of Chinese and Russian aggressive expansionism: threatening air missions into Taiwanese airspace and over 100,000 Russian troops lined up across the border from Ukraine. And then we have Iran, reportedly only weeks away from producing the amount of fuel needed to launch a nuclear bomb, and North Korea, with its recurrent, if erratic, missile tests.

The planet reeks of the stench of war.

Toward a Tripolar Geopolitical Configuration?

The United States lost, "failed miserably," in a battle against Chinese forces, reported General John Hyten, vice chairman of the Joint Chiefs of Staff. "They ran rings around us," continued the four-star general. China fired hundreds of missiles striking Taiwanese and U.S. military installations in the South China Sea, then launched a massive amphibious invasion of Taiwan, which it has long considered its breakaway province.

WAIT! WAIT! Don't run to the grocery store to buy bread and milk. Don't rush to the nearest recruiting station to enlist. At least not yet. General Hyten was speaking about a Pentagon simulated war game conducted in 2020. And the Chinese invasion of Taiwan happened, but only in a similar Air Force war simulation.

Scholars of geopolitics mostly agree that since the end of the Cold War in 1991, the global system transitioned from a bipolar (U.S. and U.S.S.R.) to a unipolar structure with the United States remaining the world's only superpower. In his 2018 book *Unrivaled: Why America Will Remain the World's Sole Superpower*, political scientist Michael Beckley argued that the United States was ahead of its major rivals and will remain so for decades. In a recent interview, Beckley reassured us that "America still has three times China's wealth and five times its military capabilities." Russia, meanwhile, holds a slight advantage over the

United States in nuclear weapons with 6,800; but while America has a nominal GDP of 20.5 trillion, Russia's economy measures only 1.6 trillion, less than half of California's.

That said, China and, to some extent, Russia have made considerable strides toward world power status and we have entered into a new phase of superpower geopolitics.[1] In a November interview, U.S. Joint Chiefs of Staff Chairman General Mark Milley said that the world was moving toward a tripolar configuration with three great powers, and that the United States will be challenged.

China's Awakening

Repeatedly defeated and humiliated by foreign powers from the mid-nineteenth-century Opium Wars through recurrent routs at the hands of Japan and Russia, the 1900 Boxer War against the Eight-Nation Alliance, and more, in the past two decades, China has awakened both economically and militarily; and as French journalist Alain Peyrefitte (perhaps echoing Napoleon) predicted in 1973, once that happened the world would tremble.

In recent years, China has built up its military (land, sea, air, space and cyber), expanding its arsenal and developing innovative military technology the likes of its hypersonic missile, which in a recent test flew undetected around the world. Its autocratic president, Xi Jinping, has made abundantly clear that he plans to gain full control over Taiwan, demonstrating China's capability to accomplish that by deploying hundreds of bombers and fighter planes into Taiwan's defense airspace throughout 2021. Anyone standing in the way of China's economic and territorial expansion, a defiant Xi said, "will have their heads bashed bloody against a Great Wall of steel."

At just two weeks away from the Beijing Winter Olympics, China will not make a move on Taiwan. But General Milley has warned that the likelihood of such an attack will increase sharply as early as 2024, perhaps 2023.[2]

---

1 Russia's humiliating defeats in September and October 2022 have brought into question its superpower status.

2 In October 2022, U.S. Navy Chief Admiral Mike Gilday and Secretary of State Blinken said that China could invade Taiwan before year's end.

Putin's Rattling Saber

While a potential Chinese attack on Taiwan may be months or a few years away, a Russian invasion of Ukraine is imminent. Just a few hours before the publication of this part of the column (January 22), Colonel Alexander Vindman said in an interview that "we are basically just on the cusp of war. I think that it is all but certain in my mind that there's going to be a large European war on the order of magnitude of World War II."

Putin's invasion and forceful annexation of Crimea in 2014 was a step in his ambitious plan to rebuild the Russian empire, which he telegraphed in the opening ceremonies of the Sochi 2014 Winter Olympics. The ceremony included a video presentation—I call it Putin's PowerPoint—in which a blonde preteen girl enumerates Russia's historical leading figures and accomplishments: Tchaikovsky, Gagarin, the Russian Ballet, the Space Station and so on. In case you missed it, the list of accomplishments included building the Russian Empire.

The slide celebrating the Russian Empire is telling. It includes an image of Russia's empire builder Peter the Great with graphics of a naval battle and St. Petersburg in the background. Another Russian celebrated with a slide of her own is Catherine the Great, under whom the Russian Empire absorbed Crimea and Ukraine.

At Sochi, the Russian Federation won more gold medals (13) and more overall medals (33) than any other country. Four days after the closing ceremony, Russian special forces seized several government buildings in Crimea where they raised the Russian flag. Ukraine had won one bronze and one gold medal, then lost a sizable chunk of its territory to the Russians.

Since the publication of part two of this column on January 22, a full-scale invasion of Ukraine has become increasingly imminent, the White House states repeatedly. Russian troops and tanks continue to cross into Russian ally Belarus in preparation for joint military exercises scheduled for February. On Sunday, the U.S. government announced that it would reduce its embassy in Kyiv to essential staff, issued a travel advisory for Ukraine, and began to deploy weapons and ammunition there, including Javelin anti-tank missiles. On Monday, the White House advised U.S. citizens to leave Ukraine and placed 8,500 troops in high alert.

Also during the weekend, less than two weeks shy of the start of the 2022 Beijing Winter Olympics, China decided to flex its muscles yet again, staging its largest incursion into Taiwanese air defense space since October 2021, with a total of 39 warplanes.

War over either Ukraine or Taiwan is likely to generate an unpredictable chain of events, perhaps leading to what some are already calling World War III.

But Is America Ready for a Global War?

There are different dimensions to war readiness. First is military preparedness, which includes the ability to recruit, train and deploy sufficient troops and support personnel, along with weapons, ammunition, and supplies. By almost all accounts, the United States has the world's most powerful military.

In case of a prolonged war, America would most certainly have to expand its active forces, but studies show that the pool of potential recruits may not be deep enough. In 2017, the nonpartisan organization Mission Readiness reported that 71 percent of the 17–24-year-old population did not meet requirements to serve in the military due to obesity, health problems and inadequate levels of education; and that only 17 percent were "qualified and available for active duty."

Since the start of the COVID-19 pandemic, matters have gotten worse. Take a look at David Brooks' recent *New York Times* column, "America Is Falling Apart at the Seams," where he paints a chilling picture of American society across generations: increasing careless driving, fistfights in airplane cabins and other forms of violence, murder, anger, fear, depression, narcissism, drug abuse and suicide.

A 2020 Reference.com article lists the qualities of a good soldier: "reliability, fearlessness, discipline, consistency, courage, motivation, and skill … prepared-(ness) to exceed their abilities, be diligent in getting tasks completed and stay focused on safety." But these qualities are in short supply in TikTok America.[3]

Recent data show that approximately 30,000 active-duty military personnel have failed to get vaccinated against COVID-19 in defiance of Defense Department orders; a few hundred have been forced out of the military.

A related form of war readiness pertains to the home front. Since the defeat of Nazi Germany and Imperial Japan in 1945, the United States has been directly involved in around 30 wars and armed conflicts, some brief like the invasion of Grenada (1983), some prolonged like the War in Afghanistan (2001–2021). But

---

3 In July 2022, reports circulated about the difficulties that all branches of the U.S. military faced in meeting their recruitment goals. Five months into the 2022 fiscal year, the Army had reached only 23 percent of its goal. Defense officials began serious discussions about using the TikTok platform as a recruitment tool.

as costly in American blood and treasure as these conflicts have been—58,000 killed in Vietnam; $2 trillion spent on the Iraq/Syria War—the American public has faced few disruptions and inconveniences, nothing comparable to the challenges and sacrifices of World War II.

The exigencies of World War II forced many sacrifices and lifestyle changes on the American public. The government imposed various forms of rationing just a few weeks after the Japanese bombing of Pearl Harbor, including tires and gasoline. Starting in May 1942 consumer products such as coffee, sugar, meats, butter, and canned foods were rationed. Americans were encouraged to walk and ride bikes to save gas, and to vacation close to home, to work where they were needed, to cultivate "Victory Gardens," to can fruits and vegetables and to mend torn items of clothing.

But we live in times of TikTok and are extremely divided and polarized. America's enemies are aware of that and factor it into their calculations as to whether to invade our allies or not.

58

Olympic Ceremonies: Spectacles of National Branding and Global Projection

(Creators Syndicate, February 5, 2022)

Sometimes I wish, if just for a moment, that I could simply enjoy what I see and hear around me: a parade, a mural, even a TV ad. But as a social and cultural historian, I carry the pleasurable burden of going beyond the simple enjoyment of things, instinctively contextualizing them in time and space, tracing their historical roots and finding meaning between the lines. That was the case earlier today when I watched the Opening Ceremonies of the 2022 Beijing Winter Olympics.

As it did in the 2008 Beijing Summer Olympics, actually in the same Bird's Nest Stadium, the People's Republic of China put on a spectacular opening ceremony combining flawless choreographies, high-tech visual displays and music ranging from traditional Chinese tunes to John Lennon's classic: "Imagine all the people / Livin' life in peace."

But much has changed in China in the past 14 years—and for that matter, in the entire world. China's GDP increased around 275 percent compared to a modest 40 percent growth in the United States. When measuring purchasing power parity (PPP), China's economy surpassed the United States' back in 2017. Supreme leader Xi Jinping continues to spearhead global economic expansionism as exemplified by the Belt and Road Initiative to build infrastructure in over 70 countries.

The Chinese have also made considerable strides as leading producers of new technologies, accomplishments telegraphed in the 2008 Beijing Olympic Ceremonies (i.e., the thunderous drumming of 2008 traditional "fou" drums synchronized with LED lights) and extravagantly magnified in today's ceremony, where the stadium floor was a giant LED screen and a massive computer-generated ice block melted digitally to reveal the Olympic rings.

Despite the torrent of visual and audible messages of harmony, global togetherness, diversity, and peace—the official slogan is "together for a shared future"—these Olympics are clouded by controversy, increasingly strident rumors of war (particularly over Ukraine), and the ugly background of wholesale human rights abuses of Uyghurs, Tibetans, and the citizens of Hong Kong.

Such violations have prompted a diplomatic boycott of the Beijing games by the United States, the United Kingdom, Australia, Canada, and several other countries. Just hours before the opening ceremonies, the world's second most populous nation, India, which has territorial disputes with China, joined the diplomatic boycott.

China sent a hard-to-read message to the world today when it used cross-country skier Dinigeer Yilamujiang as one of two athletes who lit the Olympic cauldron. Yilamujiang is a member of the Uyghur Muslim minority, which is enduring what some human rights organizations deem genocide. Xi may be taking a page from the host of the Berlin 1936 Olympics, Adolf Hitler, who tried to clean up Nazi Germany's image by ordering the temporary removal of the city's antisemitic signs and graffiti. The Berlin Olympics, historians agree, were the first to display grandiose spectacles of nationalism and international ambition, which have characterized Olympic ceremonies ever since.

China has also displayed increasing belligerence beyond its borders, particularly targeting Taiwan, who's meager four-athlete-strong delegation paraded under the International Olympic Committee-imposed name "Chinese Taipei" and a specially designed flag. Just two weeks ago, the Chinese launched their latest deployment of warplanes into Taiwanese defense airspace.

Among the other 91 delegations represented in today's ceremony was Ukraine's, whose territory is surrounded by tens of thousands of Russian troops ready to invade from the east, south and north. Ukrainians are aware of past Russian invasions and their connection to Olympic games. As athletes from around the world competed in the 2008 Beijing Olympics, Russian troops invaded the former Soviet Socialist Republic of Georgia. More recently, just a few days after hosting the 2014 Sochi Winter Olympics, Putin launched an attack on Ukraine that resulted in the annexation of Crimea.

Obviously, China will restrain from threating deployments into or near Taiwanese airspace while it hosts the Olympics. I also feel safe saying that Russia will observe an Olympic truce until at least the end of the games.[1]

Xi and Putin, who attended the opening ceremonies, have become close; some say they are even friends. Today, just hours before the start of the ceremonies, Putin and Xi met and announced to the world that "Russia and China stand against attempts by external forces to undermine security and stability in their common adjacent regions." It's 6:50 p.m. (Eastern), 10 minutes from my column deadline. After clicking the send button, I will turn on the TV again and watch, for the simple enjoyment of it, some Olympic competitions.

1 Early in March, *The New York Times* reported that U.S. intelligence had learned that Xi Jinping had asked Putin to delay the invasion of Ukraine until after the Olympics.

59

Olympic Games, Truces, and Wars (Sochi, 2014; Beijing, 2022)

(Creators Syndicate, February 26, 2022)

The primary motivation to write this column is the desire to understand and explain, as this book's subtitle says, "the unimaginable events of 2019–2022." This week's Russian invasion of Ukraine, while anticipated, ranks at the top of this period's unimaginables.

Olympic Truce I (Sochi, 2014)

I dedicated my February 5, 2022 column to the Beijing Winter Olympics with particular attention to its opening ceremony, its messages and symbolisms, contextualizing them against a backdrop of increasing international tensions and rumors of war. I connected previous Russian military attacks to past Olympic Games: the invasion of Georgia during the 2008 Beijing Olympics and the invasion of Crimea just four days after the closing ceremonies of the 2014 Winter Olympics at Sochi.

The Sochi closing ceremony revisited Russia's contributions to civilization, highlighting the music of Rachmaninov and other Russian composers, the

Swan Lake and ballet in general—falsely taking credit for the development of the waltz—and the works of Tolstoy and Dostoyevsky. But in contrast with the militaristic and expansionist overtones of the opening ceremony, the spectacle conjured images of harmony and peace: children dressed in white, doves, dreamy music. We saw children carrying sticks with flying white doves. The announcer introduced them as "the doves of peace."

Toward the ceremony's end: more happy children singing, dancing, holding hands; everything evokes the Olympic values "Peace, Tolerance, and Respect." Then, at the very end, the world was forced to endure insufferable speeches by the host dignitary and the president of the International Olympic Committee (IOC) of turn. Russia's Deputy Prime Minister Dmitry Kozak (aka Cheshire Cat), an old comrade of Russian President Vladimir Putin's, boasts: "This is the new face of Russia, Our Russia."

The Russian Federation had won the most Olympic medals with 29, followed by the United States (28) and Norway (25). Ukrainian biathlon athletes won two medals, including gold in the women's relay.

IOC President Thomas Bach spoke the closing words: "I appeal to everybody implicated in confrontation, oppression, or violence. Act on this Olympic message of dialogue and peace." On the eve of the Sochi closing ceremonies, Putin had assembled his inner circle for an all-night meeting to discuss the annexation of Crimea. Most likely present at the meeting was Kosak with his signature frozen-in-place pseudo-smile. Four days later, on February 27, Russian special forces raised the Russian flag over the building of the Supreme Council of Crimea, where it still flies.

Eight years later, almost to the day, the free world anticipates in horror that the same flag will soon fly over the Ukrainian Government Building in Kyiv. As I put the finishing touches on this column, Ukrainian President Volodymyr Zelenskyy ominously warns, "Russia will storm Kyiv tonight."

Olympic Truce II (Beijing, 2022)

In my February 5 column, I stated that I felt "safe saying that Russia will observe an Olympic truce until at least the end of the games." There were times, however, when I thought Putin would rain on Xi's parade. While the Olympians competed, the Biden administration issued several grim warnings: "Every indication we have is they are prepared to go into Ukraine (February 15)"; "We have reason to believe Russian forces are planning and intend to attack Ukraine in the coming days (February 18)."

When the games were over, Norway had earned the most medals (37); the Russian Olympic Committee (ROC)—IOC sanctions banned its athletes from competing under the country's name and flag—won 32 medals. Russian figure skater Kamila Valieva tested positive for banned performance-enhancement drugs. Ukraine carried only one medal, silver in men's aerials, outperforming a ROC skier who got the bronze medal.

On the closing ceremonies (February 20) IOC President Bach delivers another hackneyed speech. He quotes John Lennon, calling on Olympians "to give peace a chance." Three nights later, the U.N. Security Council holds an emergency meeting. Secretary General Antonio Guterres pleads with Putin: "Give peace a chance."

No chance. With the U.N. meeting still going (it is 10:00 p.m. in New York); Putin announces a "special military operation" against Ukraine (it is 5:00 a.m. in Kyiv). All hell breaks loose: missile strikes and lies, tanks roar in, propaganda spews, warplanes drop bombs, Kremlin spreads disinformation, amphibious units land, and more lies.

I do not use this kind of language but today I echo the martyred heroes of Ukraine who defiantly said, "Russian warship, go fuck yourself." Ka-Boom!

And as for Putin, he has echoed the grave mistake Hitler made in 1939, when he ordered Nazi tanks to invade Poland. This will not end well for Putin and his oligarch pals.

60

History's Ghosts Trample Roughshod over Ukraine

(Creators Syndicate, March 5, 2022)

Russian troops are advancing against several Ukrainian targets. In the past two days, they have taken possession of the infamous, out-of-commission Chernobyl Nuclear Plant and are close to capturing the southern city of Kherson, where Ukrainian soldiers and militias continue to resist. Today, they seized the Zaporizhzhia nuclear plant, Europe's largest.

A brutal bombing campaign against Ukraine's second largest city, Kharkiv (1.4 million inhabitants), has destroyed apartment buildings, schools, and sub-urban neighborhoods, leaving a toll of hundreds of civilian casualties. Western nations have denounced the indiscriminate shelling of civilian areas as war crimes.

Kharkiv is no stranger to devastating warfare and bloodshed: it was occupied by Bolshevik forces in 1917, recaptured by the White Army two years later, captured by Nazis in 1941, and retaken twice by the Red Army in 1943.

In the north, meanwhile, a 40-mile-long Russian convoy on its way to Kyiv remains suspensefully stalled; there are reports that Russian soldiers are sabotaging their own vehicles. The plan is to capture the Ukrainian capital, which Putin claims is governed by Nazis. Eighty-one years ago, real Nazis encircled the city, captured it, and inflicted over 700,000 casualties during the First Battle of Kyiv.

Ukrainian troops and civilians have mounted a courageous and effective resistance. Many civilians are arming themselves with Molotov cocktails, home-made bombs originally developed in Finland during the Winter War (1939), to be hurled against invading Soviet tanks. Soviet fake news broadcasted by then-Foreign Minister Vyacheslav Molotov claimed that bombardments over civilian areas were actually aerial drops of food. Finns derided the fake gifts as "Molotov bread baskets," and reciprocated with Molotov cocktails. Costing a few cents to make, Molotov cocktails are the poor warrior's version of the American-made Javelin anti-tank missiles, at $80,000 a pop (should I say, "a boom"?)

Kyiv is still standing but it is not clear how long it will be before it falls. Today, President Volodymyr Zelenskyy sent an apocalyptic message to the world's democracies: "If we will fall, you will fall."

There are obvious parallels between the ongoing Russian invasion of Ukraine and World War II. We hear roaring echoes of Nazi Germany's blitzkrieg (lightning war), a strategy of swift tank-and-air attacks meant to produce psychological shock and achieve quick victories. Nazis debuted that tactic against Poland in 1939; then repeated it in the Low Countries and France.

We are also seeing images reminiscent of Nazi Germany's indiscriminate attacks on civilian populations. Ukrainian men, women and children are huddling in underground shelters the way Londoners did during the Battle of London. World democracies have come together, once again, to impede the spread of authoritarian rule. As during World War II, we find on one side a bunkered, demented expansionist. On the other, a courageous President Zelenskyy, who in eight days of war has risen to Churchillian proportions.

On February 21, two days before launching attacks on Ukraine, Putin regaled his compatriots and the world with a lecture on Russian and Ukrainian history, fake history at its best. Among other things, he said that Ukraine was an artificial nation generously built by Russian Bolsheviks, an echo of Stalin's 1939 claim that Poland did not exist.

We can look even further into Russia's past. Putin is obsessed with recreating not the Soviet empire, but the Russian empire built by Peter the Great (1672–1725) and expanded by Catherine the Great (1729–1796). It was under Catherine's reign that Russia incorporated what is present-day Ukraine. In 1784, she ordered the construction of a formidable fortress in Sevastopol; 230 years later Putin's troops reconquered Sevastopol and all of Crimea.

I have no doubt that Putin will fail to restore Russia's former imperial glory. History will judge him not as the reincarnation of Peter the Great but of Ivan the Terrible (1530–1584). Ivan, who also suffered from paranoia, pursued an expansionist policy in Siberia. Domestically, he brutalized and exterminated the opposition. He died in battle at age 53 (but only on a chess board).

The clearest parallels (as well as potential consequences and lessons) are with the Crimean War (1853–1856). Tsarist Russia launched the Crimean War with the object of expanding into territories controlled by the Ottoman Empire, including the principalities of Moldavia and Wallachia, which included much of present-day Ukraine's Black Sea Coast. Russian troops faced fierce resistance from Ukrainian Cossacks and Crimean Tartars.

Great Britain and France mobilized in support of the Ottoman Empire, declaring war on the Russian Empire in March 1854. None other than Karl Marx, the future father of Soviet communism, viewed the war as a conflict between European democracy and Russian absolutism.

Putin may want to read up on that first Crimean War. Russia lost, its forces pushed to retreat and disarmed in humiliation; its Black Sea fleet and its fortress in Sevastopol destroyed, the empire's finances in shambles.

History matters, Vladimir!

61

We Know How Things Start But Not How They Are Going to End: The Russian Invasion of Ukraine

(Creators Syndicate, March 12, 19, 2022)

Growing up, perhaps because of my family's experience in early Revolutionary Cuba, my mother often said that "we know how things start but not how they are going to end." That is generally true with revolutions and wars as well. We don't know how they are going to end. That said, knowledge about previous wars offers opportunities to foresee potential scenarios and outcomes.

Of World Wars

Take for example, the two world wars. Originally called the Great War, what we now call World War I came to be known as the World War once the United States entered the conflagration in 1917. Politicians, journalists, and historians began to refer to it as WWI only after the breakout of World War II, but a few months after the 1918 Armistice the *Manchester Guardian* used the term WWII, if only in a hypothetical sense. Likewise, with "World War III," coined by *Time* magazine one month before the Japanese attack on Pearl Harbor. It has remained hypothetical since then.

Shortly after the start of Russia's invasion of Ukraine on February 24, 2022, we began to hear journalists and TV pundits use the ominous phrase "World War III," sometimes with the "nuclear" adjective attached. Known for her thoughtfulness and deep understanding of Russian and European affairs, in a March 1 interview, former National Security Council member Fiona Hill said of WWIII, "We're already in it." "We have been for some time," she underscored.

WWI was triggered by a Serbian assassin's bullet (actually two) that killed Archduke Franz Ferdinand of Austria—no one remembers that his wife, Sophie, was also killed that day. Preexisting international tensions exploded in the next few weeks leading to a global conflagration with a death toll of 9 million soldiers and 5 million civilians. That first world war began when German forces crossed Belgium with plans to take Paris. Only two days later, France, Great Britain and Russia declared war on expansionist Germany.

Twenty-one years after the end of WWI—a conflagration heralded as the war to end all wars—a second world war erupted in response to Germany's aerial bombing and invasion of Poland in September 1939. German fighter planes bombarded, and Panzer divisions encircled the capital city of Warsaw in a fashion similar to what Russian troops are now doing in Kyiv and other Ukrainian cities. A few days later, Stalin's Soviet Union invaded Poland from the other flank. Within a month, Warsaw surrendered, and Germany, Russia and Lithuania split the bounty as if it were a fresh-baked wuzetka cake—this was the third partition of Poland, the first two happening in 1773 and 1793. Thus began history's bloodiest war; all told, between 50 and 80 million deaths.

What Will Happen to Ukraine and Russia?

Every day from February 21st—the Beijing Olympics ended on the 20th—through the 24th, immediately upon waking up, I turned on the TV to find out whether the anticipated Russian invasion of Ukraine had begun. It finally happened during Prime Time (U.S. Eastern time) on the 24th, minutes after Putin announced a "special military operation" against Ukraine. The war has now entered its third week and every morning I turn on the TV with the hope of seeing Kyiv still in Ukrainian hands and President Volodymyr Zelenskyy still alive.

March 18, 2022

After three weeks of war, Putin's army has captured only one city, Kherson, off the Black Sea coast; military and civilian resistance has been just too formidable. An increasingly frustrated and angry Putin has resorted to destruction instead: more indiscriminate bombing and shelling of civilian targets—apartment buildings, schools, over 100 hospitals (most viciously maternity and pediatric hospitals), places of worship, a theater where over 100 refugees had taken shelter, and 10 civilians queuing to purchase the bread of life. Europe has not seen such levels of military brutality since WWII.

The before-and-after video that Ukrainian President Volodymyr Zelenskyy shared with the U.S. Congress and the world on Wednesday offers poignant juxtapositions of peace and war, life and death, civilization and barbarism. That video along with other images of atrocities circulating around the world have struck a primal, almost universal nerve of indignation. Ukraine and the civilized world cannot unsee the horrendous footage of that unidentified, bloodied, nine-months-pregnant Ukrainian woman ushered in stretchers out of a freshly bombed maternity hospital in the city of Mariupol. Whether in absentia or in person, alive or posthumously, Putin and his generals will eventually be tried for war crimes, and the image of that dying woman will be the prosecution's exhibit No. 1.

Years from now, historians will author countless books about this war, but they will do so with the benefit of hindsight, something that those of us who are chronicling the war as it unfolds lack. We simply do not know whether this will be a short conflict (six months to a year) or whether it will last many more years, as *Irish Times* journalist Fintan O'Toole suggested yesterday. I sense that it will end sooner rather than later.

Which Side Will Win the War?

Given Russia's military superiority in troop numbers, armament, and air power, it is possible that it will win the war in the short term, meaning that it could establish control over vast expanses of Ukrainian territory and install a puppet pro-Russia regime in Kyiv or some other major city. The odds of that happening would be sharply reduced if NATO were to establish the no-fly zone Zelenskyy has been pleading for over the last two weeks or if Ukraine were to receive the fighter planes it needs. For the time being, NATO and the United States avoid such actions. "Direct confrontation between NATO and Russia," Biden said ominously on March 16, "is World War III."[1]

Whatever the case, we are looking at a potential war of attrition. Ukrainian soldiers and civilian combatants are not likely to surrender, and Putin is pursuing, as Colonel Alexander Vindman put it, "maximalist goals," which make it hard for him to retreat and end the conflict as if nothing had happened.

Long-Term Scenarios

Longer term, Russia faces certain defeat, if not in the battlefields, in the home front, where Putin is confronting massive discontent among opposition forces, whose inspirational leader Alexei Navalny has been imprisoned since January 2021.

The thousands of opponents and antiwar protestors are the outer ring of a series of concentric circles surrounding Putin. The next circle consisting of millions of largely apolitical everyday Russians is likely to withdraw its support from Putin as foreign economic sanctions strangulate the economy, sharply cutting the average Russian's standard of living, perhaps pushing them toward hunger. Further in, stands the ring of Russian military brass; they are dissatisfied with the course of war as dictated by Putin and insubordination or a coup may be in the cards. Next is the ring of Russian oligarchs who became obscenely rich when they acquired companies, land, mines, and infrastructure that were privatized under Mikhail Gorbachev and Boris Yeltsin. They have struck a deal with Putin: you protect our fortunes, and we will support you. But we have begun to see cracks in that circle, which is likely to unravel given the consequences of prolonged economic sanctions. Closer to Putin is the ring of oligarchs of his own making, loyalists who owe their fortunes directly to him. But even they can turn on the dictator, as did the senators who stabbed Julius Caesar to death on the Ides of March in 44 B.C.

---

1 In December 2022, the United States reversed its policy when it announced preparations to supply Ukraine with highly effective Patriots Missiles.

62

Queen Elizabeth II's Passing and the U.S. Media: Reflections of a Lowercase "r" Republican

(Creators Syndicate, September 17, 2022)

Hispanic Heritage Month has just begun. It's a busy time for me as I receive numerous invitations for media interviews, public speaking, and other projects. But earlier this week, I got an unexpected media request. A reporter from my local (Orlando, Florida) CBS affiliate wanted to know my thoughts on online criticism of the British Crown following the passing of Queen Elizabeth II.

My first reaction was to say no: "I will have to pass [as in declining]," I emailed back, "I am anti-monarchical to the bone and would not have anything nice to say either about the monarchy or its relations with former colonies. I don't want to rain on the Queen's funeral procession."

The reporter must have found my answer odd. But being good at his job, he tried again, insisting that the channel was interested in representing all perspectives. I agreed to a Zoom interview later that day.

I watch a lot of news on TV, mostly CNN and MSNBC, occasionally clicking on Fox. It is interesting that Queen Elizabeth's death has united those disparate media in an apparent burst of general Anglophilic monarchism.

Coverage has been incessant and almost completely laudatory, often bordering on servility, as if we were still British subjects. I don't mean any disrespect for Her Majesty the Queen, her grieving family, and her mourning subjects. I actually admire the United Kingdom and its highly civilized people—pork pie and soccer hooliganism aside. But I found it troubling that TV reporters, correspondents, and commentators (Americans in particular) have showered, nonstop, exaggerated praise on the Queen. The coverage's main mantras: "Oh, her sense of duty"; "She has dedicated her entire life to service," yada, yada, yada.

What about this for duty and service? A "plebian" American or English woman, who works hard (and long hours) as a schoolteacher; she takes public transportation—is not chauffeured back home in a Bentley or Rolls-Royce.

Her second shift begins immediately: she must prepare the family dinner, something quick and unsophisticated (macaroni and cheese or a meatloaf)—no special French-trained chefs nor delicacies from Fortnum & Mason (est. 1707).

Then she must help her children with schoolwork—no affected tutors or exclusive boarding schools. Finally, when everybody else is sleeping, our commoner takes a quick shower—no servant attendants nor cloud-soft towels from Mitre Linen (est. 1946)—and goes to sleep in a bed whose replacement is long overdue—definitely not a Canadian handmade Hypnos bed.

There is no real vacation at the end of the school year. Our generic teacher takes a summer job just to make ends meet and perhaps buy a new mattress—no trip to Balmoral Palace to rest and play with dogs and horses.

Tell me who deserves the highest praise for sense of duty, service, and dedication. Who should wear a crown?

Why are Americans and the U.S. media so enamored with the British monarchy, from which we broke in 1776? Why such awfully laudatory news coverage? I even heard TV commentators praise the new King's humanity for shedding a tear in public and accepting an embrace from a stranger in the street. What was the expectation—that he push her back into the crowd?

Not just the United States but all Latin American countries fought for their independence, putting an end to oppressive monarchical rule, and establishing republican forms of government. We should find monarchies offensive. We don't believe in the monarchs' divine right to rule, so why do we see them as if they had that right?

We are citizens (*citoyens*), not subjects. Thank goodness for Thomas Jefferson's and Ben Franklin's Francophilia.

We claim to believe that all men (and women) are created equal, and tell our children, with some level of honesty, that they can grow up to be president. Constitutionally, the United States cannot grant titles of nobility; nor can any person holding office accept one. We do not have a House of Lords and a House of Commons.

So why have the U.S. media and the American public displayed such a monarchist spectacle?

Is this yet another manifestation of our retreat from democratic values? Is it that we so badly crave a sense of national unity and stability?

Section IX

The Oracle of History

Introduction

This closing section ties up several of the threads that run through the entire book, including the recurrent topic of history's value when seeking to understand current events and even in producing informed projections about future historical developments.

The section's opening essay "If History Is of Any Value," revisits forecasts made by several social scientists in March 2022, when the World Health Organization had just declared COVID-19 a pandemic; as well as my own prognostications about growing income and wealth inequality, increased global social and political turmoil, erosion of democracy and rise of authoritarianism, major international wars, and the potential for a second civil war in the United States.

Written in August 2022, a second essay, "Putin's Dirty War, Geopolitical Adjustments and Prospects for Future Wars," is a set of syndicated columns that examine global geopolitical realignments since 2019, the consolidation of two interlocked blocks of authoritarian nations anchored around Russia and China in a volatile standoff against two blocks of democratic states led by the United States, one in the North Atlantic and the other in the Indo-Pacific region. It concludes with reflections about the potential for the escalation and spread of the Russian-Ukrainian War, explosive turmoil in Iran, the possibility of war in

Asia over Taiwan, and the dreadful scenario of a combination of these conflicts in what some are calling a "Third World War."

A third essay, "Toward a Second American Civil War?" traces the exacerbation, since the elections of 2020, of political polarization, extremism, political violence, and other factors that may lead to that unimaginable scenario.

The book's final essay, reminds us of the complexity of historical developments, shifting trends and pendular swings by recognizing an ongoing global authoritarian wave that coexists with democratic countercurrents, and waring us of ever-present dangerous crosscurrents.

63

If History Is of Any Value: March 2020, Revisited

(Creators Syndicate, July 9, 16, 23, 30, 2022)

One of my motivations for becoming a regular columnist and going into syndication with Creators in 2020 was the realization that the COVID-19 pandemic would be a pivotal historical phenomenon with deep and long-lasting global ramifications. For the foreseeable future, I ascertained, there would be a lot to write about, and a historian's perspective might come in handy.

Among my earliest columns is one titled "What History Tells Us about COVID-19's Future Impact." Published by the *Globe Post* on March 29, 2020,[1] the World Health Organization had just officially declared COVID-19 a pandemic. Its count of worldwide confirmed cases had reached 375,498, with 16,362 fatalities; the Centers for Disease Control and Prevention was reporting 15,268 cases and 201 deaths in the United States.

---

1 The *Globe Post* uploaded an updated version of this column on September 2, 2020. This is the original March 2020 version with two extra paragraphs that had been edited out of the original published version.

Twenty-seven months later, as I sit down to write this week's column, I look up today's stats. Worldwide: 539,893,858 cases, 6,324,112 deaths; United States: 86,787,443 cases, 1,011,013 deaths.

And this is not over yet. Last week, the CDC announced that two new omicron subvariants BA.4 and BA.5 have become dominant among coronavirus cases in the United States; while less lethal, they are spreading faster and are more able to fight antibodies produced through vaccination than earlier subvariants. There will be a lot more to write about and for a long time.

Expert Predictions

At the time I wrote my March 2020 column, the editors of *Politico* magazine, *Foreign Policy*, *The Guardian*, and *Devex* surveyed various experts (*Foreign Policy* referred to them as "leading global thinkers") about the likely impact of the pandemic that was still in its infancy. With academic appointments at elite U.S. universities and positions in prestigious think tanks, those experts hailed from the social sciences: political scientists, sociologists, economists, and a few psychologists.

None of them were historians, who are trained to understand that historical phenomena are complex and interconnected, nor cultural anthropologists, who could offer informed insights on cultural change. Not surprisingly, many of the forecasts were ahistorical; some were woefully off the mark; others were, plain and simple, naive.

Many of those expert prognostications were in the fields of international relations and global economics. Stephen M. Walt, professor of international relations at Harvard University, predicted a post-COVID-19 world that is "less open, less prosperous, and less free."

Democracy, which was already on the retreat, suffered further setbacks, in some instances immediately so, as in Israel and Hungary. Established dictatorships in Russia, China, Cuba and elsewhere used the occasion to entrench themselves further and trample over the rights of their citizens.

Less open? Less free? The short-term answer is yes, but the excesses of such governments (and former President Donald Trump's) and Russia's brutal invasion of Ukraine have generated democratic countercurrents in the United States, where Trump lost his re-election bid, and across the North Atlantic, with a strengthened NATO and European Union resolved to curb the expansion of authoritarian rule, and among Asia and Oceania's democratic nations.

Walt and other surveyed experts also foresaw, prematurely so, an acceleration of China's ascendancy in the global scene. As the Harvard professor put it: "COVID-19 will also accelerate the shift in power and influence from West to East. South Korea and Singapore have responded best, and China has reacted well after its early mistakes. The response in Europe and America has been slow and haphazard by comparison, further tarnishing the aura of the Western 'brand.'"

Similarly, Kori Schake, deputy director general of the International Institute for Strategic Studies, prognosticated that "the United States will no longer be seen as an international leader."

The Western "brand," from the vantage point of July 2022, has on the contrary, regained strength: politically, diplomatically, scientifically, and militarily. And to paraphrase a misquote from Mark Twain, reports of the United States' demise as world power are greatly exaggerated.

Other consulted experts foresaw a slowdown in the globalization process. Robin Niblett, director and chief executive of Chatham House, went as far as saying that "the coronavirus pandemic could be the straw that breaks the camel's back of economic globalization." For his part, Kishore Mahbubani of the National University of Singapore's Asia Research Institute forecasted a "more China-centric globalization."

A natural consequence of globalization's slowdown, temporary as it may be, is the strengthening of political and economic nationalism and, according to some observers, the strengthening of nation-states. But Council on Foreign Relations President Richard Haass warned about yet another countercurrent: pandemic crisis-driven circumstances that may push more nations into failed state status.

Through Rose-Colored Glasses

While some of the economic and geopolitical predictions of the surveyed experts materialized (and others did not), forecasts in matters of culture, particularly political culture, and social values, have been completely off.

Yes, it is easier (albeit still tricky) to forecast economic and political developments than matters of historical and cultural change. That is why economists speak freely about future trends and some political scientists do not think twice about predicting winners in the next election.

Historians, while trigger-shy about the future, are better equipped to anticipate what may be around the corner. This is why: historians are by training multidisciplinarians; we don't look at historical phenomena in isolation but rather in their interconnectedness with their geographical, social, political, economic and cultural contexts. Historians, John Lewis Gaddis has written, "don't think in terms of independent and dependent variables. We assume the interdependency of variables as we trace their interconnectedness through time." While we do not talk about variables, we learn to identify and weigh them, instinctively and without pretense of quantification. Historians avoid the trap of the single variable (the strand) or even braiding a few strands as into a rope. We are weavers of polychromatic multitextured fabrics.

Several experts made predictions that did not come close to materializing and in some instances turned out to be the opposite of what actually happened. My objective is not to make them look bad, but rather to highlight the treacherous nature of prognostication and the ease of falling into the trap of a single variable—in this case, the worldwide pandemic.

Peter T. Coleman of Columbia University's Psychology Department applied the "common enemy" theory: the pandemic as a "formidable enemy" that "might provide us with fusion-like energy and a singularity of purpose to help us reset and regroup" generating a shift "toward greater national solidarity and functionality."

Another psychologist, Margaret Klein Salamon, spoke to *The Guardian* about the "power of shared emotion" manifested through "people calling each other up" to see how they are doing. Yet another psychologist, Sherry Turkle from the Massachusetts Institute of Technology, foresaw positive transformations in the digital world: "this is breaking open a medium with human generosity and empathy. This is looking within and asking, 'What can I authentically offer?'"

The common enemy effect did not happen; those tend to be short-lived. Remember the outburst of national unity and increased church attendance after 9/11? If bipartisan approval of a particular president is any indication of national unity, George W. Bush's soared from 51 percent to 91 percent but dropped sharply soon thereafter. And while church attendance increased (only slightly) after the 9/11 attacks, within two months it had reverted to previous levels.

In similarly optimistic terms, sociologist Eric Klinenberg, director of the Institute for Public Knowledge at New York University, categorically declared the end of "hyper-individualism." "The coronavirus pandemic," Klinenberg told *Politico*, "will force us to reconsider who we are and what we value, and, in the long run, it could help us rediscover the better version of ourselves."

A practicing journalist, Amy Sullivan, director of strategy for Vote Common Good, speculated that "maybe—just maybe" we would see an easing of the culture wars and become "newly conscious of interdependency and community."

Rather than coming together, and exhibiting higher levels of solidarity and less individualism, Americans are displaying greater selfishness, incivility, and violence, everywhere from the county road to the school board hall, from the airplane cabin to the grocery store, from Twitter to the political tribune.

Two other expert predictions that fell short caught my attention. Villanova University political scientist Mark L. Schrad anticipated a new brand of patriotism. "When all is said and done," he stated, "perhaps we will recognize" the sacrifices of doctors, nurses, and other care givers "as true patriotism, saluting our doctors and nurses, genuflecting and saying, 'Thank you for your service.'" "We will give them," Schrad continued, "guaranteed health benefits and corporate discounts, and build statues and have holidays for this new class of people who sacrifice their health and their lives for ours."

Tom Nichols, a professor at the U.S. Naval War College, concluded that the pandemic "already forced people back to accepting that expertise matters." He specifically mentioned Dr. Anthony Fauci and speculated that the crisis "may—one might hope—return Americans to a new seriousness."

Approval rates for the CDC, Dr. Fauci and other scientists leading the fight against the pandemic were high at the beginning but as the 2020 elections got closer, they dropped 30 percent among Republicans while increasing by a modest 6 percent among Democrats.

No statue for Dr. Fauci anytime soon. Hundreds have participated in protests targeting him and others have showered him with death threats. And as far as Americans becoming more serious, don't hold your breath.

My Two Cents' Worth

Like my colleagues in other disciplines, at the pandemic's onset, I ventured into some general prognostications, which I called "potential consequences." Based on a review of historical pandemics and related crises, I offered a pessimistic forecast: "If history is of any value," I wrote in March 2020, "social, political, and geopolitical tensions ... are likely to build up and perhaps explode, producing social restructuring, firing up domestic conflicts, eroding civil rights, and igniting wars."

I offered two general global forecasts: (1) increased inequality around the world, and (2) further worldwide erosion of democracy and rising authoritarianism.

Economic Inequality

"The economic disruptions of the present crisis are likely to expand income and wealth inequality and accelerate the squeezing of the middle class," I wrote in March 2020.

Both things have happened in the United States and most countries around the world, with particularly harsh and deadly consequences for the most vulnerable nations and the most susceptible inhabitants of those nations, the poor, women, children, and ethnic minorities.

Already obscene levels of inequality were exacerbated by unequal access to COVID-19 vaccines and medical treatment. According to the Global Dashboard for Vaccine Equity, as of September 2021, while high-income countries had a vaccination rate of 60 percent, in low-income countries it was a dismal 3 percent. This week (28 months after the declaration of pandemic status) the rate for high income countries is 72 percent; 20 percent for poor countries. And let's not lose sight of the fact that poorer countries have received a larger share of less-effective Russian, Chinese, and Cuban vaccines.

While worldwide death tallies reflect high COVID-19 mortality rates in high-income countries like the United States, Italy and France, a recent study published in *BMJ Global Health* examined a broader set of indicators, concluding that "The burden of COVID-19 is far higher in developing countries than in high-income countries, reflecting a combination of elevated transmission to middle-aged and older adults as well as limited access to adequate healthcare."

The economic symptoms of the pandemic-induced global recession have hurt some countries and some groups of people more than others. Income and wealth inequality have increased worldwide since 2019. This is true for the global population as a whole, among nations as well as within nations.

The pandemic reversed a trend toward the reduction of worldwide poverty that since 2000 had elevated the median income in poor countries and reduced worldwide extreme poverty rates from around 25 percent of the population to 10 percent. Various international agencies estimate that the number of people pushed into extreme poverty since the start of the pandemic hovers around 160 million. The war in Ukraine with a concomitant rise in food and fuel prices will aggravate world hunger and expand the ranks of the poor in a magnitude of tens of millions.

Women, particularly in poor countries, have suffered disproportionate harm. In 2020 alone, 13 million women lost their jobs and their incomes dropped $800 billion. Girls have also faced higher rates of disruption in their education, which spells a long-term setback in gender equality. Oxfam has also documented a higher negative economic impact on marginalized minorities in the United Kingdom and the United States.

The so-called global middle class has also shrunk. According to a July 2021 Pew Research Center report, 54 million members of the world's middle classes had slipped into poverty since the start of the pandemic. The middle-class squeeze has been particularly harsh in East and South Asia.

There is one minority that rather than suffer has experienced an unprecedented economic bonanza. You got it right: billionaires. "Billionaires," Oxfam's executive director, Gabriela Bucher, has recently stated, "have had a terrific pandemic." The assets of the world's 10 wealthiest men, including Elon Musk, Jeff Bezos and six others whose fortunes emerged from the tech sector, more than doubled to $1.5 trillion from March 2020 to November 2021, a sharper rate of growth than in the previous 14 years combined.

In defense of his fortune, on the last Friday of October 2021 (before he committed to purchase Twitter and then walked out of the deal),[2] Musk grandiosely tweeted, "My plan is to use the money to get humanity to Mars and preserve the light of consciousness." A self-absorbed libertarian with that much money and that many toys is bound to create serious global problems.[3]

Popular Protests and Authoritarian Rule

My March 2020 column also offered prognostications on the worldwide political and geopolitical repercussions of the pandemic, including a rise in authoritarianism, further erosion of democracy, a spike in civil and human rights violations, intensification of popular protests and the explosion of new wars.

"Liberal democracy," I stated then, "has been the target of unremitting attacks even in the longtime bastions of the United States, Great Britain, and France. The unholy alliance of nationalist and white supremacist masses, populist leaders, and proponents of crony capitalism is on the offensive and likely to

2 Musk began the process to acquire Twitter in April 2022. The company sued him for backing out of the deal and he completed the purchase on October 27, 2022. He immediately fired the company's top leadership and laid off 3,700 employees the following week.

3 On November 7, on the eve of the midterm elections, Musk tweeted his followers recommending they should vote for a Republican Congress.

gain ground in a context of a prolonged pandemic accompanied by months, if not years, of economic decline." The pandemic, I also wrote, was likely to fire up domestic conflicts and ignite wars.

A Worldwide Increase in Mass Protests

The Carnegie Endowment for International Peace (CEIP) has been tracking mass anti-government protests around the world since 2017, when it registered a total of 31, sparked by a variety of causes ranging from political corruption in Azerbaijan and Russia to farmers' rights in India and France. The number of protests rose sharply to 50 in 2018 and to 64 in 2019.

In 2020, the CEIP reported a major spike with a total of 89 protests, 15 of which were popular reactions to government-mandated COVID-19 lockdowns and other restrictions in the United States, Canada, Western Europe, Israel, and other democratic industrialized nations. In a handful of countries, Brazil, and Ecuador, for example, COVID-19 protests responded to inadequate government measures against the pandemic. That was also the year of massive Black Lives Matter protests sparked by the killing of George Floyd in many U.S. cities, but also in London and Paris, along with numerous popular mobilizations denouncing violence against women and ethnic minorities.

The second year of the pandemic registered a total of 75 protests, 13 of which were related to COVID-19 in countries as diverse as Australia, Mongolia, Paraguay, and Tunisia.

Democratic Recession and Depression

In 2015, political sociologist Larry Diamond coined the term "democratic recession" to describe the stalling of the worldwide trend toward democratic governance that had begun in the mid-1970s and accelerated after the collapse of the Berlin Wall (1989) followed by the implosion of most communist regimes, including the Soviet Union and the Warsaw Pact nations.

Democracy Indexes published by the Economist Intelligence Unit (EIU) since 2006 reflected a stagnant index that hovered around 5.52 between 2006 and 2016 (a country with a score of 4 or lower qualifies as "authoritarian regime"). Curiously, it was the world's most democratic regions (North America, Western

Europe, and Eastern Europe) that experienced sharper democratic decline, while Third World regions remained stagnant or saw modest improvement.

During the first and second years of the pandemic, the world has sunk—to extend Larry Diamond's metaphor—into a "democratic depression." This was largely the result of ongoing trends exacerbated by the pandemic, used by many states to justify further assaults on democracy as well as systematic violations of human and civil rights. In 2020 and 2021, many governments introduced new legislation and repressive practices to crackdown on dissidents and minority groups; persecute journalists; curb the freedoms of expression, association, and assembly; and postpone scheduled elections.

According to Human Rights Watch, the worldwide erosion of democracy has been particularly sharp in "struggling democracies and authoritarian states." EIU Democracy Index reports recorded democratic deterioration in every region of the world and an especially negative impact in Latin America.

The Democracy Index documents a sustained fall in the proportion of the world's population living in countries categorized as either "full democracies" or "flawed democracies" since 2006. In 2008, it dropped below 50 percent and fell sharply from 48.4 percent in 2019 to 45.7 percent in 2021. The number of countries categorized as authoritarian also grew from 54 in 2019 to 57 in 2020 to 59 in 2021. Countries exhibiting the steepest drops (2020 to 2021) include Afghanistan, Myanmar, Nicaragua, Nepal, Guinea, Haiti, and Venezuela.

The Americas

It may come as a surprise to some readers that the EIU Democracy Index does not presently categorize the United States as a "full democracy." That has been the case since 2016—the year when Trump was elected president—when the EIU downgraded the country to "flawed democracy." In fact, in 2021, the United States ranked 26th among 167 evaluated countries. Canada ranks 12th, a sharp decline from the 5th position in 2020, largely attributed to the reimposition of strict COVID-19 restrictions in the fall of 2021.

Latin America's democracy scores fell sharply in 2020, a development, according to the EIU, "driven chiefly by the curbing of civil liberties in response to the coronavirus pandemic." The region's Democracy Index dropped at an even sharper rate in 2021, when out of 24 countries, only 3 (Dominican Republic, Surinam, and Uruguay) showed improvement. The worst offenders have been leftist regimes in Nicaragua, Venezuela, and Cuba, the latter of which saw unprecedented peaceful mass protests in July 2021 and since the summer of 2022 that have been brutally repressed by the state. Illiberal populist governments in Brazil (Jair Bolsonaro), Mexico (Andrés Manuel López Obrador), and El Salvador (Nayib Bukele) have also contributed to the backsliding of democracy in the region. Haiti, for its part, has fallen into anarchy, with violent gangs currently threatening to take over what is left of its failed state government.

Eastern Europe

In Eastern Europe democracy was strengthened in some nations and weakened in others. Poland saw improvements in 2020 but slid back the next year. Belarus, Hungary, Kyrgyzstan, and Russia moved deeper into authoritarianism while Estonia remained the region's most democratic country. Moldova and Romania's democracy scores saw modest gains in 2021.

Alyaksander Lukashenka remained in power in Belarus through fraudulent elections in 2020; his regime imprisoned activists and journalists, effectively crushing the opposition. His Hungarian counterpart, Viktor Orbán, has used the pandemic as justification to expand his authority, declaring a national state of emergency that severely restricted the right to assembly and peaceful protest.

Putin's Russia

For several years, Vladimir Putin's increasingly belligerent Russia has suffered an erosion of democracy and seen an escalation of civil and human rights violations. In 2019 and again in 2021, Putin's regime expanded the Foreign Agents Law to silence foreigners and Russian citizens who report on government corruption, crimes, and shortcomings. With similar objectives, the Russian state has applied the Undesirable Organizations Law against international and domestic NGOs and other groups including the media and human rights organizations.

With the pandemic raging, in July 2020, Putin imposed a constitutional reform that allows him to remain president until 2036, to the ripe old age of 83. In 2021, Russians endured a hardening of repression, crackdowns on independent organizations, dissidents, and political rivals, most notably, Aleksei Nalvany, detained in January 2021 and sentenced to nine additional years in March 2022. Repression has hardened since Russia invaded Ukraine: 15,000 anti-war protesters were arrested just in the first three weeks of the war; all remaining independent media were banned; and a new law criminalizes calling the war "war" or "invasion" instead of the official euphemism "special military operation."

Asia and Australasia

In 2020, Asia and Australasia's Democracy Indexes fell to their lowest level since 2013 and had an even steeper reduction in 2021. These average scores, however, mask the reality of a combination of contradictory forces: sharp declines in countries like China, Myanmar, Afghanistan, already categorized as "authoritarian;" and a democratic countercurrent in countries with historically higher Democracy Indexes. In 2020, the EIU upgraded Japan, South Korea, and Taiwan from "flawed" to "full democracies." In 2021, the region had five full democracies, including Australia and New Zealand, while hosting seven authoritarian regimes, lowest ranking among them: Afghanistan (where the Taliban took control in 2021), Myanmar (where the military staged a coup), North Korea, Laos, and China, in that order.

International human rights monitoring organizations have denounced civil rights violations related to COVID-19 restrictions in many of the region's least democratic nations: Cambodia, China, Malaysia, Mongolia, North Korea, Singapore, Thailand, and Vietnam. At the pandemic's peak in 2020, Chinese authorities forced an estimated one half of the population into home confinement.

China and Hong Kong

Before China's president Xi Jinping abolished presidential term limits in 2018, the world's most populous nation had exhibited a dismal record of democracy and human rights. China's Democracy Index averaged 3.11 between 2010 and 2018 (4 or lower means "authoritarian regime"). Then, it dropped to an average of 2.25 in 2019–2021. This is largely the result of what numerous international organizations deem "genocidal actions" and "crimes against humanity" perpetrated against Muslims in the supposedly autonomous province of Xinjiang and the violent application of the National Security Law in Hong Kong in June 2021. Under the cover of COVID-19 exigencies, China has trampled over civil rights in Hong Kong. It forced the postponement of elections in 2020 and again in 2022, by which time repressive forces had silenced all pro-democracy opposition. The

National Security Law has been used to disband political parties, independent media organizations and labor unions.

The Middle East and Africa

The Middle East, Northern and Sub-Saharan Africa consistently rank as the least democratic regions of the world. In 2021, out of 20 Middle Eastern and North African countries, all but three ranked in the bottom category "authoritarian regime"; Tunisia and Morocco as "hybrid regimes"; and Israel as "flawed democracy." Democracy deteriorated most precipitously in Iran, Iraq, Lebanon, Sudan, and Tunisia.

With 43 nations, Sub-Saharan Africa is the region with the largest number of countries assessed yearly by the Democracy Index. More than half of those countries are ruled by authoritarian regimes. According to the EIU, 2021 was a "terrible year for democracy" in Africa. Two trends were largely responsible: (1) a rise in Jihadist insurgence and (2) an increase in number of military coups, which succeeded in Guinea, Mali, and Sudan, but failed in Niger.

64

Putin's Dirty War, Geopolitical Adjustments and Prospects for Future Wars

(Creators Syndicate, August 6, 13, 20, 27, September 10, 24, 2022)[1]

Back in March 2020, I commented on the possibility of new civil wars and international armed conflicts. Among the world's most explosive tensions with the potential to ignite into conflagrations I recognized Israel and Iran; India and Pakistan; North Korea and the United States and its Asian allies; and the United States and China over Taiwan. While none of these have burst into war, hostilities have intensified in all those cases as well as a few others: civil wars in Ethiopia (spilling over to Eritrea and Sudan), Mali, Myanmar, and Yemen; a surge in Taliban insurgency in Afghanistan; and heightened tensions between Israel and Palestine and Iran, and between China and India.

While Russia and Ukraine have been technically at war since the Russian invasion and occupation of Crimea in 2014, the latest invasion starting in February 2022 elevated what had been a low-intensity conflict with around 100 casualties per year to a massive all-out war that has brought widespread destruction, military and civilian casualties in the tens of thousands, and the displacement of

---

1 All of the columns that comprise this essay were written before August 20, 2022, with the exception of the last part "A World at Risk," published on September 24.

over 12 million Ukrainians as of July 2022. Given Putin's record of expansionist adventures, the war itself was not unimaginable, but the brutality and atrocities perpetrated by Russian troops have been indeed unimaginably barbaric.

Experts have been anticipating Chinese military aggression against Taiwan for several years. And China has, over the past three years, escalated its threatening rhetoric and expanded military exercises aimed at intimidating Taiwan, which it has vowed to bring under its control. In anticipation of Nancy Pelosi's visit to Taiwan, on August 1, China issued an ominous threat: "there will be serious consequences if she insists on making the visit." The potential for a standoff increased after August 4 when the Chinese military began live-fire drills on several locations close to Taiwan's coasts and China cut high-level military communications with the United States.

The Biden administration had objected to Speaker Pelosi's trip to avoid retaliation. On the same week, the White House announced sanctions against 39 other Putin associates, including Alina Kabaeva, his reputed girlfriend, three decades his junior. Reportedly, the United States had not sanctioned her previously out of concern that it would bring us closer to a confrontation with Russia. That the United States is trying to avoid war with Russia and China is understandable and wise. But there is also wisdom in applying the playground principle that bullies must be confronted, the earlier the better. It usually works.

Geopolitical Ramifications of Increased Russian and Chinese Belligerence

The war in Ukraine and China's growing belligerence have accelerated the formation and consolidation of two sets of parallel blocks of nations. On the one hand, two interlocked blocks of authoritarian partners and allies, one built around Russia, the other around China. On the other hand, a democratic North Atlantic block and another in the Indo-Pacific region, both anchored by the United States, which remains the only global superpower.

So much has transpired since the end of the Cold War in 1991, that it is hard to remember the short period of time when the United States was the world's only superpower. The former Soviet Union was bankrupt and China, while on a fast track to becoming an economic powerhouse, was still far from representing a substantial military threat in Asia, much less globally. Following the collapse of the Soviet Union, China continued its pursuit of economic growth, quietly watching other countries fight one another and sink into debt in the process.

No one even suggested then that the twenty-first century would be a "Chinese century." That phrase first appeared in its current definition in the title of a 1997 article published in *The Futurist*, "The Coming Chinese Century," and later in 2004 in the *New York Times* article "The Chinese Century."

Russia's Block

Putin's aggressions, particularly the unprovoked invasion of Ukraine in February 2022, respond to positions of weakness: economic, diplomatic, geopolitical. When Russia invaded and annexed Ukraine's Crimean Peninsula in 2014, the United States, the European Union, Canada, Australia, Japan, and some non-EU European nations imposed severe economic sanctions against Russian oligarchs, financial institutions, and state corporations. By all accounts, sanctions inflicted serious damage to the Russian economy. Even if a few EU member nations (i.e., Italy, Hungary, and France) opposed sanctions originally, Russia's renewed aggression against Ukraine has strengthened bonds among the world's Western democracies and Japan and South Korea.

Russia endures relative diplomatic isolation, holding on to a handful of friends and allies, among them several former Soviet Socialist Republics: a Finlandized Belarus, Kazakhstan, Kyrgyzstan, and other members of the Russian-created Commonwealth of Independent States (CIS); the Eurasian Economic Union (EAEU); and the Collective Security Treaty Organization (CSTO), a counterpart to NATO with an article (that mirror's NATO's article 5), establishing that an attack on one of its members is an attack on all; Armenia, Syria, Myanmar, Iran, Pakistan, China; and an impoverished triad of Latin American leftist dictatorships: Cuba, Nicaragua and Venezuela.

An examination of a world map helps understand Russia's geopolitical paranoia and its desire to conquer Ukraine, destabilize NATO and the EU and subvert democracy across the world. Russia is sandwiched between Europe's "full" or "flawed" democracies with which it shares a 2,665-mile-long border (by comparison, the U.S.-Mexico border measures 1,933 miles); and the United States and Japan, with which it shares water borders. With the pending finalization of Finland's admission into NATO, Russia will have 1,458 miles of land border with NATO countries, all bound by the organization's charter's mutual defense obligations. Ukraine and Georgia are at the dialog stage with NATO; if they join, the Russia-NATO border will more than double its present length.

Petrodiplomacy

So far, Russia has not faced the economic catastrophe expected from tightening international sanctions in 2022, largely because of its extant oil-generated monetary reserves and income from continued oil exports.[2] Russia is the third-largest producer and biggest exporter of oil to the global market, and the price of a barrel of oil spiked from $86.51 in January 2022 to $122.71 in June. The same Russian oil that is fueling invading tanks and armored vehicles continues to prop up Putin's regime.

Immediately upon the crossing of tanks and firing of missiles into Ukraine, Canada declared a ban on Russian oil imports; the United States followed a few days later, as did the United Kingdom. The EU's historically heavy dependence on Russian fuel sources slowed down the decision to impose its own oil sanctions until early June, when it declared a phased-in embargo against Russian and Belarusian fuel exports.

There has been much debate about the feasibility and effectiveness of such sanctions. Some argue that they will hurt Europe more than Russia because Russia has successfully expanded its oil markets, particularly in India and China. It is true that Europe will suffer much—far more than the one or two extra dollars per gallon at the pump Americans complain about—and fuel shortages and rising inflation are likely to generate social and political unrest. But in the long term, current circumstances will expand the use of clean and renewable forms of energy and nuclear energy.

Many people cringe at any mention of nuclear energy—I do not like it either—but dependence on oil and coal has already done seemingly irreparable damage to our planet and will destroy it if it persists. Germany, Western Europe's most oil-import-dependent nation, had planned to close its three remaining nuclear plants before the end of 2022, but Chancellor Olaf Scholz has recently acknowledged that it is no longer feasible. We may very well be witnessing the start of a worldwide return to nuclear energy. But then again, deadly nuclear plant disasters with long-term consequences do happen (Three Mile Island, Chernobyl, Fukushima). And then there is the problem of what to do with nuclear waste.

---

2 Still, the Russian economy has endured damage. According to a *New York Times* story of August 12, 2022 "its gross domestic product fell 4 percent from April to June, compared with a year earlier."

Shelling of the Zaporizhzhia Nuclear Plant in Russian-occupied Ukraine during the second week of August is feared to end disastrously.

China's Block

It is important to look at China and its history the way the Chinese do, with a long-term perspective of decades and centuries rather than four-year terms or quarters, the way we have come to view time in the United States. The Chinese race to become the world's largest economy and to boost its national wealth must be understood as the desire to restore China's economic greatness as the biggest economy and wealthiest country (per capita) as it was for most of the 1200s through the 1700s.

The Chinese also have a long memory, remembering economic aggressions and humiliations endured at the hands of foreign powers: the British (Opium Wars, 1839–1860), Japan (First and Second Sino-Japanese Wars, 1884–1895 and 1937–1945) and the Eight-Nation Alliance cannon-point trade impositions known as the Boxer Protocol (1901).

The resumption of civil war in China after WWII culminated in the 1949 triumph of communist forces over the Republic of China, which was forced to retreat to the island of Taiwan. Ten years later, China had a GDP of $59.92 billion (sixth in the world), but it ranked dead last (99 out of 99) in GDP per capita. Beginning in 1994, but at a much faster rate since 2006, its GDP has grown geometrically to its present level of $17.7 trillion. With GDP per capita, which is a much better indicator of the population's well-being, at $12,600, China ranks 77 out of 194 countries.

China shares land borders with countries that for the most part are friends and allies (i.e., Russia, Mongolia, Myanmar, North Korea). India (with which it has border disputes), Bhutan and Vietnam are the exceptions. Beyond its immediate perimeter, China finds a rim of democratic adversaries in Taiwan, South Korea, Japan, Australia, and New Zealand.

And let's not forget that its greatest rival, the United States, has numerous military bases in Asia and Oceania: in American Samoa, Australia, Guam, Japan, Marshall Islands, Northern Mariana Islands and South Korea. As powerful as China is, it boasts only one military base on foreign soil, in Djibouti, Africa. The United States, by contrast, has over 750 bases in over 80 countries. In 2021, China started building a secret military installation in the United Arab Emirates; it was so secret that allegedly it was unknown to the UAE government. The Biden administration warned the UAE against the continuation of the project and construction stopped.

The extent and cohesion of the Chinese block became evident in 2020, when 53 nations from Antigua and Barbuda to Zimbabwe openly supported China's violent repression in Hong Kong.

Chinese Expansionism: Eurasian Land Bridges, Debt-trap Diplomacy, and TikTok

With 3.383 million barrels per day, China is the world's seventh largest crude oil producer, but that does not even come close to fulfilling internal demand. The world's second largest economy is also second in oil consumption (15.4 million barrels a day) which means that it has to purchase the balance of what it needs from foreign sources. Last month, Reuters News reported that Russia had surpassed for the first time Saudi Arabia as China's top source of oil; it now receives 55 percent more Russian oil than last year.

Incapable of leveraging oil as part of its diplomatic arsenal, China has for about a decade used the peaceful strategy of constructing ambitious infrastructure projects around the world. Take, for example, the Belt and Road Initiative, a transportation system conceived to connect the Pacific port city of Lianyungang to Rotterdam—Attila's empire reached that far west. As of July 2020, 43 countries had signed on to the Initiative.

Its southern counterpart, the New Eurasian Land Bridge, starts in China's Pacific coast, crosses through several countries including Kazakhstan, Turkmenistan, and Turkey, where it connects with the Mediterranean (a new Bosporus) and continues to Western Europe. This is what I meant earlier when I said that the Chinese have the long-term perspective of decades and centuries. If all goes as planned, all roads will eventually lead to Beijing.

The other major Chinese expansionist tool is what Indian scholar Brahma Chellane first dubbed in 2017, "China's debt trap diplomacy." There is nothing new about this strategy, which has been deftly used for centuries by the world's commercial powers as a colonial and neocolonial weapon to gain influence and power over economically and politically weaker nations. China is well familiar with that strategy, having been on the receiving end of the scheme from the 1870s through 1940s. The Chinese remember it well, as they do the diabolical British scheme to force imports of Indian opium to get the country addicted to the narcotic extracted from the poppy flower. TikTok, which is owned by a Chinese company, has successfully addicted hundreds of thousands, if not millions, of American children and youths.

High speed trains, loans, and addictive internet platforms, not the recently unveiled hypersonic missile, are China's most formidable weapons.

Russia, China, Iran: A New Axis?

Since the start of the mid-1990s, Russia-China relations have become tighter diplomatically, commercially, and militarily. In 1996 China joined Russia and three former Socialist Soviet Republics in an alliance known as the Shanghai Cooperation Organization (SCO), with the goal of coordinating joint military exercises.

Russia and China have become even closer since the latter escalated its anti-Taiwan rhetoric in 2021 and the former invaded Ukraine in 2022. Iran, meanwhile, has established military alliances with both powers. All three nations have much in common and share similar geopolitical goals: (1) they fall under the Democracy Index's lowest category (authoritarian regimes); (2) all three endure heavy sanctions imposed by the United States and its allies; and (3) they want to undermine U.S. economic, diplomatic, and military power. This convergence of interests has cemented an alliance that some have dubbed the "New Axis."

It was not that long ago that China and the United Sates were allies, and not that further back when they were enemies. Communist China-U.S. relations became increasingly hostile after the Cuban Missile Crisis of 1962. As tense as U.S.-Soviet relations were, President Lyndon B. Johnson saw Beijing as an even greater threat than Moscow and even considered a pre-emptive military strike to stop its nuclear weapons development program. Then came the Vietnam War and Mao's Cultural Revolution which further soured Sino-American relations.

The turning point came in the 1970s in a context of increased hostilities between the United States and the Soviet Union. Both China and the United States saw rapprochement as a strategy to curb the threat of Soviet expansion. In February 1972, President Richard Nixon traveled to China and both nations signed the Shanghai Communiqué, a blueprint for the normalization of relations that culminated with the full establishment of diplomatic relations in 1979. China's threat had shrunk to the point that NATO's Southeast Asia counterpart, SEATO, disbanded in 1977.

If we think of the 1970s rapprochement as a video, it began to play in reverse in 1989 after the Chinese government's massacre of pro-democracy protesters in

Tiananmen Square. Remember the Square's 33-foot-tall foam-and-papier-mâché statue toppled by Chinese soldiers? Who can forget the so-called Tank Man who singlehandedly stopped a roaring column of tanks? He vanished into thin air and no one even knows his name.

In response, then President George H.W. Bush imposed numerous sanctions on China, including an arms sales embargo while pursuing collaborative relations with Taiwan, the primary irritant in Sino-American relations.

Sharing the goal of counterbalancing U.S. military and global economic power, in the twenty-first century, China and Russia have gradually strengthened economic links and bonds of amity. In July 2001, they signed a 20-year Treaty of Good-Neighborliness and Friendly Cooperation (extended five additional years in 2021). In 2019 and 2020, they held joint air military exercises over the Pacific. Their alliance has been further cemented since the Russian invasion of Ukraine; China supporting the military aggression, helping spread Russian war propaganda, purchasing larger amounts of Russian oil, and, according to some U.S. sources, secretly selling weapons to Moscow. Russia reciprocated, when a few days after the invasion it declared Taiwan an "unfriendly nation."

The same period has witnessed a deterioration of U.S.-Chinese relations, over several matters, first and foremost Taiwan, but also balance of trade issues, economic espionage, cyber security, intellectual property rights, and more recently, human and civil rights abuses in Tibet, Xinjiang Province and Hong Kong. Since 2018, when the Trump administration launched a trade war with China, hostilities escalated to unprecedented levels, increasing even further in 2021 over intensified threats to take Taiwan by force.

In sum, what started in the 1970s and 1980s as a strategic alliance between the United States and China to counterbalance the Soviet Union, was followed by two decades of deteriorating relations, coming full circle (only in reverse), with the current robust Chinese-Russian alliance built to counterbalance the United States.

Iran, the New Axis' Junior Partner

Iran and Russia have enjoyed decades of collaborative relations that include arms deals and Russian support for the development of Iran's nuclear program. Iran joined the Russian-led CSTO in 2007, where it holds the status of observer member state. Both countries have been military allies in the Syrian Civil War since 2011.

The China-Russia-Iran Axis has coalesced further since 2019, when all three countries began yearly joint naval exercises in the Indian Ocean. In March 2021, China and Iran signed a 25-year cooperation agreement whereby China agreed to invest 400 billion dollars in Iran in exchange for Iranian oil at guaranteed preferential prices. Later that year, Iran joined the Shanghai Cooperation Organization. Iran supported China's 2020 crackdowns in Hong Kong and has expanded collaborations with Russia since the start of the war in Ukraine, including providing drones for deadly attacks on Ukrainian civilian targets. Iran, thus, has become the bridge that cements the alliance between the Chinese and Russian blocks.

The main crack between those blocks pertains to hostile relations between India (Russian block) and Pakistan (Chinese block). China and India have border disputes of their own. Skirmishes in June 2020 in the disputed Galwan River valley, killed 20 Indian and 40 Chinese soldiers.

Pro-Democracy Blocks in Europe and Asia

Widespread human rights abuses perpetrated by Chinese authorities in Hong Kong, genocidal actions against the Uyghur ethnic minority, and escalation of belligerence toward Taiwan, on the one hand, and Russia's brutal invasion of Ukraine, on the other, have solidified two interlocked blocks of democratic nations under the leadership of the Biden administration, one in Europe, the other in the Indo-Pacific region.

This has occurred in a context of American global reengagement accompanied by a doubling in foreign U.S. favorability rates (12 democratic nation sample) from 34 percent when Trump was president to 62 percent after Biden took office. According to Pew Research Center's 2020 and 2021 Global Attitudes Surveys, trust in the U.S. president of turn jumped more than 50 points in Sweden, Belgium, Germany, the Netherlands, France, Italy, Canada, Spain, the United Kingdom, Australia, and South Korea.

Among Putin's greatest fears is the further strengthening and expansion of the thirty-member NATO military alliance. He sees Europe and the world from a nostalgic mid-1980s peak-of-Soviet-power perspective when the Russian Socialist Republic was the epicenter of a Moscow dominated empire buffered by fourteen other Soviet Socialist republics extending to the western borders of Estonia, Latvia, Lithuania, Ukraine, and Moldova. This western perimeter was protected by the Iron Curtain, a wall of Warsaw Pact nations, stretching from Poland in the north through Czechoslovakia, Hungary, and Romania, all the way to Bulgaria. And in the Scandinavian region, a border buffered by a Soviet Union-dominated Finland, whose foreign and military policies were for decades dictated from Moscow.

That is a far cry from the current situation in which NATO includes all former Warsaw Pact members, and all three former Soviet Baltic states; and where Sweden and a long de-Finlandized Finland are close to joining the military alliance. More alarmingly, from Russia's perspective, NATO is open to incorporating the two former Soviet Socialist Republics of Georgia and Ukraine.

If Putin's intention was to stop the expansion of NATO, invading Ukraine has backfired miserably and rather than allowing him to reconstitute the former Soviet Union will likely push the old Iron Curtain closer to Moscow.

While there is no equivalent to NATO in Asia and Oceania, a series of military alliances and increasingly tight multination organizations have cemented a democratic block to counterbalance China and North Korea. In October 2020, the United States and India signed the Basic Exchange and Cooperation Agreement (BECA) that established long-term strategic and military agreements between the two nations. The following year, Australia, the United States, and the United Kingdom, finalized AUKUS, a military pact for the Indo-Pacific region. The G-7, for its part, has forcefully and unanimously condemned China's human rights record and in December 2021, as Russian forces gathered across Ukraine's borders, the United States hosted the first of two Summits for Democracy, a global gathering to discuss "the challenges and opportunities facing democracies in the 21st century."

In June's NATO meeting in Madrid, member nations hosted democratic allies from the Indo-Pacific region (Japan, South Korea, Australia and New Zealand). On that occasion, NATO recognized that China's "stated ambitions and coercive policies challenge our interests, security and values." It is premature to say, but we may be witnessing the gestation of a new SEATO, closely aligned with NATO.

Non-Democratic Allies

The gathering storm is not as clear cut as a standoff between democracies and authoritarian regimes. As united as the world's democracies are, in times of war and rumors of war, they are forced to explore and cultivate alliances even with authoritarian states. Remember that Stalin's Soviet Union was an Allied Power during World War II. The Biden administration, if not seeking collaboration in the battlefield, is at least strengthening bonds with undemocratic partners that can supply the West with oil and other strategic wartime necessities.

In November 2021, presidential candidate Joe Biden promised to turn Saudi Arabia into a "pariah" if elected. And on the closing days of the 2020 presidential campaign, Democratic presidential nominee Biden criticized President Trump's friendly policies toward dictatorships in Russia, Belarus, and North Korea and uttered a statement that he probably regrets: "you see what is happening from Belarus through Poland to Hungary, and the rise of totalitarian regimes in the world." While Poland and Hungary were veering in an undemocratic direction, they were and remain U.S. allies and NATO members.

But that was then, and now Russia is at war with Ukraine; and average gas prices in the United States rose dramatically from $3.00 per gallon in June 2020 to $5.00 in June 2022. The United States and its allies are wooing potential undemocratic allies, the more oil rich the better. Feeling increasing domestic pressures to help bring down the price of gas, Biden traveled to Saudi Arabia in July 2022, where he met with Prince Mohammed bin Salman, who reportedly had been ignoring White House phone calls. Biden did not go as far as participating in a ceremonial sword dance—as Trump had done in May 2017—but bumped fists and exchanged smiles with the dictator.[3]

There are encouraging signs toward democratization in Poland, which is aiding Ukraine's war efforts and has taken on the lion's share of Ukrainian refugees, 1.25 million as of August 2022. In Hungary, Orbán's regime remains firmly in control; and NATO member Hungary has been shy about sanctions against Russia, with whom it seeks to maintain friendly relations. The United States and Europe's democracies will be forced to look the other way to avoid pushing Hungary closer into Putin's orbit.

A World at Risk

While unlikely to occur soon, the world faces the possibility of a Third World War, a worst-case scenario that could destroy the earth and its human inhabitants. Unlike in 1945, when the United States was the only country that had developed nuclear weapons, in 2022 a total of seven nations (U.S., Russia, U.K.,

---

3 U.S.-Saudi Arabia relations got colder when OPEC, in coordination with Russia, decided to cut oil production in October 2022 and Biden warned Saudi Arabia about "consequences."

France, China, India, Pakistan and North Korea) have acknowledged having them (and Israel is widely believed to have them), a worldwide total of around 13,000 nuclear heads.

On August 15, the journal *Nature Food* published a new study which concluded that a nuclear war between India and Pakistan would kill an estimated 2 billion people worldwide; and 5 billion (nearly two out of every three human beings) would die in case of an all-out nuclear war between Russia and the United States. Most of those deaths would be from starvation caused by a nuclear winter resulting from soot accumulation in the atmosphere blocking sunlight.

But let's set aside the madness of a nuclear circular firing squad going off and focus on the three most volatile areas of conflict and potential war: the ongoing war in Ukraine, the potential of war over Iran's nuclear program, and over Taiwan if the Chinese were to attack it.[4]

Putin has demonstrated that he is unstable and unpredictable and there is no telling whether he will go through with his threats of going nuclear. Just this week, he issued another televised nuclear war warning. "This is not a bluff," he said. Even when his troops were on the offensive, he was thinking and acting like a cornered beast; he is not likely to back away and be satisfied with the status quo antebellum.

That status quo antebellum is even less acceptable to Ukrainians who have endured systematic brutality (murder, torture and rape of civilians) at the hands of Russian invaders. Ukrainians rightly want to restore their borders to where they stood before 2014. And then, there is the expectation of reparations to indemnify and help reconstruct Ukraine.

The first three weeks of September have proven disastrous for the Russian military as Ukraine launched successful dual counteroffensives to recapture Kharkiv in the northeast and Kherson in the south. Russian forces have lost vast extensions of territory on both fronts. On September 10, Ukrainians recaptured the railway hub city of Izum, an advance that *New York Times* reporters saw as

---

4   Following the original publication of this column on September 24, 2022, North Korea embarked on aggressive military actions, including the firing of six ballistic missiles between September 25 and October 6, one of which flew menacingly over Japan, moving the United States to call an emergency meeting of the U.N. Security Council. On October 6, 12 North Korean warplanes flew close to the South Korean border. Then on November 2, it launched a record 23 rockets, one landing near South Korea's water border, prompting South Korea to respond with three precision-guided missiles.

"igniting a dramatic new phase" in the war. It is premature to suggest that these victories mark a turning point, but mighty Russia is currently on the run.[5]

Putin is also running out of fresh troops, announcing earlier this week the activation of 300,000 reservists. Crowds of demonstrators immediately gathered in Moscow and other cities with chants of "no to war" and "send Putin to the trenches." The announcement has sparked a mass exodus of Russians to bordering countries, Finland, Georgia, even Mongolia.

There are intelligence reports that Russia is also running out of ammunition and weapons; and that it may have enough to last only six more months. Some reports claim that Putin's Russia made a deal to purchase artillery weapons and shells from North Korea's fellow dictator Kim Jong-un.

I still hold on to the belief, as I wrote shortly after Putin announced the start of his "special military operation" that this will not end well for him and his oligarchs; and that as I foresaw on March 19, "whether in absentia or in person, alive or posthumously, Putin and his generals will eventually be tried for war crimes."

On another front, despite advances in U.S.-Iranian nuclear negotiations this summer, there are some areas of concern, including increased tensions and the possibility of a confrontation between the United States and Iranian-backed militias in Syria. Those militias targeted U.S. forces on August 15, and the United States responded two weeks later with air attacks.

Precisely this week, tens of thousands of Iranian women and men have taken to the streets in protest of the killing of 22-year-old woman Mahsa Amini apparently at the hands of the regime's so-called morality police. Is this Iran's George Floyd moment?[6]

With regards to China's potential aggression against Taiwan, a historical perspective reminds us that the Chinese have, for decades, followed the strategy of "peaceful" or "silent" rise in pursuit of reestablishing themselves as an economic superpower.

While Xi and other Chinese leaders see gaining control over Taiwan as necessary and a matter of national honor, they remain rational global players who are, for the time being, unwilling to risk China's multi-billion worldwide investments and access to the United States and Europe's markets.

---

5 During the last week of September 2022, Ukrainian forces continued to liberate vast Russian-occupied territory and on October 1 forced Russian troops to retreat from the strategic city and railroad hub of Lyman.

6 The U.S.-based rights monitor HRANA reported that up to October 15, Iranian police had killed at least 233 Iranian demonstrators.

It is telling that China, if it ever did, is not openly selling weapons to its Russian ally. All saber rattling aside, China's policy toward Taiwan echoes John Quincy Adam's early nineteenth-century Cuba "ripe fruit" policy. Why shake the mandarin tree, when the laws of political and physical gravitation will eventually land Taiwan on Chinese ground.

65

Toward a Second American Civil War?

(Creators Syndicate, September 3, 2022)

This book began with essays and columns written between May and September 2020 that traced parallels between the Antebellum and Civil War and America's contemporary increasingly radicalized and violent political environment. In a July 2020 column entitled "All History is Contemporary: A 20/20 Look at the Antebellum and Civil War," I identified seven parallels (1) political and partisan polarization, (2) passing or marginalization of political compromisers, (3) rise in political extremism, (4) loss of confidence in government institutions, (5) intensified nationalism, (6) escalating political vitriol, and (7) racial violence.

In a May 2020 column, while addressing the social unrest and violence in the wake of George Floyd's killing, my historian's intuition moved me to write "the smell of civil war is in the air." In July, I used with much hesitation the phrase First Civil War ("First" in quotation marks).

Closer to the 2020 elections, in September, I forecasted that "once the results are in, racial, ethnic, gender, geographical, cultural, and partisan hostilities will intensify, as they did in November 1860." "Given Trump's record of denouncing rigged elections and mass electoral fraud, and his persistent calls for political violence," I continued, "it is hard to imagine the scenario of a dignified concession and exit from power. Blood will be spilled, not between two armies but in a low-intensity conflict that could last years. May my historian's intuition fail me this time." Two weeks later, I anticipated "greater problems than figuring out hanging chads [as in 2000], and larger, angrier mobilizations of partisans during any recount. This time, they will not be in preppy clothes. Some will be armed."

How close are we to a second civil war? All of the seven factors enumerated above have actually intensified since November 2020. Political polarization has worsened since the last elections and moderate Republicans have been systematically purged from Republican Party leadership, replaced by Trump loyalists who must kiss his royal ring and embrace the "big lie" to survive politically.

Of the ten Republican congresspeople who voted to impeach Trump in January 2021, Liz Cheney and three others have been defeated in primary elections at the hands of Trump-endorsed candidates; Adam Kinzinger and three others decided not to run; and only two won their primaries. According to BallotPedia as of September 1, out of 200 Republican candidates endorsed by Trump, all but 17 had won their primaries or special elections.

Regarding confidence in government institutions, Gallup Poll surveys show that the public's trust sank to new lows in 2022. The percentage of Americans who trust the presidency (a great deal/quite a lot) dropped from 38 to 23; confidence in the Supreme Court, which on June 24 reversed Roe v. Wade, fell from 36 to 25; already in the basement of public trust at 12 percent, faith in Congress declined to 7 percent. Trust in the electoral system also stands at historic lows; and the FBI's favorability has eroded sharply in the eyes of many Republicans since the execution of a search warrant in Trump's Mar-a-Lago resort on August 8. Some have called for the Bureau's defunding. Others are instigating violence against its agents and some have responded to that call.

Political violence is rampant and manifests itself in a variety of ways. The unimaginable events of January 6, 2021, were in a category of their own: a coordinated military-style assault on the U.S. Capitol by several thousand individuals, including militia members of the Proud Boys and Oath Keepers. One has to go back to the American Revolution and the Civil War to find uprisings or a rebellion of such magnitude.

Some acts of violence are explicitly political, for example, the June 2017, Alexandria, Virginia, shooting of House Majority Whip Steve Scalise and three others by an anti-Trump gunman, or the throwing of a Molotov cocktail into the

Democratic Party headquarters of Travis County, Texas in October 2021.[1] And then there are acts of violence that are political because they respond to the politicization of social and cultural beliefs such as antisemitism and white supremacy. Take for example the 2018 deadly terrorist attack in the Tree of Life synagogue in Pittsburgh, or the mass shooting targeting Black shoppers at a Buffalo, New York supermarket this spring.[2]

Will the United States break into a second Civil War? According to a July article in *Science*, half of Americans believe that it will happen and soon. And in the days following the raid at Mar-a-Lago, the internet has been glowing with right-wing calls for civil war. This Thursday, Wisconsin GOP gubernatorial candidate Tim Michels called on people to "be ready to get out on the streets with pitchforks and torches." We are certainly moving in that direction.

1 Three other 2022 incidents stand out: In June, police arrested an armed man outside of Supreme Court Justice Kavanaugh's home; in July, another man with a handgun showed up in front of the home of Congresswoman Pramila Jayapal, threatening her with racial slurs; and on October 28, a man broke into the home of Speaker Nancy Pelosi, where he attacked her husband with a hammer.

2 In a speech on September 20, 2022, in Youngstown, Ohio, Trump warned of "big, big problems" in the event of him being indicted.

66

The Global Authoritarian Wave, Democratic Countercurrents and Dangerous Crosscurrents

(Creators Syndicate, December 10, 2022)

When it comes to the preservation of democracy, I can sound like a broken record. Democracy is very fragile; it must be protected, I tell my students and anyone willing to listen. The erosion of democracy and the urgency of protecting it are, in fact, recurring topics in my weekly columns.

While in the past 15 years, the global trend has pointed toward increasingly authoritarian and undemocratic rule (China, Russia, Belarus, Cuba, Venezuela, Myanmar, etc.), in the past two years, the world has witnessed some encouraging countercurrents, pendular swings toward democracy in the United States, Western Europe, Poland, Hungary and Brazil, to name only a few cases.

But undemocratic crosscurrents persist. In the past week alone, former President Donald Trump issued a disturbing message calling for the "termination of all rules, regulations, and articles, even those found in the Constitution," to redress the "massive fraud" he claims robbed him of reelection.

Even more bizarre were this week's revelations of a thwarted right-wing, QAnon-connected plot to overthrow the German government and replace it with an obscure minor aristocrat.

Also this week, Peru's democratically elected left-of-center president, Pedro Castillo, was impeached, arrested and removed from office, following his failed attempt to overstep his constitutional powers and dissolve the Congress and impose a new constitution, which would have been the nation's 14th since its independence.

Lingering Trumpism

Nearly two years into Trump's antidemocratic administration, the American electorate expressed its repudiation in the 2018 midterm elections, giving Democrats control over the House of Representatives with a net gain of 41 seats and 7 new governorships; and in November 2020, voted him out of office. The anti-authoritarian countercurrent's latest manifestations were the recent midterm electoral defeats of Trump-endorsed, election-denial candidates, including Mehmet Oz, Herschel Walker and four other senatorial candidates, and Doug Mastriano, Kari Lake and nine other MAGA gubernatorial candidates.

While Trump appears to have lost all chances of becoming the Republican Party's 2024 presidential nominee, the anti-ideological ideology of Trumpism still dominates the party and he retains enormous loyalty and popularity among the party's base. This authoritarian crosscurrent is bound to survive Trump's political, and perhaps his biological, life.

German Putschism, Then and Now

Not that long ago, Germany epitomized fascism, the worst manifestation of Western dictatorial rule and expansionism ever. The ambitious and temporarily successful Third Reich, however, had humble roots in a 1923 failed putsch in the unlikely stage of a Munich beer hall, where Hitler and his Nazi confederates tried to seize power by force. Hitler was tried and sentenced to five years in prison but not 10 years had passed before he was named German chancellor. The rest of the story needs no recounting.

There is some irony in the fact that what had been Europe's most horrific and destructive dictatorial nation has become the continent's most solid democratic bastion.

Authoritarian putschism has, however, reared its ugly head in Germany as evidenced by Wednesday's arrest of 25 plotters belonging to the heavily armed right-wing organization Reichsburger (Reich citizens) which was seeking to install a lower aristocrat, Prince Heinrich XIII, as German head of state. In August 2020, members of the Reichsburger group attempted to storm the German Parliament building to seize control (January 6-style), some responding to QAnon rumors that none other than Donald Trump had traveled to Berlin to liberate the German people. I can almost hear the Wagnerian score to this opera of the absurd.

Peruvian Presidents (Six in as Many Years)

After leaving dictatorial Cuba in the summer of 1962, my family resettled in Peru, where Army General Ricardo Pérez Godoy had just staged a coup d'état installing himself as the nation's 47th president. Six years later, another coup—the 12th in Peru's history—removed president No. 49.

In 1992, President Alberto Fujimori staged a coup against/and in his own favor, imposed a new constitution and ruled with an iron fist until 2000. In the last 22 years, Peru has had 20 different presidents (six since 2016). Of the eight living former presidents, all but one have either been arrested or convicted of serious crimes or have been impeached (two of them twice). Another one killed himself in anticipation of his arrest for corruption charges. Talk about "candidate quality."

One of the legacies of the 1993 Fujimori constitution is the ease with which presidents can dissolve the national congress and the ease with which Congress can impeach presidents. Fujimori dissolved Congress in 1993, and Martín Vizcarra did the same in 2019. Congress impeached Fujimori in 2000 on grounds of "permanent moral incapacity," then unsuccessfully impeached Pedro Pablo Kuczynski (2017), and Vizcarra twice in 2020, successfully on the second try.

This past week, Peru lived through constitutional warfare: anticipating a third set of impeachment proceedings against him, Pedro Castillo moved to dissolve Congress on December 7; he was impeached and arrested by the National Police.

Democracy is, indeed, fragile, in countries where it has been historically weak, in places still recovering from authoritarian rule and in its long-term bastions. Watch for those dangerous crosscurrents.

Epilogue: Deadlines, Periodization and This Book's Title

(December 19, 2022)

Before I became a syndicated columnist, I always had, going back to 1992, a book deadline hanging over me, a manuscript that I had to deliver to some press by a date we had mutually agreed on. After publishing my most recent book, *Key to the New World* in 2018, I found myself for the first time in my career, free from any deadlines. It felt good not to owe any manuscript to anyone.

But alas, when I signed up with Creators Syndicate in August 2020, I brought upon myself regular weekly column deadlines: every Friday, week after week, by 7:00 p.m. With few exceptions I have fulfilled my weekly obligations punctually, skipping just a few weeks in the past two and a half years.

A year into syndication, I decided to collect my columns and publish them as a book. And in December 2021 agreed to yet another deadline when I signed the contract for this book with Peter Lang Publishers. Since then, I've had to contend simultaneously with my weekly columns' and this book's deadlines. Originally due in March 2022, we agreed to extend the deadline so I could add columns on pressing unfolding topics such as the Russian invasion of Ukraine and social turmoil in Cuba and write a closing section (Section IX) in which I could wrap up the book's major themes.

Periodization is an important historical skill; historians learn to organize our books and scholarly articles by dividing them into periods, not just arbitrary periods (say ten- or fifty-year intervals) but into blocks of time dictated by pivotal moments of change. I started writing regular columns in 2020, precisely because I recognized that the United States and the world were entering a distinct period when the COVID-19 epidemic became a pandemic. In March of that year, I gave one column the rhetorical title: "Pivotal Moment? What History Tells Us About COVID-19's Future Impact." Then came the killing of George Floyd, followed by mass demonstrations and social unrest, in the United States and abroad. That was an election year in the United States, the most conflictive and rancorous ever. Then came the Big Lie and January 6, 2021. And Russia invaded Ukraine in February 2022.

This book's original working title was "All History Is Contemporary History," a quote from Italian historian Benedetto Croce. But just as I was wrapping up this project in October 2022, I decided on a title that more accurately (and powerfully) reflected the book's overarching theme: 2019–2022 are more than years of pivotal change, they are the start of a distinct period when the world started to turn upside down.

When will this period end? And will the world ever turn right side up again? I can't tell.

Index

Q

About the Author

Luis Martínez-Fernández is a historian, university professor, nationally syndicated columnist, and public speaker whose fields of expertise include Latin America, the Caribbean, Cuba, education, world cultures, and Latino/Hispanic politics and culture. He is Pegasus Professor of History at the University of Central Florida and an award-winning columnist with Creators Syndicate.

His books include *Fighting Slavery in the Caribbean, Revolutionary Cuba: A History*, widely acclaimed as the most comprehensive and systematic study on the subject ever written, and *Key to the New World: A History of Early Colonial Cuba*, winner of the 2018 Florida Book Awards bronze medal for nonfiction and the 2019 International Latino Book Awards gold medal in history.